THE DESIGNER'S DESKTOP MANUAL

SECOND EDITION

For more fine books from F+W Media,
visit www.fwbookstore.com.

Distributed in Canada by Fraser Direct
100 Armstrong Avenue
Georgetown, Ontario, Canada L7G 5S4
Tel: (905) 877-4411

Distributed in the U.K. and Europe by
David & Charles, Brunel House, Newton Abbot,
Devon, TQ12 4PU, England
Tel: (+44) 1626-323200, Fax: (+44) 1626-323319
E-mail: postmaster@davidandcharles.co.uk

Distributed in Australia by Capricorn Link
P.O. Box 704, Windsor, NSW 2756 Australia
Tel: (02) 4577-3555

Library of Congress Cataloging-in-Publication Data

ISBN: 978-1-4403-0300-5

Design: Fineline
Cover design: Emily Portnoi

THE DESIGNER'S DESKTOP MANUAL

SECOND EDITION

JASON SIMMONS

HOW BOOKS
Cincinnati, Ohio
www.howdesign.com

CONTENTS

Operating Systems and Applications

Whether you're a die-hard Mac fan, love the flexibility of Unix, or prefer the universal acceptance of Windows, your computer simply won't function without an operating system—and it pays to ensure you know your way around that system as many hours of frustration can result from not being able to find a particular function or option. The following pages provide you with a beginner's guide to the two main operating systems used by designers the world over, Apple's OS X and Microsoft's Windows. If you are used to Windows, we'll show you how to get started with a Mac, and vice versa.

While many of you will be familiar with, or even expert in, a number of different applications, it's usual for designers to posses less working knowledge of software outside their core area of skills. However, today's designers should attempt to address this issue as it's not unusual to find yourself in a situation where you need to create a piece of work using an application you've not used before. To get you started, an overview of the primary design applications is given with annotated guides to the interface and tips on how to get the job done.

A MAC USER'S GUIDE TO PCS

Many Mac users would rather go back to alcohol markers and Letraset than use a PC—but such narrow-mindedness is ill-advised. The problems that beset PCs in the past—viruses, stability problems, compatibility issues, poor build quality—have largely been addressed thanks to a mixture of the maturing of the operating system and its attendant "ecosystem," and a recognition on the part of top- and mid-tier manufacturers that they had to improve the user experience.

Indeed Windows 7 features a number of tools and design touches that might be very familiar to Mac users, including Gadgets—much like OS X's Widgets only placeable on the main desktop—and even a recently re-designed task-bar with seems to have a lot in common with the Mac's Dock.

Consider too that while the desktop-publishing revolution began on the Mac, all the major print and online publishing packages are now also available for Windows. A modern PC, therefore, is as valid a choice for design work as a Mac, with two caveats. First, type rendering on older systems using "nondesign" applications tended to be less sophisticated than that with Mac OS X. Obviously, one wouldn't necessarily expect precise typographic rendering and control when not using specific DTP applications such as QuarkXPress or InDesign, but things have improved. For example, text rendering in the most recent version of Word is particularly impressive.

The second proviso relates to color. Thanks in part to Windows' more business-focused heritage, colors appear punchier; for this reason you need to make consistent use of gamma correction and color profiles to ensure accurate color throughout the workflow, just as you would on a Mac.

CONTROL KEYS
Control/Ctrl

On a PC, Ctrl does the equivalent job of Mac's Command/Cmd in most circumstances, issuing keyboard shortcuts to active applications. Common shortcuts such as X, C, V, and P (for cut, copy, paste, and print, respectively) work as expected.

Alt

Look across the menus of most Windows' applications and you'll notice that one letter in each is underlined. Tap Alt to access any menu, then press the relevant key to initiate whatever menu item you've chosen. You can access almost any menu item or select almost

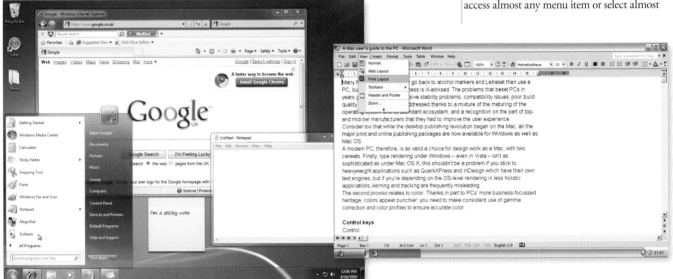

all onscreen options directly from the keyboard using Windows or Vista. This facility is particularly popular with "power users" who need to work fast with the minimum number of mouse clicks.

WINDOWS

The main use of the key marked with the Windows symbol is to pop up the *Start* menu, from which you can navigate, using arrow keys, to any option within the *Start* menu. It's also used a lot for shortcuts, such as Win+E for a new Explorer window, or Win+R which opens the *Run* dialog box.

FILE STRUCTURE

By default, Windows creates three visible folders in the root of your main hard disk: *Documents and Settings* (which holds your user data, as with *Users* under Mac OS X); *Program Files* (analogous to Mac's *Applications*) and *WINDOWS*, which holds your system and its settings.

INSTALL/UNINSTALL

Unlike the Mac, Windows has a native uninstaller utility. *Add or Remove Programs* is part of the *Control Panel*.

BASIC TROUBLESHOOTING AND HOUSEKEEPING

Older PCs, in order to ensure smooth operation, used to require regular reorganization of the data on their hard disks, a process known as degfragmentation. Modern PCs—and most external hard drives—organize their data using NTFS (New Table Filing System) which, like Mac OS's system, needs this far less frequently. Unlike the Mac, however, Windows ships with a utility to perform the operation (*Disk Defragmenter*) should you feel the need.

Force quit

Tap *Control-Alt-Delete* and the *Task Manager* appears. From here you can inspect running processes, and click *End Process* to force Windows to quit it. Always exercise caution however, and don't shut down any processes unless you're sure they've actually crashed.

A PC USER'S GUIDE TO MACS

There's a popular misconception that an Apple Macintosh is so different from a Windows-driven PC that anyone familiar with the latter would find using a Mac almost impossible. This is wrong on many levels. Not only is the hardware practically identical now that Apple have switched from PowerPC to Intel chips, but the "user experience" is also very similar.

Like Windows, Macs employ a graphic user interface—windows, icons, menus, and pointers—sometimes shortened to WIMP. In both platforms, documents are stored in folders, work is created using applications, and settings are made using *Preferences*. There are, however, some differences between the two platforms. Here are some examples.

CONTROL KEYS

Command ⌘

This is the main command modifier on the Mac, and in many circumstances takes the place of Control under Windows. Common shortcuts such as X, C, V, and P—for "cut," "copy," "paste," and "print," respectively—work as expected. Command-Tab on the Mac provides the same functionality as Alt-Tab under Windows.

Control (ctrl)

Often used simply as an additional modifier for keyboard shortcuts, one of Control's most essential roles comes into play if you only have a one-button mouse or trackpad, now increasingly rare thanks to the introduction of Apple's Magic Mouse, with its "two-button" functionality. Hold Control when you click to emulate a "right-click" in order to bring up contextual menus.

Alt (alt) or Option (opt)

One of Alt's main roles is to help type accented characters; Windows' use of Alt to navigate menus has no Mac equivalent.

FILE STRUCTURE

The root level of a Mac's hard disk contains four folders:
• Applications—where installed software and utilities reside
• Library—which contains configuration and support files
• System—in which the operating system (OS) and associated files are found
• Users—which contains all the files you create

It's a good idea to retain Users' basic file structure—Documents, Pictures, Music, and so on—which is imposed by the system, but you can add your own additional folders if you wish.

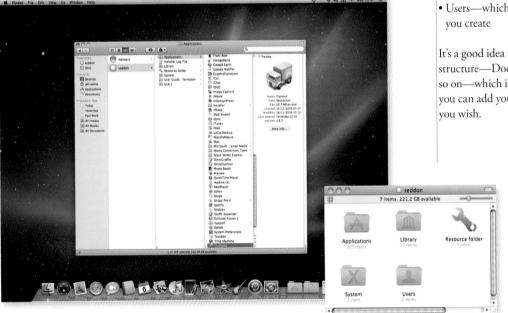

Mac OS X structure overview

THE DOCK

Similar to, though not the same as Windows' Taskbar, the Dock allows you to launch applications, minimize windows, and store links to folders and documents; simply drag items in and out.

PREVIEWING IMAGE FILES

There's a really quick and easy way to preview images in the Finder without opening them all individually. Simply select a range of images and hit the spacebar. A preview window automatically opens within the Finder, allowing you to scroll through each image in turn. Hit the spacebar again to close the preview window.

CONTROL-ALT-DELETE

Pressing Command-Control-Escape on the Mac brings up a window that allows you to force quit troublesome applications.

INSTALLING APPLICATIONS

It's rare that any application or utility for the Mac isn't supplied with its own installer app, which makes installations very simple. It's good practice to install all applications in the main applications folder, but if you wish to run the application in just one user account there is an additional applications folder within the User folder for each account.

QUITTING APPLICATIONS

Unlike Windows, closing an application's last active document does not exit the application. You need to quit manually from the application menu to quit the software.

BASIC TROUBLESHOOTING

If your Mac is misbehaving, first try repairing permissions (open Disk Utility, click on your hard disk, then click Repair Disk Permissions), then restart from your install CD/DVD, holding down the C key. Pick Disk Utility from the Utilities menu and then repair your hard disk.

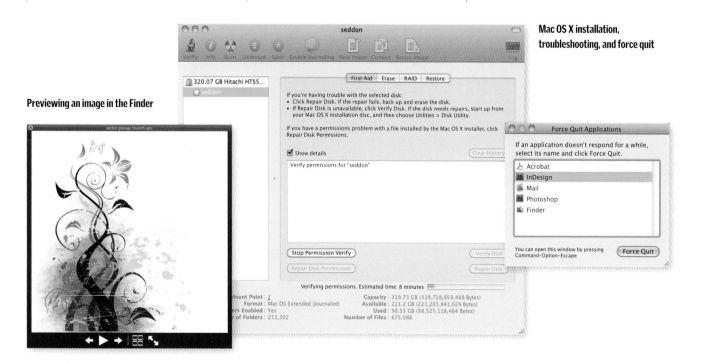

Previewing an image in the Finder

Mac OS X installation, troubleshooting, and force quit

HOW COMPUTERS DISPLAY AN IMAGE

Look closely at any screen—no matter whether it's a flat-panel screen, a boxy CRT monitor (less commonly used these days), or a television—and you'll see small blocks of color, known as pixels (short for picture elements). Look closer still, and you'll see that these colors are made up of even smaller blocks of pure red, green, and blue light—all at differing intensities.

Displays use this system—known as the "additive" color system—of mixing together red, green, and blue light to create the gamut, or range, of colors we see on-screen. Such a system relies on our mind's ability to perceive adjacent blocks of pure color either as different hues, shades, or tints.

The practical upshot of this is that while you might think the photograph you see on-screen uses continuous tones of color, in fact it's just a trick that exploits our eyesight's relatively poor ability to resolve fine detail. The image is really made up of a fine matrix of blocks of color, a little like a 21st-century equivalent of a Roman mosaic.

COLOR PERCEPTION

Today's computer monitors are sufficiently sophisticated to display more colors than our eyes are able to distinguish, but that doesn't mean the colors you see on-screen are necessarily "accurate"—it's all a question of perception.

Let's think of a printed page for a moment. In simple terms, the colors in this book were created by mixing different intensities of cyan, magenta, yellow, and black inks. This is known as the "subtractive," CMYK model. And while color-matching systems such as Pantone® help ensure color consistency from screen to page, additive and subtractive systems construct colors in different ways, with each displaying a different gamut of colors. For example, it's quite usual for print designers previewing CMYK colors on-screen (using simulation systems such as those in Photoshop) to be disappointed by how dull the colors appear.

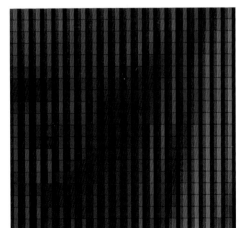

A screen up close

On-screen images are made up of thousands of points of red, blue, and green light. These combine to produce an image with millions of colors, hues, and shades, but the illusion breaks down as it is magnified. The example shown here is a flat screen rather than a CRT.

PC display

The importance of calibration

Macs and PCs have slightly different approaches to displaying colors, and because of this, the same image will look different when viewed on each system. Proper color calibration can minimize these problems.

Mac display

To make the matter more complicated, PCs and Macs may display slightly different color gamuts, with images appearing darker on a PC than on a Mac. Consistent and sensible use of color profiles can help to reduce this effect.

ANTI-ALIASING

Computer displays are still only capable of displaying relatively coarse detail compared with the printed page, so anti-aliasing—a system of reducing the jagged appearance of edges—is used. This is particularly apparent in text rendering. In addition, modern systems can use sub-pixel rendering (anti-aliasing with colored blocks) to exploit the inherent misregistration of flat-panel screens and increase the resolution of a display.

TFT-LCD and CRT
The days of the cathode ray tube (CRT) monitor being regarded as the first choice for accurate color work are over. Manufacturers are no longer producing monitors that use this out-dated technology, and as a result thin film transistor (TRT) monitors are now predominant. All liquid crystal display (LCD) monitors use TFT technology to improve image quailty, and the products available today are well up to the task of displaying accurate on-screen color. Regular color calibration is of course essential if color accuracy is to be maintained over time. This can be achived best through the use of specialist calibration hardware such as LaCie's "blue eye" device.

Anti-alias off   Anti-alias on

Anti-aliasing
The illusion of smooth edges is provided using a system called anti-aliasing. Single pixels of color are tinted to blend between the foreground and background elements, fooling the mind into ignoring the jagged edge that would otherwise be obvious.

BITMAPS AND VECTORS

As discussed earlier, all computer monitors display images by using a grid of colored dots called pixels. At a basic level, we can create patterns, text, and even images simply by switching some of these pixels on (white) or off (black), as we could do with a sheet of graph paper, a black pen, and infinite patience. Exchange the black pen for a big box of crayons in thousands of different colors, and you have the ability, in theory at least, to create images that, when viewed from a sufficient distance, look like continuous-tone photographs.

BITMAP IMAGES

Bitmap images, such as those created by a digital camera for example, are created using finite grids of colored pixels—and unsurprisingly the fewer pixels that make up the image, the less detail there is. You can reduce detail by removing pixels from an image, but you can't add detail that's not already there simply by adding new pixels. The best you can do is use a process called interpolation, which calculates pixel values between existing pixels during an image enlargement and fills in the gaps. There are various tools that can interpolate images, including Photoshop's *Resample Image*, found in the *Image Size* dialog window, but such tools can only approximate missing detail, and results will vary depending on the content of the image.

This, then, is the main drawback of bitmap images—there is a finite level of detail available. Their use of fine grids ensures that they can show very subtle changes in color, texture, and detail, but scale an image up too far and pixellation—blocks of color replacing the smooth gradations—will occur.

Bitmaps

Bitmap, or raster images, are created using colored blocks or pixels. Subtle shifts in tone, color, and detail are possible, which makes them perfect for photographs.

Resolution

A bitmap image at a low resolution will lack fine detail. Attempting to scale-up bitmaps beyond their original size leads to poor results, although there are workarounds that can help to a point.

VECTOR IMAGES

Contrast this with vector images which are constructed from a series of connected points defined by mathematical coordinates. Rather than slavishly drawing a number of lined-up black pixels to create a line, as for a bitmap image, a vector representation of the same line is described simply as two points, the beginning and the end, joined by a line.

This system has two advantages: vector file sizes are much smaller than bitmap files (think of just two data points rather than many thousands of individual pixels), and vectors are resolution-independent. This latter characteristic means that you can scale vector images up or down with no loss in quality, which is not the case with bitmap images.

The drawback is that it's possible but not practical to create photo-real images using vectors. They are better suited to simpler shapes and flat colors as found in type, company logos, and certain types of artwork. Remember, however, that since computer displays use a bitmap system, you never truly "see" vector images. Instead, you see a "rasterized"—or preview version of the vector—created inside the computer. The vector data remain pure as far as scaling, storage, and manipulation are concerned, but are rasterized—converted to a series of lit pixels or droplets of ink—during display or output, usually at the maximum resolution of the display or printer concerned.

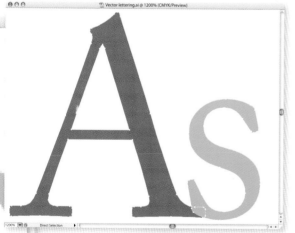

Detail
More anchor points will be generated as more detail is added to a vector graphic. This can increase the file size enormously, to the point where it may be beneficial to convert the vector image to a bitmap.

Vectors
Vector graphics use a series of points and lines to describe an image that is resolution-independent, so the graphic can be scaled up or down with no loss of quality. This makes vector graphics perfect for type, logos, and bold illustration work.

THE QUARKXPRESS WORKSPACE

Before InDesign appeared on the scene, QuarkXPress was the dominant page makeup software. Any professional designer involved in most types of layout design would almost certainly have used QuarkXPress, and for a while layout files were ubiquitously referred to as "Quarks." This position has changed since the release of Adobe's Creative Suite and in particular InDesign, but it's important to acknowledge that QuarkXPress is still an incredibly powerful design and layout tool which, 20 years ago, helped to pioneer the whole DTP revolution and turn the publishing industry on its head.

The latest release of QuarkXPress, version 8, attempts to level the playing field in the battle with InDesign by touting itself with the slogan "Revolutionizing Publishing. Again." and has a number of new features that distinguish it from previous versions.

The first thing that strikes anyone familiar with QuarkXPress is the redesign of the user interface. Those users that prefer to keep changes of this kind to a minimum in order to lessen the need for retraining need not panic as the changes are mainly to the top level workspace, with other dialogs and palettes remaining the same. Notably, there is a new set of command icons positioned at the bottom of the active document window which allows you easily to move between pages, toggle the master and page view, view split screens, and export your layout. The main toolbox has also been restructured with just eight tools displayed. In previous versions the text and picture box tools were separate, but these have now merged into one. This means you can add either text or an image to the same pre-drawn container, or simply drag and drop a file directly into the layout. QuarkXPress 8 will automatically create the type of container needed, which is a great productivity enhancement.

PEN TOOL

QuarkXPress 8's *Pen* tool has been given a serious overhaul and now works in a similar way to the same tool that appears in Adobe Illustrator. Lines are created using Bézier paths made from a series of control points. A pop-out menu allows you to add, delete, and convert the control points, which makes it much easier to create non-standard rules and shapes directly within the QuarkXPress document rather than having to create them in an alternative application and then import them to your layout.

TEXT HANDLING

Support has been added for hanging punctuation and punctuation alignment, which is great news for exacting typographers. Attributes can be added on a paragraph basis rather than to the whole story which is particularly useful when several sizes of font are being used. Another popular addition, much requested over the years but now a reality, is the ability to create multiple baseline grids within the same document which can be applied to different master pages or text boxes. Grids can also be linked to a paragraph style, so if line spacing is edited the baseline gird changes too.

SYNCHRONIZATION

A great feature retained in this release is the ability to synchronize the content of both text and picture boxes, including all attributes, between different layouts in a project. To achieve this, access the *Shared Content* palette where the synchronization can be customized to include item and content attributes, or content only.

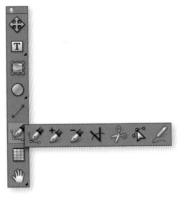

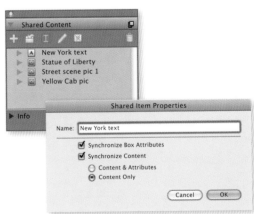

Pen tool options and the *Shared Items Properties* palettes

QuarkXPress workspace

THE INDESIGN WORKSPACE

Since the release of the first incarnation of InDesign CS, which shipped toward the end of 2003, InDesign has gradually established itself as the weapon of choice for the majority of graphic designers working with layouts. The largely panel-based user interface and tool set provides designers with an extremely intuitive workspace, and InDesign's feature set has grown over subsequent versions to include pretty much everything that one needs to create an efficient workflow for creating any kind of layout. The latest release of InDesign CS5 (version 7.0) has added some real gems to its feature set. The Adobe website (www.adobe.com) is of course the best place to read and learn about the new features, but covered here are a few that really stand out.

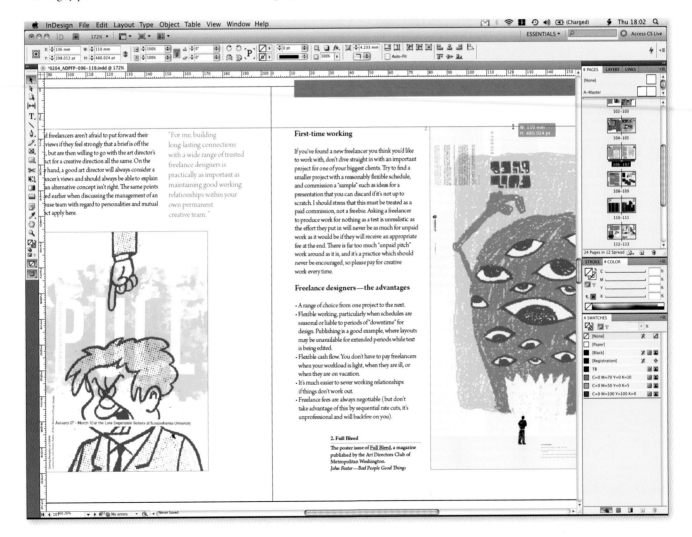

MULTIPLE PAGE SIZES

Designers have long requested the ability to create different page sizes within a single document, and this is now possible. Simply select a page with the new *Page* tool and change the settings in the *Control* panel.

LAYERS PANEL

Adobe have changed the way the *Layers* panel works, making it similar to the Illustrator *Layers* panel. The individual objects that reside on each layer, along with their stacking order, can now be revealed in the *Layers* panel using the new disclosure triangles. The stacking order can be changed directly within the panel, and objects can be locked or hidden individually.

CONTENT GRABBER

The new *Content Grabber* appears in the form of a translucent target whenever you move the cursor to a position above a placed image. Clicking on the target allows you to select and move the content of a frame with the *Selection* tool still selected, meaning you don't have to keep switching tools. The option can be switched off if you prefer it not to appear.

SWATCHES IN CONTROL PANEL

Color swatches can now be applied to strokes and fills directly from the *Control* panel, freeing up more screen space.

Spanning multiple columns

This is one feature that designers have been waiting for for a long time—the ability to run a headline across multiple columns of a single text box without affecting the running text. This is a really useful new feature introduced with the release of InDesign CS5 and one which will be welcomed by designers who like to keep their artwork free of too many separate text boxes. The option to run the selected text across two or more columns, and to add space before and after the same text selection, can all be set from one palette, accessed from the drop-down menu at the top right of the screen.

Selecting a color directly from the Control panel

The new Layers panel

The new Content Grabber tool

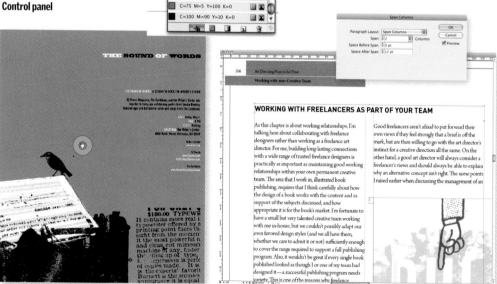

THE ILLUSTRATOR WORKSPACE

Adobe Illustrator has long been seen as the sister product to Photoshop, using vectors rather than pixels for creating graphics. Although the differences between Illustrator, Photoshop, and InDesign have become blurred over the years, Illustrator is the leading tool for creating complex vector-based images—only CorelDRAW, popular with PC users, comes close to Illustrator's dominance of the market. Illustrator's interface has in the past contained some small quirks that didn't crop up in Photoshop or InDesign, although functionality in cross-over areas was, of course, similar. The release of CS5 has seen some of those features, for example the functionality of the *Layers* panel, absorbed by other members of the CS Suite.

USING ILLUSTRATOR

Illustrator graphics are created using polygon shapes and the *Pen* tool. Each shape or path can be manipulated and colored in much the same way as in Photoshop or InDesign, and many tools, palettes, and commands are very similar to their CS counterparts.

Vector graphics are usually used for razor-sharp line work—resolution independent images that need to stay crisp no matter how much they are enlarged. But the distinction between Illustrator's vector files and Photoshop's bitmaps becomes indistinct once you start feathering vector graphics or stylizing them with filters that were, until recently, strictly off limits for vector graphics. Even when feathered, distorted, warped, sketched, and extruded, the original image remains completely editable and scalable.

The Illustrator workspace

TRACING IMAGES

The *Live Trace* tool can be used to transform a photograph or other bitmap image into a vector graphic. The *Tracing Options* allow you to specify the numbers of colors, detail, and accuracy of the resulting artwork.

The quality of the original image, and the conversion settings greatly affect the finished result, but with practice it is possible to start with a washed-out and grainy bitmap image and achieve an exciting graphic masterpiece. In fact, turning a low-quality bitmap into a high-quality, scalable vector can save the day if no other images are available.

3D GRAPHICS

Using the 3D Effects *Extrude & Bevel, Revolve,* and *Rotate,* it is possible to add depth and perspective to flat graphics. Arguably the controls will never match those in a dedicated 3D-rendering application such as Cinema 4D, and the surface rendering is relatively unsophisticated, but when a graphic designer requires a basic 3D effect for a print project there is no need to leave the Creative Suite.

Effect > 3D > Extrude and Bevel is the primary 3D tool, allowing a flat shape to be stretched into an object that can be rotated around the X, Y, and Z axis. It's perfect for making 3D type or adding perspective.

SAVING AND EXPORTING

The main formats for Illustrator files are the proprietary .AI or vector .EPS. Printers will accept Illustrator files as final artwork, usually for packaging designs when the complex meshes are packed full of rich graphics, but little type.

Illustrator files can be imported or placed into Photoshop or InDesign, but the simplest and quickest way to transfer graphics is to simply cut and paste between the applications. Its integration with Flash has also improved considerably, making even Illustrator more appealing for web designers.

Blending

The *Blend* tool transforms separate shapes and colors into a seamless blend. Specify the number of steps in the blend, or the distances between each stage. The effect is live, so altering the target shapes will update the blend.

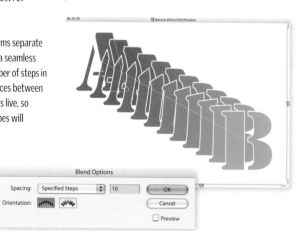

THE PHOTOSHOP WORKSPACE

Photoshop has in many ways become more than simply an application—it has entered common language usage in the same way that some brand names are used generically. If an image has been retouched it is now generally said to have been "photoshopped." There is no real challenger to this fine software, at least in terms of the professional market. For those of us who require fewer features there is the cut down version of Photoshop, Adobe Elements, but there are very few professional designers who do not own a copy of Photoshop.

WORKSPACE OVERVIEW

One of the neatest innovations added to Photoshop since the release of CS4 is the *Adjustments* panel. Instead of manually creating adjustment layers, clicking on the relevant icon in the *Adjustments* panel creates a new adjustment layer and allows you to make the changes you require from within the same panel. It's a much neater way of working and can save a lot of time if you process a lot of images. Furthermore, there are a number of presets available for the most commonly used adjustments.

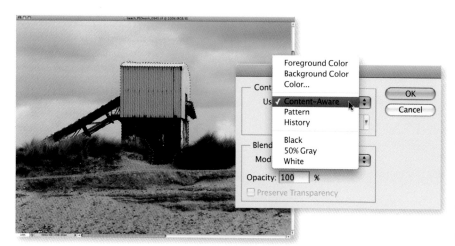

Content-Aware fill

With only a minimal amount of work, the rusty old mine building has been removed from the image. The selection doesn't need to be particularly accurate as you can carry out additional work with the *Spot Healing Brush* tool which can also be used in *Content-Aware* mode.

CONTENT-AWARE FILL

With the release of Photoshop CS5, image retouching has become a whole lot easier, thanks to the inclusion of the truly amazing *Content-Aware Fill* features. It is now possible to simply make a rough selection around any object in an image and fill that selection with the *Content-Aware* option to miraculously remove it and replace the space with newly generated background. In our example shown on this page the building has been selected with a little extra of its surrounding image included in that selection. Filling the selection using *Content-Aware* has produced the image shown to the right. Apart from one or two small areas that were touched in using the *Spot Healing Brush*, which can also be used in *Content-Aware* mode, that was all the work needed. What would have taken hours can now be achieved in minutes!

THE BRIDGE WORKSPACE

As the nerve center for all activities within the Creative Suite set of applications, Bridge performs an important function. Essentially an image browser for viewing and selecting large numbers of images, Bridge can add a great deal to your productivity. Here are some of the key features in the CS5 version.

FASTER PERFORMANCE

Bridge has become increasingly responsive through each subsequent version, which will please anyone who handles a large amount of material. This isn't really a new feature as such, but it'll certainly benefit anyone with an older, slower workstation.

BRIDGE STACKING

To help you navigate your way through large collections of images, Adobe have included a "stacking" feature to aid organization. If you have a series of images that are similar, or are perhaps intended to be seen as a group of images from which to make a selection, you

can multiple select them in the *Content* pane and *Group as Stack* from the *Stack* menu. The affected images stack themselves in the *Content* pane, taking up the space previously occupied by one image. You can still view them all by either scrolling the small slider that appears at the top of the stack, or by clicking on the number button at the top left

of the stack, which indicates how many images the stack contains. Clicking this button expands the stack so all images can be viewed simultaneously in the *Content* pane. Incidentally, all images in a stack can be viewed together in the preview pane whenever a complete stack is selected.

PREVIEW MAGNIFIER

This is a useful feature for zooming in on details when viewing an image in the *Preview* pane. If you move the cursor over a preview you'll notice it changes to a magnifier icon. Click on the preview and a magnifier window rather like a traditional "loupe" appears, allowing you to examine small details of an image with ease. It's now possible to create multiple magnifier window above a single image with multiple clicks.

Bridge workspace, *Stack* menu, and *Preview* pane

THE ACROBAT WORKSPACE

Despite the fact that Acrobat is in itself an extremely powerful and feature-rich software package in its own right, many of us simply treat it as an application we use to "look at PDFs." While this may be true of Acrobat Reader, which can be downloaded without charge from the Adobe website and is intended exactly for that purpose, there's a lot

more to the full version of Acrobat that ships with every different version of the CS Suite. PDF files can be split, combined, shared, annotated, read aloud, electronically signed, the list goes on. PDF files that have been generated for use as repro-ready artwork can be pre-pressed as well.

COMBINE FILES

Multiple PDFs can be combined into one single PDF package. This option—similar to joining paper documents together with a paper clip—allows a group of documents to be treated as one, while maintaining individual security settings and digital signatures. It's ideal for proposals, legal

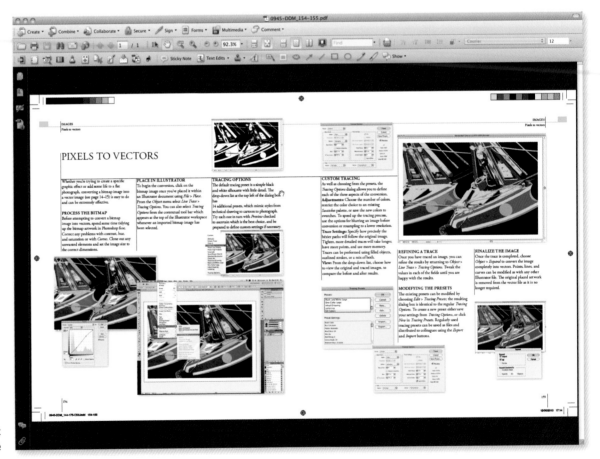

Acrobat interface

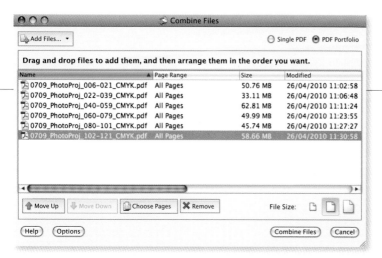

Acrobat's *Combine Files* palette

documents, project binders, and the like. In addition to this the function is very useful when different elements of a design project are put together by different members of a team. At the end of the workflow a design manager can combine all the constituent parts of a project together in one cohesive document for despatch to a printer.

REVIEW AND COMMENT

It's extremely easy to annotate a PDF using the built-in tools. Notes can be added as "sticky notes," and the properties of the notes, for example the color, can be changed for different types of comment. It's the digital equivalent of marking-up a laser, but it's a lot quicker to distribute your thoughts.

Furthermore, it's extremely easy to send your PDFs to colleagues or clients for review using the *Send for Shared Review* facility provided by the acrobat.com website.

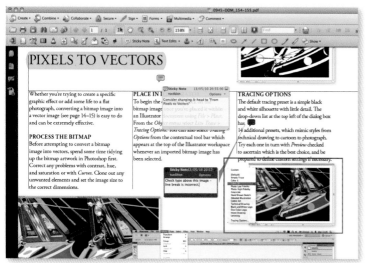

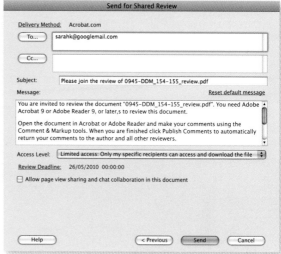

THE DREAMWEAVER WORKSPACE

Dreamweaver is the preferred production tool for most web designers. The program provides direct access to web-page code, and offers a huge amount of scope to those that take the time to learn its abilities. It is, at heart, a tool for assembling content created in other software. Use it to bring your design elements together in a web layout, but don't start without having a plan first.

WORKSPACE OVERVIEW

The main document window can be set to show your visual layout, the code that produces that layout, or both at once with a horizontally split display. This *Split* view option lets you edit the code in the top half and play with the layout in the bottom. When you start using Dreamweaver, two of the most important palette windows are

Insert and *Properties*, found just above and just below the document window. Another palette worth noting is the *Site* window, used when you set up a new site and add pages and media to it. This helps manage your different pages, the images you use, and the links from one page to another.

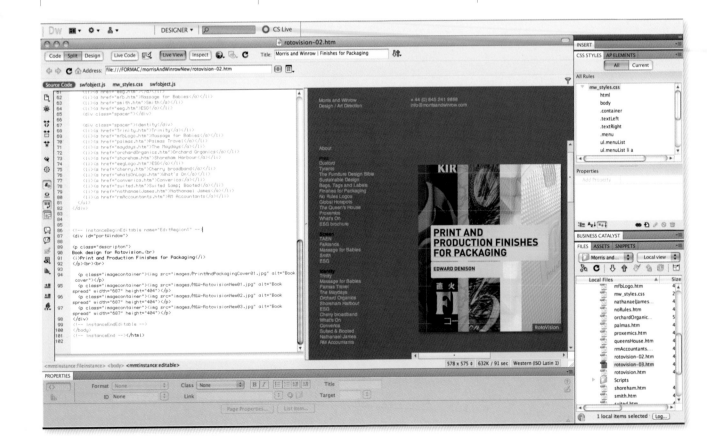

MAKING LAYOUTS

You can start with a blank page or with a ready-made structure. Choosing *File > New* opens the *New Document* window; here you'll find a long list of options in the *Layout* section.

When first creating layout structures in Dreamweaver, use the *Insert* toolbar. (Choose *Window > Insert* if it isn't visible.) With the *Layout* tab active, click in the *Design* view page and then click the *Draw Div* icon. Alternatively, drag it from the toolbar into your page where you want it to float. A "div"

is essentially a container that can be used to hold text, graphics, and anything else you like. You can resize it and move it around the page to suit your design vision.

Use the *Properties* palette to alter the properties of your page and anything that you select in it. (Choose *Window > Properties* if you can't see it.) The div container that you just created can be scaled and positioned numerically and given a fill color via the *Properties* palette.

INSERTING CONTENT

Switch the *Insert* toolbar to the *Common* tab to find buttons for inserting table structures (best reserved for handling formatted tabular data), images, Flash movies, and other items. Click the *Images* button (sixth from the left) and pick your web-ready image, or click the drop-down menu of the *Image* button and choose one of the image-related options.

Dreamweaver overview, *Assets* palette, and insert options

THE FLASH WORKSPACE

Flash has a special place in the heart of a great many web developers, since it opened up the possibility of developing rich media content through a relatively familiar design environment. That, however, is only scratching the surface of what this tool can do. Flash includes a complete programming language of its own, ActionScript 3, which makes it possible to create interactive content that displays on any web browser with the (free and widely installed) Flash player plugin. The files you work on in Flash are called .flas, while the versions you publish for the web—which can be placed in a web page using IMG tags just like a JPEG—are called .swfs and cannot be opened for editing. They are "published" by Flash, and it's also possible to create standalone applications, for example as an interface for an interactive CD-ROM.

WORKSPACE OVERVIEW

Given the breadth of possibilities Flash offers, and some of the amazing Flash designs you've seen on the internet, you'd be forgiven for being quite underwhelmed by the interface. At first glance, there isn't even a toolbox—don't worry, it's there, but by default it lives on the far right.

The important point is that what you're looking at is only ever the surface of Flash, and it looks and feels very much like any other vector graphic editor—Illustrator, for example. Only the timeline, beneath the stage, which allows you to create frame-based animations, hints at anything more.

BUILDING PROJECTS

As mentioned, Flash projects can be exported in a number of ways, but the classic one is a web graphic. As such you can open Flash and use the standard shape tools to draw a graphic, before saving it as a .swf. In practice,

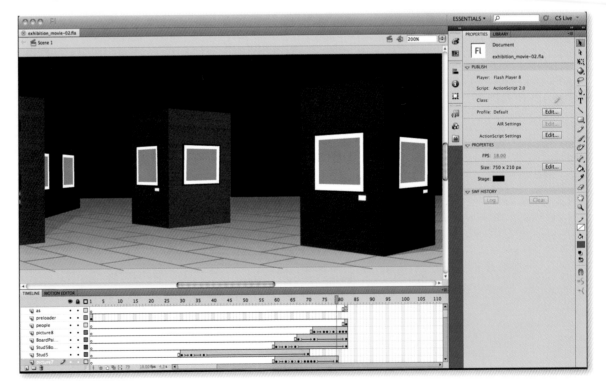

however, you're only likely to be using Flash if you want to create animated or interactive graphics, so there are some other considerations, and you'll be asked about these when you click *File > New....*

If you're creating a project for the web, choose Flash File (ActionSctipt 3.0) unless you have a good reason to use the older language. That might be familiarity with the older language, or the size of the installed base, but since Flash Player 9, the first to play AS3-based files, has been around since 2006 it is now installed in 99% of browsers.

The other options are for more specialist purposes; Adobe AIR is a platform for creating desktop software, and mobile will help you program Apps for a number of smart phones.

Once you've created your new file, you should set the pixel size using the *Modify > Document* command.

INTERACTIVITY

Working in an organized fashion is the key, and Flash will help you with that. The first part of this is the naming of various features on the stage so that they can be called and directed by the scripts. These are also logged in your *Library* panel so you can duplicate them, or in Flash-parlance, "create other instances" of them.

Flash will also keep you organized in the ActionScript window. You can add actions to frames on the timeline—it's best to create a separate layer and name it "actions"—then pop open the ActionScript window and simply start typing. Flash will format your code for you so you know it's going well, as well as providing a complete reference. This is

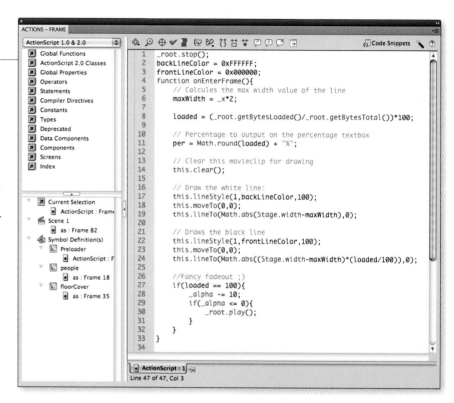

vital; if you're planning on programming in ActionScript—or any language, for that matter—it's crucial not to be proud about help files. No one can possibly be expected to remember all the functions and syntax in any language; the help pages should be referred to constantly to ensure you're using the (many) provided tools and functions correctly. Believe it or not, a lot of designers pick up scripting very fast, and come to love it.

KEYBOARD SHORTCUTS

Despite the improved interfaces of most applications, such as tabbed palettes, fly-out menus and contextual "ctrls," the most efficient way to work in any application is with keyboard shortcuts. Learn the ones you'll use the most to significantly speed up your workflow.

COMMON TO ALL APPLICATIONS

New	Ctrl/Cmd N
Open	Ctrl/Cmd O
Save	Ctrl/Cmd S
Save as	Shift/Ctrl/Cmd S
Print	Ctrl/Cmd P
Export PDF (in Creative Suite)	Ctrl/Cmd E
Undo	Ctrl/Cmd Z
Redo	Shift/Ctrl/Cmd Z
Select all	Ctrl/Cmd A
Select/deselect	Ctrl/Cmd Click
Cut	Ctrl/Cmd X
Copy	Ctrl/Cmd C
Paste	Ctrl/Cmd V
Zoom in	Ctrl/Cmd =
Zoom out	Ctrl/Cmd –
Close window	Ctrl/Cmd W
Quit	Ctrl/Cmd Q

QUARKXPRESS

Navigation

Zoom In	Ctrl ⇧ Click or Drag
Zoom Out	Ctrl ⌥ Click
Fit spread in window	⌘ ⌥ 0
Use page grabber	⌥ Drag
Change pages	⌥ Page down/Page up
To stop screen redraw	⌘ period
To force screen redraw	⌘ ⌥ period

Objects

Move object (item tool) 1pt	Any arrow key
Move object (item tool) 0.1pt	Any arrow key ⌥
Move picture (content tool) 1pt	Any arrow key
Move picture (content tool) 0.1pt	Any arrow key ⌥

Step and repeat	⌘ D
Select through stack of items	⌘ ⌥ ⇧ Click
Bring to front	F5
Bring forward one level	⌥ F5
Send to back	⇧ F5
Send backward one level	⌥ ⇧ F5

Text

Get text	⌘ E
Select whole word	Double click
Select whole line	Three clicks
Select whole paragraph	Four clicks
Select whole story	Five clicks
Select to end of text	⌘ ⌥ ⇧ Down arrow
Select to beginning of text	⌘ ⌥ ⇧ Up arrow
Increase font size by 1 point	⌘ ⌥ ⇧ >
Decrease font size by 1 point	⌘ ⌥ ⇧ <
Increase leading by 1 point	⌘ ⇧ "
Increase leading by 1/10 point	⌘ ⌥ ⇧ "
Decrease leading by 1 point	⌘ ⇧ :
Decrease leading by 1/10 point	⌘ ⌥ ⇧ :
Increase kerning/tracking by 10/200 em	⌘ ⇧ }
Increase kerning/tracking by 1/200 em	⌘ ⌥ ⇧ }
Decrease kerning/tracking by 10/200 em	⌘ ⇧ {
Decrease kerning/tracking by 1/200 em	⌘ ⌥ ⇧ {
Baseline shift up by 1 point	⌘ ⌥ ⇧ =
Baseline shift down by 1 point	⌘ ⌥ ⇧ –
Increase horizontal scaling by 5%	⌘]
Decrease horizontal scaling by 5%	⌘ [
Indent here	⌘ \
Right indent	⌥ →|
New line (without starting a new paragraph)	⇧ ↵
Inch marks (smart quotes checked)	Ctrl ⇧ "
Foot marks (smart quotes checked)	Ctrl '
Symbol font	⌘ ⌥ Q
Zapf Dingbats Font	⌘ ⌥ Z
Nonbreaking hyphen	⌘ =
Soft hyphen	⌘ –
Em dash	⌥ ⇧ –
En space	⌥ Space
Insert page number of previous text box	⌘ 2
Insert page number of current text box	⌘ 3
Insert page number of next text box	⌘ 4
Copy paragraph formats to selected text	⌥ ⇧ Click
Open Style Sheets Dialog Box	⌘ Click on style name
Display edit style sheet pop-up menu	Ctrl Click on style name
Apply No Style, then style sheet	⌥ Click on style name

Images

Get picture	⌘ E
Increase scaling by 5%	⌘ ⌥ ⇧ >
Decrease scaling by 5%	⌘ ⌥ ⇧ <
Scale box and contents	⌘ Drag
Constrain box shape and scale contents	⌘ ⇧ Drag
Maintain aspect ratio of box and contents	⌘ ⌥ ⇧ Drag
Scale box only, proportionally	⌥ ⇧ Drag
Center picture	⌘ ⇧ M
Fit picture to box	⌘ ⇧ F
Fit picture to box, maintaining aspect ratio	⌘ ⌥ ⇧ F

Miscellaneous

Show guides	F7
Snap to guides	⇧ F7
Move guide, when not using item tool	⌘ Click Drag guide
Delete ruler guides	⌥ Click on Ruler
Open modify dialog	Double click with item tool
Font usage	F13
Picture usage	⌥ F13
Drag and drop text	Ctrl ⌘ Drag
Drag and copy text	⇧ Ctrl ⌘ Drag

ADOBE INDESIGN

Tools

Selection Tool	V
Direct Selection Tool	A
Pen Tool	P
Type Tool	T
Pencil Tool	N
Line Tool	\
Rectangle Frame Tool	F
Rectangle Tool	M
Rotate Tool	R
Scale Tool	S
Shear Tool	O
Free Transform Tool	E
Eyedropper Tool	I
Gradient Tool	G
Button Tool	B
Scissors Tool	C
Hand Tool	H
Zoom Tool	Z

Navigation

Actual size	⌘ 1
Fit page to window	⌘ 0

Fit spread to window	⌥ ⌘ 0
Use page grabber	Space bar or ⌥
Next page	⇧ ‡
Next spread	⌥ ‡
Previous page	⇧ ‡
Previous spread	⌥ ‡

View

Show/hide baseline grid	⌥ ⌘ '
Show/hide document grid	⌘ '
Show/hide guides	⌘ ;
Snap to document grid	⇧ ⌘ '
Snap to guides	⇧ ⌘ ;
Show/hide frame edges	Ctrl ⌘ H
Show/hide text threads	⌥ ⌘ Y
High quality display	Ctrl ⌥ ⌘ H

Objects

Move object by default measurement	Any arrow key
Move and duplicate	⌥ Any arrow key
Move x10	⇧ Any arrow key
Move 1/10	⇧ ⌘ Any arrow key
Move 1/10 and duplicate	⌥ ⇧ ⌘ Any arrow key
Move x10 and duplicate	⌥ ⇧ Any arrow key
Step and repeat	⌥ ⌘ U
Select through stack of items	⌘ Click
Bring to front	⇧ ⌘]
Bring forward one level	⌘]
Send to back	⇧ ⌘ [
Send backward one level	⌘ [
Group	⌘ G
Ungroup	⇧ ⌘ G

Object editing

Place text/picture	⌘ D
Paste into	⌘ V
Increase image scale by 5%	⌥ ⌘ ,
Decrease image scale by 5%	⌥ ⌘ .
Increase font size by 1pt	⇧ ⌘ ,
Decrease font size by 1pt	⇧ ⌥ ⌘ .
Increase font size by 5pt	⌥ ⌘ ,
Decrease font size by 5pt	⌥ ⌘ .
Center content	⇧ ⌘ E
Fit content proportionally	⌥ ⇧ ⌘ E
Fit content to frame	⌥ ⌘ E
Fit frame to content	⌥ ⌘ C
Move to next word	⌘ Right arrow
Move to previous word	⌘ Left arrow
Move to start of the line	Home

Move to next paragraph	⌘ Down arrow
Move to previous paragraph	⌘ Up arrow
Reset horizontal text scaling	⇧ ⌘ X
Reset vertical text scale	⌥ ⇧ ⌘ X
Drop shadow	⌥ ⌘ M
Clipping path	⌥ ⇧ ⌘ K
Make compound path	⌘ 8

ADOBE ILLUSTRATOR

Tools

Selection	V
Direct selection	A
Magic wand	Y
Lasso	Q
Pen	P
Add anchor point	=
Delete anchor point	−
Convert anchor point	⇧ C
Type	T
Line Segment	\
Rectangle	M
Ellipse	L
Paintbrush	B
Pencil	N
Rotate	R
Reflect	O
Scale	S
Warp	⇧ R
Free transform	E
Symbol sprayer	⇧ S
Column graph	J
Mesh	U
Gradient	G
Eyedropper	I
Paint bucket	K
Slice	⇧ K
Scissors	C
Hand	H
Zoom	Z
Toggle Fill/Stroke	X
Swap Fill/Stroke	⇧ X

Navigation

Fit window	⌘ 0
Actual size	⌘ 1
Use page grabber	Space bar or ⌥

View

Show/hide guides	⌘ ;
Lock guides	⌥ ⌘ ;
Show grid	⌘ '
Snap to grid	⇧ ⌘ '
Snap to point	⌥ ⌘ '
Show/hide edges	⌘ H
Show/hide rulers	⌘ R
Show/hide bounding box	⇧ ⌘ B
Show/hide transparency grid	⇧ ⌘ D
Show/hide text threads	⇧ ⌘ Y
Preview	⌘ Y
Overprint preview	⌥ ⇧ ⌘ Y
Pixel preview	⌥ ⌘ Y

Objects

Move object by default measurement	Any arrow key
Move and duplicate	⌥ Any arrow key
Move x10	⇧ Any arrow key
Move x10 and duplicate	⌥ ⇧ Any arrow key
Select down through a stack of objects	⌥ ⌘ [
Select up through a stack of objects	⌥ ⌘]
Reselect	⌘ 6
Paste in front	⌘ F
Paste in back	⌘ B
Bring to front	⇧ ⌘]
Bring forward one level	⌘]
Send to back	⇧ ⌘ [
Send backward one level	⌘ [
Transform again	⌘ D
Transform each	⌥ ⇧ ⌘ D
Group	⌘ G
Ungroup	⇧ ⌘ G
Lock selection	⌘ 2
Unlock all	⌥ ⌘ 2
Hide selection	⌘ 3
Show all	⌥ ⌘ 3
Repeat pathfinder	⌘ 4
Make clipping-mask	⌘ 7
release clipping-mask	⌥ ⌘ 7
Make compound path	⌘ 8
Release compound path	⌥ ⌘ 8

Paths

Join	⌘ J
Average	⌥ ⌘ J
Average and join	⌥ ⇧ ⌘ J

KEYBOARD SHORTCUTS

PHOTOSHOP

Tools

Marquee tools	M
Move tool	V
Lasso tools	L
Magic wand tool	W
Crop tool	C
Slice tools	K
Healing brush/patch/color replacement tool	J
Brush/pencil tool	B
Stamp tools	S
History brush tools	Y
Eraser tools	E
Gradient/paint bucket tool	G
Blur/sharpen tools	R
Dodge/burn/sponge tool	O
Path/direct selection tool	A
Type tools	T
Pen tools	P
Rectangle/ellipse/polygon/line/shape tools	U
Notes/audio annotation tools	N
Eyedropper/color sampler/measure tools	I
Hand tool	H
Zoom tool	Z
Default colors	D
Switch foreground/background colors	X
Toggle quick mask	Q
Toggle screen modes	F
Toggle preserve transparency	/
Decrease brush size	[
Increase brush size	]
Decrease brush hardness	{
Increase brush hardness	}
Previous Brush	,
Next Brush	.
First brush	<
Last brush	>

View

Proof colors	⌘ Y
Gamut warning	⇧ ⌘ Y
Fit on screen	⌘ 0
Actual pixels	⌥ ⌘ 0
Show/hide target path	⇧ ⌘ H
Show/hide grid	⌘ '
Show/hide guides	⌘ ;
Show/hide rulers	⌘ R
Lock guides	⌥ ⌘ ;

Select

Deselect	⌘ D
Reselect	⇧ ⌘ D
Inverse	⇧ ⌘ I
Add to current selection	⇧ and selection tool
Subtract from current selection	⌥ and selection tool
Refine mask	⌥ ⌘ R

Editing

Paste in place	⇧ ⌘ V
Paste into	⌥ ⇧ ⌘ V
Fill	⇧ F5
Free transform	⌘ T
Transform again	⇧ ⌘ T
Last filter	⌘ F
History step forward	⇧ ⌘ Z
History step backward	⌥ ⌘ Z
Extract	⌥ ⌘ X
Lens correction	⇧ ⌘ R
Liquify	⇧ ⌘ X

Adjustments

Image size	⌥ ⌘ I
Canvas size	⌥ ⌘ C
Levels	⌘ L
Auto tone	⇧ ⌘ L
Auto contrast	⌥ ⇧ ⌘ L
Auto color	⇧ ⌘ B
Curves	⌘ M
Color balance	⌘ B
Hue/Saturation	⌘ U
Desaturate	⇧ ⌘ U
Invert	⌘ I
Open dialog while retaining last settings	Add ⌥ to shortcut

Layers

New layer	⇧ ⌘ N
Layer via copy	⌘ J
Layer via cut	⇧ ⌘ J
Merge layers	⌘ E
Merge visible	⇧ ⌘ E
Bring to front	⇧ ⌘]
Bring forward	⌘]
Send backward	⌘ [
Send to back	⇧ ⌘ [
Create clipping mask	⌥ ⌘ G
Release clipping mask	⌥ ⇧ ⌘ G

DREAMWEAVER

Editing

Find and replace	⌘ F
Insert line break 	⇧ Return
Insert nonbreaking space	⌘ ⇧ Space
Add selected items to library	⌘ ⇧ B
Toggle design view and code editor	⌥ →
Toggle property inspector	⌘ ⇧ J
Indent	⌘ ⌥]
Outdent	⌘ ⌥ [
Format > None	⌘ 0
Paragraph format	⌘ ⇧ P
Apply Headings 1 to 6	⌘ 1 to 6
Edit style sheet	⌘ ⇧ E

View

Toggle standard view	⌘ ⇧ F6
Toggle layout view	⌘ F6
Toggle live data mode	⌘ R
Toggle live data	⌘ ⇧ R
Toggle design and code view	⌘ '
Toggle visual aids	⌘ ⇧ I
Server debug	ctrl ⇧ G
Refresh design view	F5
Rulers	⌘ ⌥ R
Show/hide grid	⌘ ⌥ G
Snap to grid	⌘ ⌥ ⇧ G
Head content	⌘ ⇧ W
Selection properties	⌘ ⇧ J
Page properties	⌘ J

Coding

Validate markup	⇧ F6
Open quick tag editor	⌘ T
Open snippets panel	⇧ F9
Show code hints	⌘ Space
Indent code	⌘ ⇧ >
Outdent code	⌘ ⇧ <
Insert tag	⌘ E
Edit tag (in design view)	⌘ F5
Select parent tag	⌘ [
Select child	⌘]
Balance Braces	⌘ '
Toggle breakpoint	⌘ ⌥ B
Go to line	ctrl ,

Images

Insert image	ctrl ⌥ I
Change image source attribute	Double click
Edit image in external editor	ctrl Double click

Frames

Select a frame	⌥ Click in frame
Select next frame or frameset	⌥ Right Arrow
Select previous frame or frameset	⌥ Left Arrow
Select parent frameset	⌥ Up Arrow
Select first child frame or frameset	⌥ Down Arrow

Tables

Insert table	ctrl ⌥ T
Select table (with cursor inside table)	ctrl A
Merge selected cells	ctrl ⌥ M
Split cell	ctrl ⌥ S
Increase column span	ctrl ⇧]
Decrease column span	ctrl ⇧ [

Layers

Select a layer	ctrl ⇧ Click
Select and move layer	⇧ ctrl Drag
Add or remove layer from selection	⇧ Click layer
Resize selected layer by pixels	ctrl Arrow keys
Resize selected layer by snapping increment	ctrl ⇧ arrow keys
Make same width	ctrl ⇧ 7
Make same height	ctrl ⇧ 9

Hyperlinks

Check links sitewide	ctrl F8
Check selected links	⇧ F8
Create hyperlink	ctrl L
Remove hyperlink	ctrl ⇧ L

Previewing and debugging in browsers

Preview in primary browser	F12
Preview in secondary browser	⇧ F12
Debug in primary browser	⌥ F12
Debug in secondary browser	ctrl ⌥ F12

Site map

View site map	⌥ F8
View site files	F8
View as root	ctrl ⇧ R
Link to new file	ctrl ⇧ N
Link to existing file	ctrl ⇧ K
Change link	ctrl L
Remove link	ctrl ⇧ L
Show/Hide link	ctrl ⇧ Y
Show page titles	ctrl ⇧ T

Site management

Connect/Disconnect	ctrl ⌥ ⇧ F5
Refresh	F5
Create new file	ctrl ⇧ N
Create new folder	ctrl ⌥ ⇧ N
Open selection	ctrl ⇧ ⌥ O
Rename file	F2
Get selection from remote site	ctrl ⇧ D
Put selection on remote site	ctrl ⇧ U
Check out	ctrl ⌥ ⇧ D
Check in	ctrl ⌥ ⇧ U

Panels/palettes

Insert bar	ctrl F2
Properties	ctrl F3
Answers	⌥ F1
CSS styles	⇧ F11
HTML styles	ctrl F11
Behaviors	⇧ F3
Tag inspector	F9
Snippets	⇧ F9
Reference	⇧ F1
Databases	ctrl ⇧ F10
Bindings	ctrl F10
Server behaviors	ctrl F9
Components	ctrl F7
Site	F8
Assets	F11

Using this reference with a PC

These shortcuts are shown using Mac symbols. If you are using a PC replace ⌘ with Ctrl, and ⌥ with Alt.

Creative Suite window commands

The follow commands work across the entire Creative Suite range of applications, but on a Mac may clash with your current Exposé settings. Exposé can be modified under System Preferences.

Actions	Opt+F9
Align	⇧ F7
Appearance	⇧ F6
Attributes	F11
Brushes	F5
Color	F6
Gradient	F9
Graphic styles	⇧ F5
Info	F8
Layers	F7
Pathfinder	⇧ F9
Stroke	F10
Symbols	⇧ F11
Transform	⇧ F8
Transparency	⇧ F10
Character	⌘ T
OpenType	⌥ ⇧ ⌘ T
Paragraph	⌥ ⌘ T
Tabs	⇧ ⌘ T

Customizing shortcuts

Many applications include the option to customize keyboard shortcuts. InDesign even has a set of presets to mimic the shortcuts in QuarkXPress, useful for those who regularly use both applications.

SETTING APPLICATION DEFAULTS

A digital environment with a familiar and well-organized user interface is a real time-saver. Many applications allow you to go beyond the usual general preferences dialog window to a point where tool, document, and object settings can be set up exactly as you want them.

INTERFACE

The first step is to open an application, but not a document. Personalize the palettes and toolbars to suit your needs—if you rarely use the *Transparency* palette in InDesign, for example, then hide it, and so on. Double-clicking on many tools will allow their behavior to be defined—in Photoshop choose *Window > Tool Presets*. Keyboard shortcuts have largely been standardized across the CS applications, but these can be user-defined to replicate those from other applications, and most mainstream design applications allow customization of the menu configuration for different workspaces.

TYPE

The default font on creating a document will vary between applications, and while a standard font such as Times or Helvetica is normal, it's possible to change the default type to your preferred font and input values for point size, leading, and so on. When using InDesign, insert your preferred default values into the *Control* palette; when using QuarkXPress, insert them into the *Measurements* palette. These choices will be the defaults whenever a new document is created. The same goes for colors, strokes, and runarounds; in fact, anything with a definable value can be given a default setting, but remember to enter those values without opening a document.

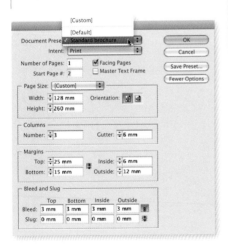

Document Presets

InDesign and Photoshop allow you to add your own selections to the list of Document Presets. From the *New Document* dialog window, input values before saving to the preset list. All applications will store default settings when they are added without opening a document, and this applies to preferences as well as interface and tool settings.

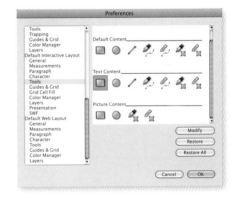

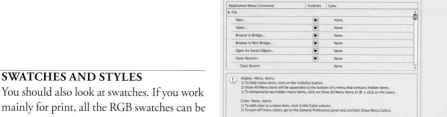

SWATCHES AND STYLES

You should also look at swatches. If you work mainly for print, all the RGB swatches can be removed from the palette. Add any often used CMYK colors, plus any corporate spot colors or recurring colors such as a rich black. Take the time to name the swatches to avoid confusion, and ensure all the colors will separate properly. *Character*, *Paragraph*, and *Object* styles can also be treated in the same way—remove what you don't need and add any style you often return to.

RESTORING DEFAULTS

Once palettes, tools, and defaults are as you want them, it's worth making a duplicate of the application's preferences file, or to save the Workspace or Palette Set. These preferences can be transferred between computers, and should there be a problem with the application, it's a simple matter of replacing the preferences file with the archived copy to restore any settings from a previous installation.

DOCUMENT DEFAULTS

As an alternative, you can set defaults on single documents by entering values without an object selected. This can be useful for making templates and other repeatable documents. If you choose body text as a default text style for example, it is a simple matter for anyone to click, start typing, and be confident that the correct font, size, and colors are being used.

Organizing color swatches
Mistakes with color mixing can be minimized with a personalized *Swatches* palette; remove what you don't need and add what you do. You can do the same for *Character, Paragraph*, and *Object Styles*.

Setting defaults for documents and templates
Settings can be defined at document level by inputting values without having an element selected. These become the default choices for any new objects.

Creative Suite workspaces
Adobe Creative Suite users can define multiple custom workspaces for different types of jobs. Menu items, keyboard shortcuts, and palette locations can be set and saved for later use or for transfer to other workstations with the same software installed. QuarkXPress users are also able to save Palette Sets for use in different workspaces.

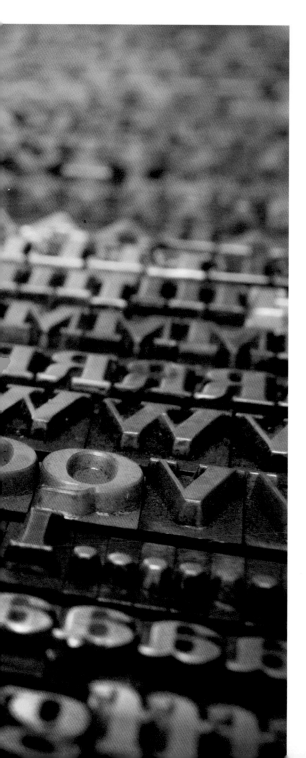

Type

With few exceptions, designers use some form of type everyday. Type is a very powerful communication tool and by making a well-considered choice of body text and display face, a designer can suggest a range of moods, emotions, or tones. In a way, it's only in the event of an ill-conceived selection of a typeface that the viewer really notices the impact that an inappropriate choice can have—using a childlike and quirky typeface for a business report, for example, would be a disaster, regardless of the content.

This chapter begins by explaining some of the jargon of typography and breaking down a character set into its component parts. Guidelines for choosing display and body text fonts are given, along with tips for putting them to use—how wide should a column be, how much space between lines, and so on. Practical tutorials explain how to manipulate and control your type within the major layout applications, how to set up your type exactly as you want it, and then streamline the process for future use with style sheets.

Finally, technical considerations when choosing typefaces are discussed, and the strengths of each font format are laid bare. The many problems that can occur between the designer's desktop and the printed sheet are dealt with and solutions offered.

THE ANATOMY OF TYPE

A good tradesman understands exactly how to use all the tools and materials they have at their disposal in order to produce the best results. It's the same for graphic designers. To understand typography properly, it's important to have a good working knowledge of letterforms and their properties.

WHAT IS A FONT?

A font is the complete set of characters, or glyphs, that make up a typeface. That means all the regular letter and number characters, punctuation marks, all additional symbols and special characters, and the often numerous italic and bold weights. Strictly speaking, there's a distinction to be made between a "font" and a "typeface." Typeface designates the visual appearance or style of type, while font designates a specific version of a typeface. Therefore 12pt Garamond is a font, and 14pt Garamond is a different font, but both are the same typeface. The term font is from the middle French *fonte*, which contextually means "[something that has been] melt[ed]," harking back to the days of hot-metal typesetting.

FONT METRICS

All fonts when set are aligned horizontally along a *baseline*. They have a *cap height*—the distance from the baseline to the top of an upper-case letter—and an *x-height*—the distance between the top of the lower-case "x" and the baseline. *Ascenders* and *descenders* are the parts of a font's character, which correspondingly extend above the x-height to the cap height, or below the baseline. These measurements are called the *ascent* and the *descent*. Along with other distinctive features of the design of the typeface family, these characteristics play a significant role in defining the visual impact and flavor of any one font.

Terminology

The terminology used for different components of a type character is extensive, and it is important that you are aware of the commonly used terms. This diagram indicates the main naming conventions.

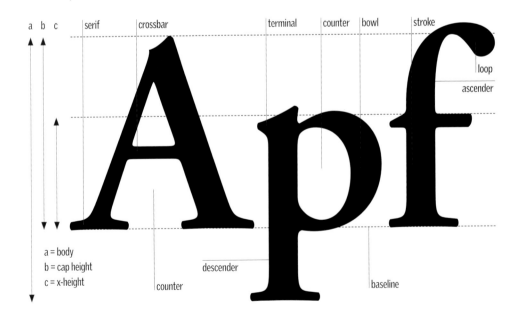

a b c   serif   crossbar   terminal   counter   bowl   stroke

loop

ascender

a = body
b = cap height
c = x-height

descender

counter

baseline

Font Font Font

The whole of this line is set in the same font size, 21 point.

This example clearly illustrates that the "size" at which different fonts appear varies considerably across different font families. For the font spotters among you, we've used, in order of appearance, Adobe Garamond Pro, Griffith Gothic Regular, Rockwell Regular, Helvetica Medium, Bauer Bodoni Roman, Bell Gothic Bold, Centaur Regular, Compacta Roman, Weiss Medium, BaseTwelve SerifB, ITC Fenice Light, OCRA, Sabon Roman, and lastly, FoundryFormSans BookOSF. The main factor that affects how large a font appears is its x-height (see diagram below left). The larger the x-height, the larger the font appears in relation to others.

If type is to read well when set, the intercharacter spacing must be visually correct. The technique used to adjust this spacing is known as kerning. This can involve either reducing or enlarging the space between certain pairs of characters. Kerning is particularly useful when setting type at larger sizes, when the spacing is more obvious visually. Shown here are some of the character pairs that often require kerning.

AT	AY	AV	AW	Ay	Av	Aw
FA	TO	TA	Ta	Te	To	Ti
Tr	Tu	Ty	Tw	Ts	Tc	LT
LY	LV	LW	Ly	PA	VA	Va
Ve	Vo	Vi	Vr	Vu	Vy	RT
RV	RW	RY	Ry	WA	Wa	We
Wo	Wi	Wr	Wu	Wy	YA	Ya
Ye	Yo	Yi	Yp	Yq	Yu	Yv

CHOOSING A TYPEFACE

Typefaces, or fonts as they are often called, are probably the most fundamentally important ingredient available to a graphic designer. The appearance, and therefore the "feel," of any piece of graphic design you produce will be governed largely by your choice of font. There's now such an enormous choice available to designers that in some ways the task of choosing the right font has become harder. The reality is that, among the thousands of available choices, only a relative handful are actually of a quality suitable for use when engaging in professional design work.

For this reason it's worth spending time putting together a list of fonts that you feel are first and foremost well designed, but also appropriate for the various types of project that you generally work on. This will help when choosing a suitable font to use at the beginning of a new project as you won't have to trawl through so many choices to arrive at the most appropriate option. This is not to say that you should subsequently restrict yourself to just those choices, but it will help you to focus during the early stages of a new design brief. If, after some deliberation, you feel it's appropriate to widen the range of fonts to choose from, go ahead and do so.

TYPES OF FONT
Sans serif fonts

Sans serif fonts lack the counterstrokes of serif fonts, and are visually much cleaner and modern in feel. The punchier look of sans serif fonts means they are good for large headlines or for short runs of printed text, such as in a table or over well-spaced paragraphs of limited length. It's the more uniform nature of sans serif fonts that make them a little harder to read as the individual characters are visually less distinct. Having said that, some sans serif fonts do work well in body copy, particularly if they have a generously sized x-height. They are also easier to read on low-resolution screens than serif fonts because fewer pixels are required to display them, so often appear on websites that specify the display font.

Helvetica 45
Grotesque
Eurostile
FoundryForm
Dax Condensed

Serif fonts

These are easily identified because of the short serifs, or counterstrokes, at the ends of ascenders, descenders, stems, and so on. Serif fonts are generally regarded as the best choice if an air of authority is appropriate to your design as they are more classical in feel than sans serif fonts. Serif fonts also tend to be easier to read for long periods so are the most popular choice for novels or newspapers. I've heard it argued in the past that serif fonts look more old-fashioned than sans-serif fonts. For some font families this may well be true, but it is a generalisation and really doesn't stand up to test.

Bembo Regular
Egyptienne 55
Meridien Roman
Modern No 216
Memphis Medium

CHOOSING A TYPEFACE

Script fonts

Script fonts are closely related to calligraphic type forms, and are generally not suitable for body text due to their complex letterforms. They have their uses, however, and are normally used for ornamentation.

Decorative or display fonts

Display fonts are rarely suitable for use as body text as, by their very nature, they are not so easy to read at smaller point sizes. They can work well when used for headlines, but must obviously complement the font chosen for the body text that follows. If you want to make a typographic statement, on a poster or a cover for example, a display font may be a suitable choice.

Künstler Script

Pepita Regular

Snell Roundhand

Radio AM

Linoscript Medium

AG Book Stencil

Armada Bold

Caslon Open Face

Dot Matrix 2

MASON BOLD

Frankfurter

SOME DESIGN RULES FOR CHOOSING AND USING FONTS

• Always think carefully about who your design is aimed at when choosing a font. The demographic of the assumed readership is very important, not just in terms of the styling, but also in terms of how suitable the font will be for reasons of clarity. Older readers or children merit special consideration in this area.

• Think carefully about font sizing, and keep the relationships between headlines, text headings, body text, and captions distinct.

• Never use dozens of fonts when two or three fonts or font weights will do the job.

• Take care when combining serif and sans serif, and test combinations of differing fonts to find which work well together for you. Keep notes of the best combinations for future reference in the form of type sheets.

• Make sure that any font families that you choose have sufficient weights and styles for your project. Not all families include italics for example—an essential ingredient if you are engaged in any kind of book design where names must be picked out in italic.

• When designing with more than one font family, compare the physical characteristics of each to make sure they combine well. Look at the body width, cap- and x-height, and at how the relative weights of the fonts compare in terms of emphasis.

FONT FORMATS

There are a number of widely used yet incompatible font formats—historically making font selection full of potential disaster. While modern operating systems, and more advanced and flexible font formats have made it simpler to choose the right format for your setup, it's useful to know what's available.

Purchasing fonts

All major type vendors now have an online presence and offer their products in all available formats for Mac or Windows compatibility. OpenType formats are now widely available, and are a wise investment due to their compatibility across platforms and because of their greatly expanded character sets.

Postscript Type 1

During the mid-1980s, Adobe's development of the Postscript Type 1 format was an important aspect of the desktop-publishing revolution. Type 1 fonts consist of a printer font (vector) and screen font (bitmap)—for the font to work properly both are required. When one of these components is missing, jagged or replacement fonts may be displayed.

Mac and PC versions of Postscript Type 1 fonts are not multi-platform so if your workflow contains both Mac and PCs you will need two versions of the font files, ideally from the same foundry and bought at the same time to minimize differences between the two systems. Despite the many advances in System development since the early days of desktop publishing, Type 1 fonts still function on the newest platforms, but beware of occasional changes to kerning and/or baseline positioning if you switch systems.

Multiple Master

Multiple Master fonts are still found lingering on some legacy systems and were an extension of Adobe's Postscript Type 1 format, but have now been superseded by the much newer OpenType format. Their advantage over other formats was due to the inclusion of a matrix of options within a single font file. This meant users could create a range of typeface styles of different widths, weights, and proportions without compromising the quality of the original characters, all with one Multiple Master font. Fonts in this format are no longer commercially available from regular sources.

TrueType

Apple and Microsoft launched the TrueType format in the early 1990s. Both screen and printer fonts are combined into a single file making them less likely to become corrupted when compared with Type 1 fonts. Many system fonts are TrueType, and a TTF file will work on both Windows and Mac OS X systems.

TrueType fonts include spacing and hinting information, and support a character set of up to 65,000 glyphs, but in reality most foundries include just the western character sets. Despite the potential of TrueType fonts, they are not widely used by professional graphic designers because they can be problematic when exported to the PDF/X format. There are ways around these problems but it is safer to go for the Postscript or OpenType options.

OpenType

Announced in 1996, and a collaboration between Microsoft and Apple, OpenType fonts are the most modern of the formats available. OpenType fonts contain all the information required in a single file, and the same file will work on both Mac OS X and Windows 2000/XP, making them ideal for multiplatform workflows. Up to 65,536 glyphs can be included in an OpenType font, many include language variations, punctuation, ligatures, alternate characters, and swashes.

Applications need to be Unicode compliant, a standard for the consistent display and usage of character sets across all computer platforms, in order to use OpenType fonts. Versions of QuarkXPress earlier than 7.0 do not support OpenType.

Mixing formats

While there are no barriers against installing Postscript, TrueType, and OpenType fonts on the same system, having the same font (or even a font with the same name) in more than one format can cause conflicts which cause fonts to become inactive. A common example of this is Helvetica Neue on Mac OS X, which is installed in the system font library in the TrueType format, and often installed by designers as a Postscript or OpenType font elsewhere. The best solution is to use a font manager, such as Apple's Font Book, to ensure only one version at a time is available.

Glyphs

These two glyph palettes from InDesign show the character sets from the Postscript Type 1 and OpenType versions of Myriad and Myriad Pro respectively. The extended character set of the OpenType font shows the full range of options, previously only available by purchasing "expert" fonts in addition to the regular character sets.

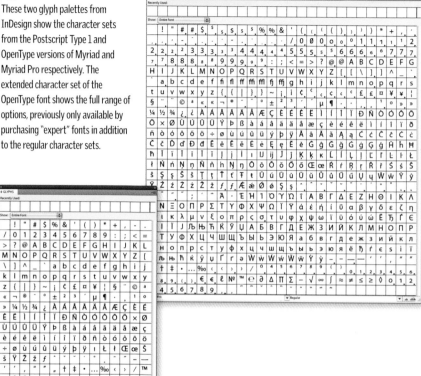

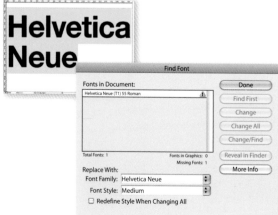

MANAGING TYPE ON A MAC

If you use Mac OS X there are several locations where fonts are installed, and each of these folders sits within a specific hierarchy in terms of activation. Also, it's essential that certain fonts are installed correctly if OS X is to function, so be careful not to delete or move any of these. The following list is a breakdown of each of these locations.

Local Domain/Library/Fonts
Installed fonts that must be available to all users should be placed in this folder. All applications running under OS X will have access to these fonts.

User Domain/Users/[Your user name]/ Library/Fonts
Installed fonts available only to the user logged on to the system should be placed in this folder. Once again, all applications running under OS X will have access to these fonts. Fonts installed using Font Book (see opposite) can be copied directly to this location.

System Domain/System/Library/Fonts
This folder contains fonts used by the operating system and it's important that required fonts are not removed. The required fonts are shown in the accompanying screen shot to the left. If you are keen to pare down the list of fonts displayed by running applications, non-essential fonts can be removed from the folder.

Classic Domain/System Folder/Fonts
This folder contains fonts linked specifically with the Classic environment, which is no longer support by newer Intel Macs and will only run on Macs using a PowerPC processor. Again, the essential fonts must not be removed, but others can be deleted if you wish to cut down the font lists displayed by applications. The required fonts are shown in the second screen shot to the right.

Applications fonts/Library/ Application Support
As part of their installation procedure, applications sometimes install their own collections of fonts, some of which are essential for correct functionality. Adobe supply a large number of fonts with the Creative Suite (not all essential) which are placed in an *Adobe/Fonts* folder inside *Application Support*. These fonts are available only to the applications that installed them.

Duplicate fonts can be stored in different folders, but it is not recommended. However, if this is the case the hierarchy in which the above folders activate fonts is as follows:

1. **Applications fonts**
2. **User fonts**
3. **Local fonts**
4. **System fonts**
5. **Classic fonts (PowerPC Macs only)**

FONT ACTIVATION

Font Book is the font management tool supplied as part of OS X since version 10.3. It's a fairly basic utility, and doesn't offer as many features as provided by third-party applications, but it does help resolve issues with duplicate fonts. Font Book can also validate installed fonts, and allows you to create font "sets" for specific projects that you can switch on and off as required. Font Book is useful for anyone who does not require a more heavy-duty, third-party, font-management solution.

Extensis provide the applications most familiar to Mac users, in the shape of the much improved Suitcase Fusion 2 and Universal Type Server 2, both of which offer robust auto-activation functionality via plug-ins for fonts used with InDesign, Illustrator, and QuarkXPress.

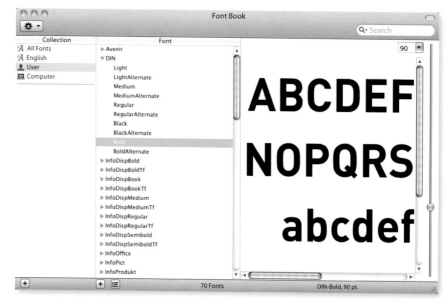

The main application windows for font-management tools Font Book (above) and Suitcase Fusion 2

MANAGING TYPE ON A PC

Installing fonts on to a Windows system is managed through the Control Panel. Upon installation, font files will be copied to the Fonts folder on your hard drive for use by the system.

Installing fonts

To begin, from the *Start* menu select *Control Panel* and then the *Appearance and Themes* category. From the *See Also* panel at the left of this screen choose *Fonts*. From the *File* menu select *Install New Font*. Navigate to the drive and folder that contain the fonts you want to add. Select the fonts, using the Ctrl key to select more than one, then click OK. You can also simply open up the font folder and drag the fonts into it to install them.

Uninstalling fonts

Follow the procedure for installing fonts, up to the point of choosing *Fonts* from the *See Also* panel. Now select the fonts you want to remove from the list, using Ctrl to select more than one. Either move the fonts out of the folder, choose *Delete* from the *File* menu, or simply press Delete, to remove them permanently.

Activating fonts

On older Windows machines, there is no need to activate fonts installed on a PC as fonts are always on. Windows 7 makes it possible to deactivate and reactivate a font without deleting it from the system, by right-clicking on its three-letter preview and choosing *Hide* or (if it's already grayed out) *Show* from the font's pop-up menu.

Protected fonts

Windows File Protection runs as a background process on Windows and monitors certain files. It prevents the unauthorized replacement of essential system files; when it detects that a protected file has been changed, the original is restored. Protected files include the following fonts that ship with Windows: Micross.ttf, Tahoma.ttf, Tahomabd.ttf, Dosapp.fon, Fixedsys.fon, Modern.fon, Script.fon, and Vgaoem.fon.

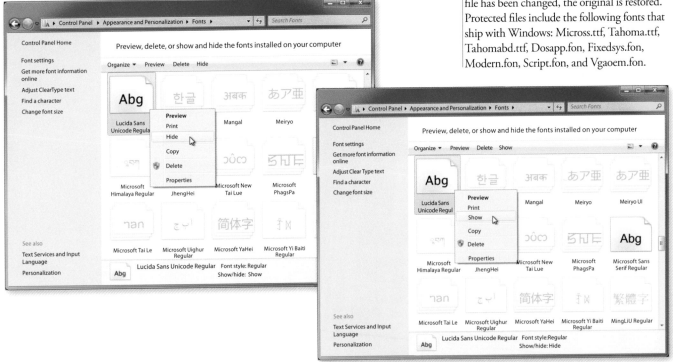

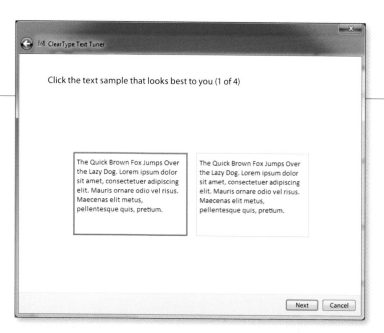

ClearType

Windows XP has a system-wide, font-rendering and smoothing application called ClearType. Using sub-pixel rendering, ClearType can greatly enhance the appearance of type on flat-panel screens. Download the ClearType Tuner PowerToy from http://download.microsoft.com to activate and fine-tune your ClearType settings, through the *Appearance and Themes* control panel.

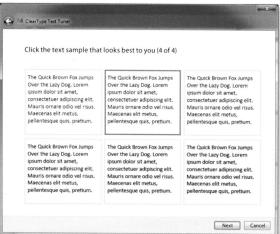

Control panels for installing, uninstalling, and controlling the on-screen appearance of fonts

MANIPULATING TYPE

Today, type controls are pretty much standard across most design and layout applications—in fact the Creative Suite (CS) applications have almost identical controls. There are differences when it comes to controlling the finer parts of your type, and this is where the strengths and weaknesses of each application really show through.

Character controls

Font point size, leading, kerning, tracking, and baseline shift are controlled through the Character palette in CS applications, or the Measurements palette in QuarkXPress. Most controls are obvious and require little explanation: simply type a value, or click the arrows to increase or decrease a value. Fonts can be distorted using the controls for horizontal scaling, vertical scaling, and skew, or by creating faux bold and italics. Generally, these tricks should be avoided as it's not good typographic practice to significantly alter the shape of a font's characters—it's far better to select one with the full range of widths and weights.

Difference in increments

Users of QuarkXPress and InDesign (or other CS applications) will notice minor differences when manipulating type between the two applications, with the most noticeable difference being kerning units. QuarkXPress kerns in units that are 1/200 of an em, InDesign kerns in a much finer 1/1000 of an em. Typing QuarkXPress values directly into InDesign will result in overtight text; the simple solution is to change InDesign's kerning value to 20/1000 em in the Units & Increments preferences.

Advanced kerning

While the basic Character palette has ample controls for managing the space between individual pairs of characters, there are further tools for automatically removing ugly gaps or clashes. It's achieved using the *Optical Kerning* feature in the CS applications. Rather than using the fonts in-built kerning tables (known as metrics) to handle the spacing of letters, the software will take over and adjust the kerning based upon shape and aesthetics. While not always perfect, visible improvements are often apparent, especially at larger point sizes.

QuarkXPress has had a similar feature for a long time, but it's less well known and often overlooked. *Kerning Table Edit* under the *Utilities* menu makes it possible to customize

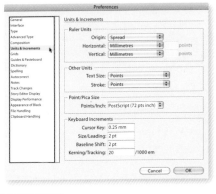

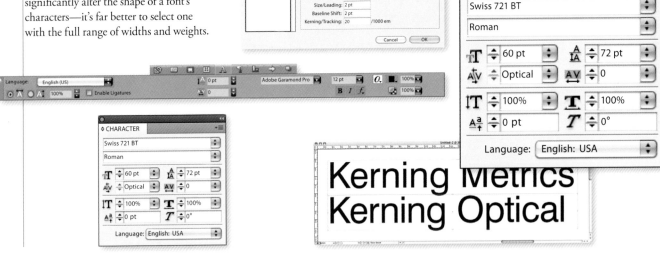

a kerning table. Changing a value in *Kerning Table Edit* will affect every instance of the character pair in the document, whilst the original font file will remain unchanged.

Paragraph controls

To go beyond manipulating individual letters and words to styling whole blocks of text, use the *Paragraph* palette in InDesign, or the

Paragraph Attributes dialog in QuarkXPress by going through *Style > Formats*. Alignment of text, either range left, right, centered, or justified, is controlled using buttons or pull-down menus, as is the option to lock text to the baseline grid (see below). Indents to the first line, last line, or paragraph can be added using the appropriate fields, along with spaces before and after each paragraph— very useful for making a list more readable.

Drop caps can be added by specifying the character depth and number of characters, although for particularly large drop caps it is usually better to set a single letter with a manually adjusted text wrap.

Baseline grid

Any document with large amounts of text set over multiple columns will benefit from having a baseline grid. Each column of text, and the lines within, will have the option to automatically line up with each other, demonstrated by the blue rules shown here, creating a neater look without the need for precise measuring. Once the leading of your text has been decided, go to the application

preferences and after setting the position of the first line, transfer the leading information to the baseline grid settings. Baseline grids are usually described in millimeters, while leading is in points, but you can input the data in any form of measurement and the software will perform the necessary conversion calculations. As mentioned above, text can be locked to sit on a baseline grid by clicking the icon in the *Paragraph* controls.

Left and above: Character palettes and kerning controls
Right: Paragraph controls
Far right: Baseline grid controls

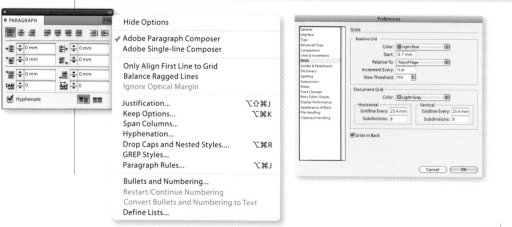

MANIPULATING TYPE

Balancing ragged columns

Justification will adjust word spacing, letter spacing, and glyph scaling (see pages 58–9) to fit text neatly within lines. Resist the urge to give the software more range with the minimum and maximum values, or text full of gaps and distorted letter shapes will appear.

Hyphenation is another method of creating tidy columns of text, breaking words with hyphens, and wrapping the remainder of the word to the next line. Parameters for controlling the frequency of hyphens, the length of the words in which they can appear, and where within the column, allow type to be controlled very precisely. Hyphenation is used less frequently today due to more advanced microtypographic controls.

InDesign shows its true strength with the optional *Adobe Paragraph Composer* and the *Balance Ragged Lines* option. Rather than looking at each line of text in isolation, the entire paragraph is studied and line breaks are adjusted dynamically to create the most visually pleasing text shapes. The results are not always perfect, and the feature can be switched off if preferred.

Vertical alignment

Vertical alignment of text is linked to the object in which the text is placed, such as to the top, middle, or bottom of a text frame. Access the controls using *Object > Text Frame Options* in InDesign, or *Modify > Text* in QuarkXPress. Each side of the frame can have a different indent, in addition to and separate from any paragraph indents already set. Vertical alignment can be set to top, center, bottom, or justified—although irregular shaped boxes or intruding text wraps will cause this setting to default to top alignment.

The first line of text within the box can also be offset, to allow for irregularly spaced headers. InDesign adds controls for defining which part of the font is used for measuring

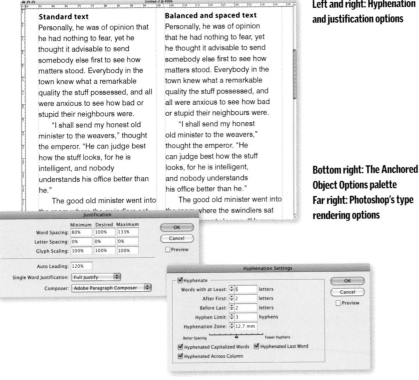

Left and right: Hyphenation and justification options

Bottom right: The Anchored Object Options palette
Far right: Photoshop's type rendering options

the offset—the cap height, x-height, or leading for example. Additionally each text box can have its own, and unique, baseline grid. Similar to the document baseline grid described previously, the custom baseline can also be set relative to the box, page, or margins, making it very flexible and perfect when working with large box-outs.

Embedding graphics

Adding a graphic to a line of text, so it reflows with the copy and remains relative to the lines of text is deceptively simple. With the object tool use Cmd/Ctrl+C to copy the object, switch to the *Text* tool and place the cursor in the correct position before using Cmd/Ctrl+V to place the object as a glyph. Once in place there are simple controls for adjusting the position relative to the surrounding text. In addition many of the regular type controls can be used with the object as well. Use *Text Wrap* or *Runaround* to knock text away from the graphic as normal. InDesign has additional controls for anchoring the object relative to the spine of the document, frame, columns, or margins.

Type on a line

Most applications support type flowing along a line or the edge of an object. The relevant tools in InDesign, Illustrator, and QuarkXPress are fairly straightforward, and provide most options that the average layout might require; click on a line with the *Type on a Path* tool to set the start point, insert your text, and choose how you wish the text to orientate itself against the path's direction. Options allow you to set how the type reacts to curves in the baseline, which part of the text is aligned to the path, and even to flip the text completely.

Photoshop's *Warp Text* tool is not strictly "text on a path," but it can give the same impression. Type can be distorted to follow a preset arc, wave, or outline, and adjusted for the amount of distortion, while still remaining fully editable. While such tricks are frowned upon by serious typographers, the effects can be useful for matching type to a photomontage background.

Photoshop's type rendering

Unlike most typographic applications, Photoshop is bitmap based and deals in pixels rather than vectors. Because of this there are controls to fine-tune type anti-aliasing, especially useful at small point sizes where legibility can be lost due to a lack of resolution. The choices are *None*, *Sharp*, *Crisp*, *Strong*, and *Smooth*. Each minutely adjusts the appearance of the type edges, and while one option may work for a certain font in a certain size, it will look too bold or weak in another. The only option is to experiment.

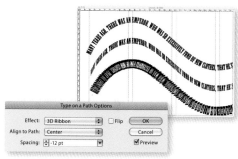

CREATING NEAT BODY TEXT

Whether in a newspaper, book, or on the back of a breakfast cereal packet, any large portion of text must be readable. Words, sentences, and paragraphs should flow without interruption. There are no hard and fast rules when it comes to setting body text—each font is different, and each situation unique. For example, Adobe Caslon sets small for its point size, so it can be used with tight leading. On the other hand ITC Stone Serif sets large so it needs looser leading. If both fonts are set using the same values they appear markedly different. Below are some basic guidelines that will help when setting body text.

Black on white

If setting text over more than one or two paragraphs, consider using black text on a white page. This combination provides the most contrast, and doesn't tire the eye.

Hyphenation

Hyphenation is the subject of many heated discussions between designers and proofreaders. Hyphenated text can be beautifully smooth to look at, but with too many broken words the natural reading flow will be repeatedly disrupted. Modern layout applications, with sophisticated text-handling software, have made the use of hyphens to create balanced text columns far less common.

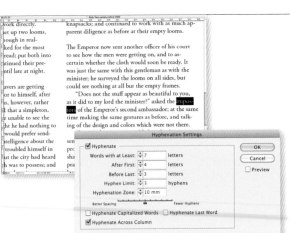

Where to start

When beginning a new project, it does no harm to take a look at similar publications to find a starting point, but don't think that you can't develop and improve on what has been done before through creative font choices and layout innovations.

Optical Margin Alignment

Punctuation and irregular letter shapes (such as a capital "T") are traditionally set by a computer so they line up at the edge of a column, right on the guide. Optical Margin Alignment in InDesign goes a step better by moving these glyphs to slightly outside the guide, where they visually appear to create a smooth column edge, even if in reality they are not.

Be average

For your first attempts at body text use the application defaults as your basis. Different fonts will need different treatment, as in the examples above, so begin in the middle and make adjustments in small steps. Remember that changing one element, such as the leading, will affect the feel of another area, such as word spacing. After spending hours searching for the perfect body text font, don't immediately ruin it by distorting the letter shapes or spacing—if the font isn't right find an alternative.

Usage

The project you are working on will affect many of your choices. Cookery books are read at arm's length and need to be clear. They need a large text with plenty of leading, with markers in the text created using bold numbers or subheads. At the other extreme, magazines are read close in, usually in short chunks. This means narrower columns, and smaller point sizes, can be used.

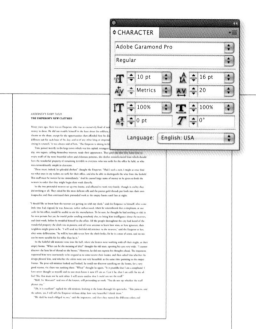

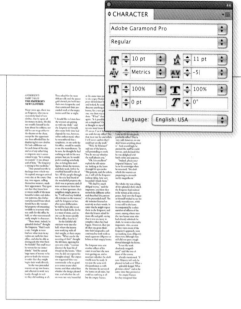

Paragraph composer

The type controls in InDesign are extremely sophisticated, rivaling even hand-set text. With *Paragraph Composer* and *Balance Ragged Lines* activated, long columns of text will have ragged edges balanced by wrapping words and making microtypographic adjustments to type. Controls for defining the freedom InDesign is given to make adjustments are in the *Justification* dialog window, where the amount of variation on glyph scaling, letter spacing, and word spacing can all be set as maximum and minimum amounts.

Long reading

To set text that is comfortable for reading over long periods, your watchword is "medium." Start with a size of around 9 point text with 11.5 point leading and work from there. You should use a wide column, ideally 10 to 12 words wide, and one or two columns on the page to create the right aesthetic. Tracking and word spacing should be left at an average setting, although wider columns will need looser spacing and more leading. Wider columns can also accommodate justified text without too much risk of large gaps or rivers appearing.

Short reading

Common in magazines, small amounts of text can be set smaller and tighter, with as many as six narrow columns to a page. Aim to get a minimum of five or six words to a line, and if you use a font with an above average x-height it will appear larger than its real point size, so improving legibility. Tracking and word spacing can be tightened up, and always set tight columns with flush text—usually flush left, ragged right for western languages.

Read it

The only way to check the readability of your text is to, you guessed it, read it! Or better still, get someone else to read it. Ideally your tests need to be printed on the press and paper stock you will be using for the finished job, but failing that a laser printer proof is far better than reading on-screen. A proper test requires a real story as well, not Latin (or "Klingon") placeholder text.

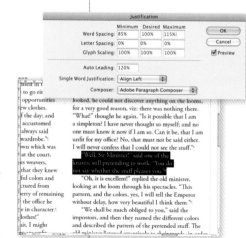

GLYPHS AND HIDDEN CHARACTERS

If, in the course of your design work, you set a lot of body text, sooner or later you'll need to access some of the lesser used characters, whether it's accented letters or mathematical symbols. Built-in utilities can help with this. Windows' Character Map or Mac OS X's Character and Keyboard Viewer—activated through the International system preference pane by clicking on the flag icon at top right of the screen—provide pretty much everything you're likely to need. Failing those there are a wealth of third-party utilities such as PopChar (www.ergonis.com/products/popchar/), which make the process even easier. High-end DTP applications have their own glyph palettes as well.

Easiest of all, though, is our handy reference table, which gives you the Mac and Windows keyboard shortcuts for common symbols and diacritical marks, along with the HTML entities for those characters. Windows users should hold down the Alt key and type the numbered code shown using the numeric keypad at the right of the keyboard.

			Mac	Windows	HTML
Punctuation					
Left single quote		'	alt]	0145	&lsquo;
Right single quote		'	alt shift]	0146	&rsquo;
Left double quote		"	alt [	0147	&ldquo;
Right double quote		"	alt shift [	0148	&rdquo;
Single low quote		,	alt shift 0	0130	&sbquo;
Double low quote		„	alt shift W	0132	&bdquo;
Left double guillemet		«	alt \	0171	&laquo;
Right double guillemet		»	alt shift \	0187	&raquo;
Inverted exclamation mark		¡	alt 1	0161	&iexcl;
Inverted question mark		¿	alt shift /	0191	&iquest;
Dagger		†	alt t	0134	&dagger;
Double dagger		‡	alt shift 7	0135	&Dagger;
Prime (feet)		′	[no shortcut]	2032	&prime;
Double prime (inches)		″	[no shortcut]	2033	&Prime;
Degrees		°	alt shift 8	0176	&deg;
Diacritical					
Acute		´	alt E	"On a Mac, these diacritical	
Grave		`	alt `	marks can be combined with any	
Circumflex		^	alt I	other character; type the	
Diaerisis		¨	alt U	combination shown, then the	
Tilde		~	alt N	character you wish to accent."	
Uppercase C cedilla		Ç	alt shift C	0199	&Ccedil;
Lowercase C cedilla		ç	alt c	0231	&ccedil;
Uppercase O with stroke		Ø	alt shift O	0216	&Oslash;
Lowercase O with stroke		ø	alt o	0248	&oslash;
Uppercase AE		Æ	alt shift '	0198	&AElig;
Lowercase ae		æ	alt '	0230	&aelig;
Scharfes s		ß	alt S	0223	&szlig;
Uppercase A with grave		À		0192	&Agrave;
Uppercase A with acute		Á		0193	&Aacute;
Uppercase A with circumflex		Â		0194	&Acirc;
Uppercase A with tilde		Ã		0195	&Atilde;
Uppercase A with umlaut		Ä		0196	&Auml;
Uppercase A with ring		Å	alt shift A	0197	&Aring;
Uppercase E with grave		È		0200	&Egrave;
Uppercase E with acute		É		0201	&Eacute;

Uppercase E with circumflex	Ê		0202	&Ecirc;	
Uppercase E with umlaut	Ë		0203	&Euml;	
Uppercase I with grave	Ì		0204	&Igrave;	
Uppercase I with acute	Í		0205	&Iacute;	
Uppercase I with circumflex	Î		0206	&Icirc;	
Uppercase I with umlaut	Ï		0207	&Iuml;	
Uppercase O with grave	Ò		0210	&Ograve;	
Uppercase O with acute	Ó		0211	&Oacute;	
Uppercase O with circumflex	Ô		0212	&Ocirc;	
Uppercase O with tilde	Õ		0213	&Otilde;	
Uppercase O with umlaut	Ö		0214	&Ouml;	
Uppercase U with grave	Ù		0217	&Ugrave;	
Uppercase U with acute	Ú		0218	&Uacute;	
Uppercase U with circumflex	Û		0219	&Ucirc;	
Uppercase U with umlaut	Ü		0220	&Uuml;	
Uppercase N with tilde	Ñ		0209	&Ntilde;	
Uppercase Y with acute	Ý	[no shortcut]	0221	&Yacute;	
Lowercase A with grave	à		0224	&agrave;	
Lowercase A with acute	á		0225	&aacute;	
Lowercase A with circumflex	â		0226	&acirc;	
Lowercase A with tilde	ã		0227	&atilde;	
Lowercase A with umlaut	ä		0228	&auml;	
Lowercase A with ring	å	alt A	0229	&aring;	
Lowercase E with grave	è		0232	&egrave;	
Lowercase E with acute	é		0233	&eacute;	
Lowercase E with circumflex	ê		0234	&ecirc;	
Lowercase E with umlaut	ë		0235	&euml;	
Lowercase I with grave	ì		0236	&igrave;	
Lowercase I with acute	í		0237	&iacute;	
Lowercase I with circumflex	î		0238	&icirc;	
Lowercase I with umlaut	ï		0239	&iuml;	
Lowercase O with grave	ò		0242	&ograve;	
Lowercase O with acute	ó		0243	&oacute;	
Lowercase O with circumflex	ô		0244	&ocirc;	
Lowercase O with tilde	õ		0245	&otilde;	
Lowercase O with umlaut	ö		0246	&ouml;	
Lowercase U with grave	ù		0249	&ugrave;	
Lowercase U with acute	ú		0250	&uacute;	
Lowercase U with circumflex	û		0251	&ucirc;	

Lowercase U with umlaut	ü		0252	&uuml;	
Lowercase N with tilde	ñ		0241	&ntilde;	
Lowercase Y with acute	ý		0241	&ntilde;	
Lowercase Y with umlaut	ÿ		0255	&yuml;	

Currency + mathematics

Dollar	$	shift 4	0036	&#36;	
Cent	¢	alt 4	0162	&cent;	
Pound	£	shift 3	0163	&pound;	
Euro	€	alt 2	0128	&euro;	
Yen	¥	alt Y	0165	&yen;	
One quarter	¼	[no shortcut]	0188	&frac14;	
One half	½	[no shortcut]	0189	&frac12;	
Three quarters	¾	[no shortcut]	0190	&frac34;	
Plus or minus	±	alt shift =	0177	&plusmn;	
Multiplication	×	[no shortcut]	0215	&times;	
Division	÷	alt /	0247	&divide;	
Is approximately equal to	≈	alt X	8773	&asymp;	
Is not equal to	≠	alt =	8800	&ne;	
Greater than	>	shift .	shift .	&gt;	
Less than	<	"shift ,"	"shift ,"	&lt;	

Other

Trademark	™	alt 2	0153	&trade;	
Registered trademark	®	alt R	0174	&reg;	
Copyright	©	alt G	0169	&copy;	

USING NON-ROMAN ALPHABETS

The familiar QWERTY keyboard layout is fine for writing in any language that uses the 26-character Roman alphabet, but if you want to write with a different glyph system, you'll need to make some changes.

FONTS AND ENCODING

The most basic requirement is that your computer can display non-Roman characters. This depends, broadly, on two things: a suitable font and a suitable way of encoding. All modern operating systems come preinstalled with fonts to handle many different scripts. Best of all are OpenType fonts, the huge glyph range of which can pack up scripts for dozens of languages in one font file. Unicode is the most reliable encoding technology when dealing with multiple scripts; both InDesign and QuarkXPress support both.

POINT AND CLICK

Later editions of Mac OS X feature character palettes (*System Preferences > International*) that allow you to enter small quantities of non-Roman text, including a dedicated panel for Japanese Kana. Simply select the script, and you can choose whether to pick the character based on sorting by category or radical (see below).

CHANGING KEYBOARD LAYOUT

For more frequent text entry, you need to change your keyboard layout. The process is similar in Windows and Mac OS X; simply go to *Control Panel > Regional and Language Options* (Windows) or the International pane of System Preferences (Mac OS X) and add a new language. Ordinarily, this will switch your keyboard layout to match the new language, although Windows offers a little more control by allowing the keyboard to be specified independently of the language. OS X's Keyboard viewer may help you learn the new layout. Switch between keyboard layouts using the Language bar in the Taskbar (Windows) or the icon in the menu bar (Mac OS X), or use keyboard shortcuts.

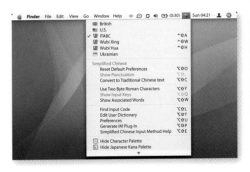

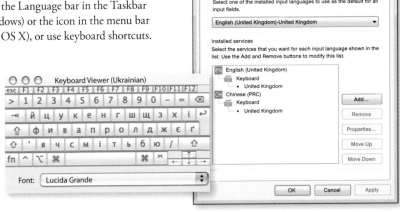

INSERTING PICTOGRAPHIC GLYPHS

Pictographic languages such as Chinese and Japanese create the thousands of glyphs used in written language by combining a number of "radicals"—fundamental strokes that are formed together to create stylized pictures. These are entered on a Roman keyboard in essentially two ways: either by entering constituent strokes manually, to "add up" to a completed character, or by typing the Roman-alphabet-equivalent of the foreign word, and have it converted. Here, for example, we're using the Mac OS X's ITABC input method to write "I am Chinese" in Simplified Chinese; just type the word, tap the space bar, then select the correct pictogram from the list, either by pointing and clicking, or tapping the appropriate number.

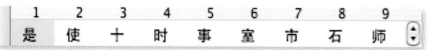

PROOFREADING MARKS

If your studio does a lot of book or magazine work, at some point you're likely to encounter proofreader's marks. Even with computerized spelling and grammar correction, errors still creep into text, and a human eye is still the best way to check that the copy makes sense. After the author has submitted the text, a proof of the text—known as a galley proof—is sent to a copy editor who will check for errors. Any corrections are marked using a standardized set of symbols, one in the side margin and another in the text itself. Traditionally, printer errors would be marked in red and author corrections in blue, but the informal production processes brought about by desktop publishing has led to this practice falling out of fashion for many.

Different studios have different methods of working and it's not uncommon for designers to find themselves inputting text corrections from a marked proof, so it's worth knowing the most common proofreading marks, or at least having a reference for them. The list presented here includes those marks in common usage today. Many symbols have become redundant with the disappearance of metal type, and these have been omitted for the sake of simplicity.

DESCRIPTION			
Set in roman type	Rom	Transpose the letters or words	TR
Set in italic type	ITAL	Delete letters or words	⌐
Set in bold type	BOLD	Delete letter and close word	⌐
Set in lower case	LC	Remove space	⌒
Set in upper case	CAP	Insert space	#
Set in small capitals	SC	Ignore correction	STET
Make superscript	Ꮴ	Begin new paragraph	⌐
Make subscript	₂	Don't begin new paragraph	⌐

Insert new matter	⅄	Range right	FR
Insert period (full stop)	⊙	Range left	FL
Insert comma	⌀	Center	]C[
Insert apostrophe	५	Move up	⌐ ¬
Insert question mark	?	Move down	⌊ ⌋
Insert colon	⊙	Horizontal alignment	═
Insert hyphen	/=/	Vertical alignment	‖
Insert en dash	÷N		
Insert em dash	÷M		
Insert parentheses	(/)		
Insert brackets	[/]		

Galley proof

Reading text on a galley proof makes it far easier to spot mistakes, and it's not as tiring as reading on-screen. Corrections are marked in the margin and on the text, often in a red. A common proofreading trick is to use a sheet of paper or rule to show only one line of text at a time, the intention being to slow down the reading pace and prevent scan reading.

ISO-5776

The International Organization for Standardization has specified a set of 16 symbols for proofreading and marking corrections, in English, French, and Russian. In addition, or as a replacement, many studios have adopted their own symbols, often specifying them in an internal style guide.

USING STYLE SHEETS

Using style sheets to format text for all but the smallest of projects is good practice for numerous reasons. First, style sheets allow the application of complex styling to large amounts of text with just one click of a mouse or assigned keystroke, saving hours of time on large jobs. Secondly, they provide consistency throughout a project, as the task of applying all the required attributes to, for example, a heading or a caption is left to the style sheet rather than the designer—who may overlook an element of the styling. Thirdly, if you decide to change a style halfway through a project, all you have to do is edit the style sheet, and all the previously styled text will be updated with the revised attributes automatically and consistently.

Some designers argue that setting up style sheets for small projects with only a limited amount of text causes unnecessary work. This may be true to a certain extent, but if you have any repeated text styling within a document or across multiple items, say for example a range of press advertisements, creating style sheets is worth the effort.

Creating style sheets

If you use InDesign, style sheets are created via the *Paragraph Style* and *Character Style* palettes. In QuarkXPress you access the appropriate palette by selecting *Edit > Style Sheets*. The principles by which style sheets are created are similar in both applications.

It is important to make the distinction between *Paragraph* and *Character* styles. *Paragraph Style* affects all text within the paragraph, while *Character Style* can be applied to individual words or characters. Notice in the example screen shots shown

InDesign CS5 Character Styles and Paragraph Styles palettes

here that TXT-1—the main body text style—is a *Paragraph Style*, while TXT-italic is a *Character Style* used to pick out italicized words and phrases within the body text. When creating a new style sheet, decide on the required styling by first creating sample setting on the page with all the required attributes applied. This is a useful visual exercise in itself as part of the design process. When you create the new style make sure you have the sample selected, and the new style sheet will match its attributes, saving you the trouble of entering the settings for

a second time. Remember also that one style can be based on another, for example first paragraphs and second paragraphs with a first line indent. If the original, or "parent," style sheet is edited, the changes will also apply to the related style sheets.

QuarkXPress 8
Style Sheets palettes

TYPE AND COLOR

Type is meant to be read easily, and while most designers are happy to spend hours setting beautiful headlines and flowing copy, the effect the chosen and applied color may have on the readability of the text can sometimes be overlooked.

If readable text is your main priority, it is best to set black text on a white background. This provides the most contrast, and there is little that can go wrong during printing. Should small mistakes be spotted at the last minute, new printing plates can be produced quickly and for less than the cost of a full color plate change.

Not every black is the same, however, so ensure your body text is set using plain black and not registration black, or any other black mix. Any slight misregistrations in printing, and these are quite common no matter how hard the printers try to prevent them, will cause the colors used in a black mix to peep out and give a fuzzy, rainbow edge to your fine type.

Razor-sharp type

On occasion you may want to print colored text, in which case you should avoid fonts with very fine detail in the serifs or counters, and stick to strong, highly readable sans-serif faces such as Frutiger. For type with a sharp edge, keep at least one of the cyan, magenta, or black ink values set to 100%: type printed purely with lighter tints may exhibit a soft edge where the dots of ink meet.

Keep the number of inks used to a minimum to reduce the risk of misregistration problems. Ideally, don't use more than two inks to mix your type color, and keep one of these solid. If you really do need to set some small, highly detailed text in a mid-range tint, it is best to consider using a special spot-color ink to prevent it turning into a mush of tiny dots.

White out

When working with white type out of a dark background, the rules are the same as above, but apply them to the background rather than the type. The fewer inks used in the background, the less likely you are to get colored halos at the edge of your type when printed. For white type out of a black background, use a mix of 100% black and 40% cyan (sometimes referred to as a Rich Black) to keep the background dense with minimal chance of misregistration. If you must use a multi-tinted background, spend time setting the trapping properly.

Black type

Single-color black type is the most readable. Adding colors to the black mix increases the likelihood of colored halos appearing at the edges of the letters, and of counters filling in.

White type

When working with white type on a colored background, keep the number of inks used to a minimum: you could end up with colored text, or no text at all. For a white type out of solid black, a mix of 100% black with 40% cyan gives the most dependable results.

Colored backgrounds

Black type over a colored background can be kept sharp simply by not using black in the color mix of the background. In addition, mix tints using values of cyan, magenta, and yellow. For example, 10% cyan, 8% magenta, and 8% yellow will give a cool, light gray background, and black type printed over the top will remain crisp without the screen dots below affecting it.

An image with lots of contrast or detail will make type hard to read. Use a semi-opaque white panel—created either in InDesign or Photoshop—to reduce the contrast. Solid black type will be the most readable.

Finally, by default your layout application will have black type set to overprint any backgrounds. Leave it that way—unless you have a very good reason to knockout any ink below—and you won't get fine white lines at the edge of the type.

Tinted panels

Use a semiopaque white panel over images to reduce their strength and make type set over them clearer. Black text will give the best results for readability and crisp edges.

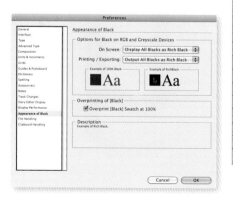

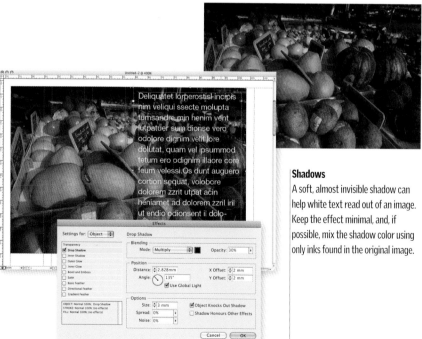

Shadows

A soft, almost invisible shadow can help white text read out of an image. Keep the effect minimal, and, if possible, mix the shadow color using only inks found in the original image.

CUSTOM TYPEFACES

No matter how many fonts you have, eventually you'll want something tailored for a specific job. If you're just thinking about a few words or so, this is fairly easy to achieve. To begin, try to pick a font with a design that's visually as close as possible to the final design idea to minimize the amount of work you have to do.

Font tweaking
Custom fonts can be altered to create something tailored to a specific job. For single headings, this is achievable with a minimum of time and effort.

Creating Outlines
In Illustrator or InDesign, set your text, then select it with the *Direct Selection* tool and choose *Type > Create Outlines*. The letters will be converted into regular, editable bézier paths. The objects will have the same stroke and fill settings as when the shapes were text, although the stroke width will crop into the fill areas slightly differently.

In Quark, set your text, then select it with either the *Content* tool or *Type* tool. Choose *Item > Convert Text to Boxes* whilst using the *Content* tool and you'll be able to convert the entire content of the frame to outlines. If you use the *Type* tool you'll be able to convert selected text to either unanchored or anchored outlines. Versions of QuarkXPress prior to 7 were not so adept at this conversion process, but now all software pacakges handle the process well.

Editing Outlines
To customize the letterform shapes in Illustrator or InDesign use the *Direct Selection* tool or the *Pen* tool and modify the outlines as you would with any regular outline graphic. To get at the elements of a converted chunk of text, choose *Object > Compound Paths > Release*.

In Quark use the *Item* tool to select and edit the points and paths of the outlined letters as bézier-drawn shapes. To break words into individual letters use *Item > Split > Outside Paths*. Each letter, and any counters, will be treated as a separate object and can be moved, replaced, or filled with imported graphics or text.

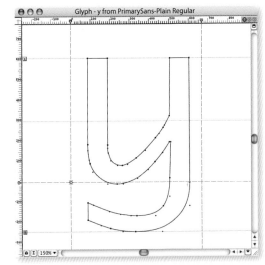

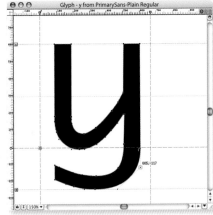

Photoshop

For certain effects, such as elaborate blends of type and image, Photoshop may be a superior method of editing your text. Choose *Layer > Rasterize > Type* to convert your type into pixels, and from that point onward you can treat it as an ordinary image. It's a good idea to keep a copy of your original text in a channel or separate layer in case you need to return to your starting point.

For warped, bowed, and distorted text, choose *Layer > Type > Warp Text* to access a range of effects that can be applied to text whilst keeping it fully editable.

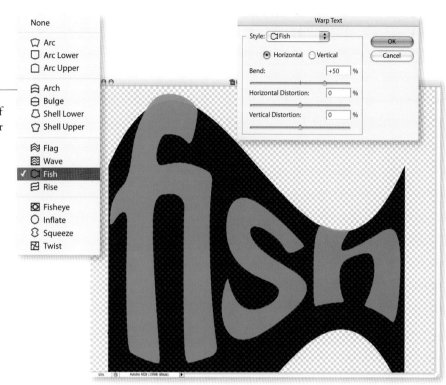

Creating new fonts

If you want to go a step further and make a custom typeface, you'll need a dedicated typeface-creation program. FontLab Studio and Fontographer are the tools of this particular trade. You can get both at www.fontlab.com, but be prepared to put some time into learning the software and then crafting each character in your new typeface. You'll end up with a real working typeface at the end of your efforts, but it isn't a quick job by any means.

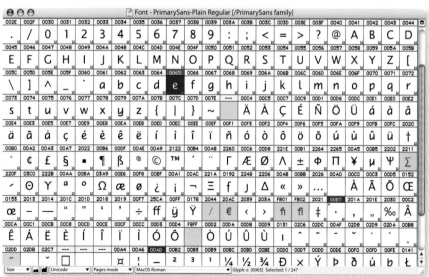

USING FONTS FOR PRINT

Sending final layouts to the printers is often a stressful process, as there are many things that can go wrong. While on-screen and inkjet proofing can help to calm your fears and reassure you that all is as it should be, font problems can creep in where you least expect them. Here's a rundown of the most common issues that crop up from time to time with fonts—and the solution.

The printed text looks completely different

If you're sending InDesign or QuarkXPress files to the printer, along with fonts and images, this problem is likely to occur when a font file is missing or has been installed incorrectly. If you have supplied the fonts correctly—both the printer and screen fonts if you are still using Postscript Type 1 format—there is very little you can do to prevent the problem occurring again. Run tests to determine if the problem was a one-off or a recurring error, if the latter replace the font file. Alternatively supply final PDFs to the printer.

The printed text is similar, but not exactly the same

It is possible you have a font that is missing completely (see above). InDesign's built-in, font-rendering engine can mimic missing type so well that you may have just not noticed the substitution. Ensure that you have enabled *Highlight > Substituted Fonts* in the *Composition* tab of InDesign's *Preferences* to avoid this. It is also possible that you have two fonts with the same name, and they have been substituted. Check for duplicates, especially in those fonts used by the operating system—a good example of this is Helvetica Neue, which is a system font for Mac OS X, but also installed by many designers. As the system font will always take precedent over a user font, the only fix is to remove the offending font from the system and use a type manager, such as Font Book or Suitcase Fusion 2, to ensure only the font you want to use is active.

Black text has appeared as four-color text

If activated, InDesign's *Color Settings* will adjust your document colors to match the settings for the destination printer. While this is normally a good thing, it also performs the unexpected action of changing all the black text to a black mix using all four of the CMYK colors. One solution often given is to select *Text as Black* from the *Output* panel when printing, but this will turn all of the text in the document to black. If the destination printer you're using is causing significant problems with the appearance of the black text ouput, try temporarily switching to the *Emulate Adobe InDesign 2.0 CMS OFF* setting in the *Color Settings* control panel. This may change the appearance of other colors or imported images so it's a compromise.

THE EMPEROR'S NEW CLOTHES
Many years ago, there was an Emperor, who was so excessively fond of new clothes, that he spent all his money in dress. He did not trouble himself in the least about his soldiers; nor did he care to go either to the theatre or the chase, except for the opportunities

THE EMPEROR'S NEW CLOTHES

Many years ago, there was an Emperor, who was so excessively fond of new clothes, that he spent all his money in dress. He did not trouble himself in the least about his soldiers nor did he care to go either to the theatre or the chase, except for the opportunities then afforded him for

The impostors requested him very courteously to be so good as to come nearer their looms; and then asked him whether the design pleased him, and whether the colors were not very beautiful; at the same time pointing to the empty frames. The poor old minister looked and looked, he could not discover anything on the looms, for a very good reason, viz: there was

The printed text has a fuzzy edge

If you are printing text made of tints of the CMYK colors, the letters will be made purely of dots, and no solid ink. From a reading distance this can make them to appear to be slightly soft at the edges. The solution is to ensure at least one of the CMYK colors in your mix is at 100%, giving a razor-sharp edge to at least one of the separations.

It's also worth checking that the *Color Settings* are set appropriately for the destination printer and that there are no feathering or shadow effects applied to the type within the layout application.

The printed text has a colored halo

This is likely to be because of misregistration, where one of the colored CMYK plates has shifted out of sync slightly during printing. Misregistration is increasingly uncommon as printing technology continues to improve; but the best way to avoid the problem completely is to limit yourself to creating combinations of colors for type and background using only one or two of the CMYK inks. Also experiment with your trapping settings or use a spot color if you need to match an exact hue.

White text has filled in

White text out of a richly colored background can fill in if ink bleeds into the white areas, or plates become slightly misaligned. The problem is similar to the previous example, but in reverse. Minimizing the number of CMYK colors used to mix the background will reduce the potential misregistration problem. Trapping may also provide a solution, especially if the text is running over an image.

So the two pretended weavers set up two looms, and affected to work very busily, though in reality they did nothing at all. They asked for the most delicate silk and the purest gold thread; put both into their own knapsacks; and then continued their pretended work at the empty looms until late at night. So the two pretended weavers set up two

"We shall be much obliged to you," said the impostors, and then they named the different colors and described the pattern of the pretended stuff. The old minister listened attentively to their words, in order that he might repeat them to the Emperor; and then the knaves asked for more silk and gold, saying that it was necessary to complete

The impostors requested him very courteously to be so good as to come nearer their looms; and then asked him whether the design pleased him, and whether the colors were not very beautiful; at the same time pointing to the empty frames. The poor old minister looked and looked, he could not discover anything on the looms, for a very good reason, viz: there was

USING FONTS ON A WEBSITE

Choosing the fonts to use on a website is not as simple as when designing a printed page. Web pages can display different fonts, but embedding fonts without third-party tools creates extra work and is not straightforward. If you choose an unusual font, there is little chance that a visitor to your website will have it installed on their computer. Indeed many users will only have whatever came with their operating system and web browser. At worst, the result will be ugly; at best, boring.

There are some fonts, or families of fonts, that you can use safely and be certain that almost every other computer will have a close approximation preinstalled. These include two nearly universal serif and sans-serif fonts called Times Roman and Helvetica. Both PCs and Macs include about 15 matching font sets beyond those two, but many portable devices are not so blessed. If you want to make sure that text appears in a predictable way, specify the font you want and then list others that are acceptable alternatives: <font face="Verdana, Arial, Helvetica"> No serifs here</font>. In the example below we want the phrase "No serifs here" to appear using Verdana, a sans-serif font ideal for use on a computer screen. If that is not available, we'll settle for Arial or, at a push, Helvetica. Whatever happens, the visitor should not see text formatted with a serif font.

Font size is something else to watch out for. While you can specify the size of fonts on

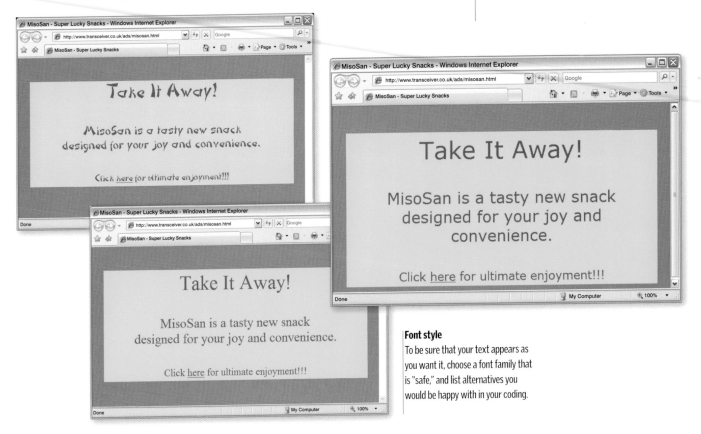

Font style
To be sure that your text appears as you want it, choose a font family that is "safe," and list alternatives you would be happy with in your coding.

a web page, there are lots of ways to do it—the most accurate involves CSS—but none of them will guarantee that every viewer of your page will get exactly the same results. Try to design your pages to flow, rather than attempting to maintain a rigid structure.

You may need to use a specific font, perhaps to enforce a brand. You might use this on labeled buttons on a navigation toolbar or to provide headings to web pages. Create an image in a package like Photoshop and add the text, formatted in your chosen font, as a layer. Save the image in JPEG format and insert it into the web page. Because it is an image, it will appear the same to every visitor, regardless of the fonts installed on their computers.

A labeled button

Selecting larger font size

CASCADING STYLE SHEETS

In the early days of the world wide web, HTML pages stood alone; all the formatting information—such as it was—was contained within the page itself using simple tags such as <B> and </B> to start and end a section of bold text.

Web page elements, often called tags, represent elements such as headings, paragraphs, lists, tables, and images. Using Cascading Style Sheets (CSS), it is possible to customize their appearance heavily, even to the point at which you dictate where they appear on the page.

You can store the styles in the page itself or use a separate file. The first option, which uses an internal style sheet, is fine for very small projects. However, it is more flexible to use an external style sheet, because many pages can make reference to it and you only need to edit one file to make broad, site-wide style changes.

HTML, the mark-up language used to create web pages, was built to provide a formal structure to documents. It was never intended to provide flexible layout options, and CSS was added later to separate display and formatting workflow from content.

A popular way to create flexible, well-designed web pages is to sketch an idea for a layout, or mock one up in Photoshop, and then identify the hierarchical structure. Use HTML to create a plain-looking document, with the most important items at the top, then edit the CSS file and allow it to dictate the page's layout. If you use Dreamweaver in design view, you can do a lot of this within the one application.

CSS can create hierarchical headings and elements to describe a page, including block quotes, emphasized text, and even arbitrary document divisions that you can define

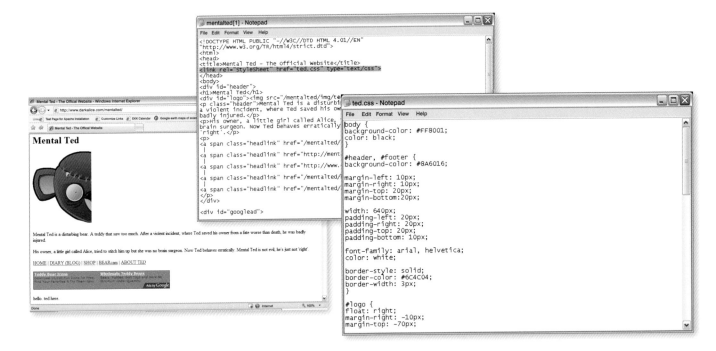

yourself. This page can then be linked to a style sheet, which provides all of the site's page formatting and layout.

When you create a style, avoid naming it according to its appearance. It makes more sense to use a description of its function. For example, you might identify a box of text on a page as "redbox" and enter the appropriate formatting into the style sheet. However, if you later change the box's background to blue, you end up with a confusing set of descriptions and definitions. It would have been better to identify the boxout as "importantbox."

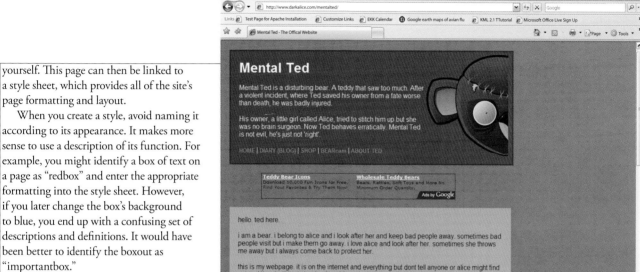

Color

Color plays an enormous part in our lives. From a young age we all have a favorite color, enjoy brilliant blue skies, and pay attention when we see a red warning sign. Color is a key tool for a designer—a way to express emotion and feeling without the need for imagery. But we also take color for granted, expecting the vibrant color on our screens and swatch books to translate into print without a hitch. Color reproduction, however, can be where many of the problems with print design occur—from washed-out hues or over-dark shadows, to patchy fills and uneven gradients.

By knowing the potential pitfalls of print reproduction, and building a working environment that deals with them, you can be assured your print jobs will be more to your, and your clients, liking. The first step is understanding the transformation colors go through as they move from screen to print, and why the two systems are almost completely opposite from one another. Setting up a managed, color-profiled workflow will give you more control over the production process, as will having a quality-control filter with on-screen and print proofing.

RGB vs CMYK

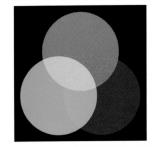
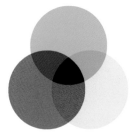

To truly understand how an image or color on your screen will transfer to print, you need to understand the differences in how RGB and CMYK colors work. The principles of how a computer monitor displays an image are covered on pages 12–13, but here we must go into how primary colors mix together and why RGB and CMYK are almost exact opposites.

MIXING LIGHT AND PIGMENT

Most of you will know that RGB colors are made from red, green, and blue light, but it's often very difficult to visualize RGB colors and how they interact. For example, mixing red and green to get yellow is completely alien to most people. On the other hand, mixing cyan and yellow pigment to get green is learned at an early age. The confusion arises because in RGB we are mixing light, and the more we use, the brighter the image becomes; it's what is called an "additive" color system. CMYK (cyan, magenta, yellow, and black—the K stands for key), on the other hand, is "subtractive," so the more pigment we use, the darker the image will become.

Everything you photograph, scan, or see on-screen will be in RGB. To print an image, however, you need to convert it to CMYK, but that conversion can cause problems because not every RGB color can be recreated in CMYK, some are beyond the reproduction capabilities of the CMYK pigment, and are known as "out of gamut."

OPPOSITES

The closest opposite to RGB red we can produce is cyan pigment; for RGB green it is magenta, and for RGB blue it is yellow. Try inverting the colors in Photoshop to test this for yourself. To get the opposite of black (no light), we use white (no ink).

The limitations of printing become apparent when it comes to mixing black using the cyan, magenta, and yellow pigments. In theory, the three inks should combine to make black. The reality, though, is that the pigments have insufficient strength to produce a pure black, so a fourth color is introduced, black, to add density. On a properly separated color image there will be plenty of tone in the CMY channels, but black should only appear in deep shadow. Incidentally, black ink is made using carbon, and it is the cheapest ink to produce. It is therefore always preferable to use pure black ink rather than a more expensive mix of cyan, magenta, and yellow.

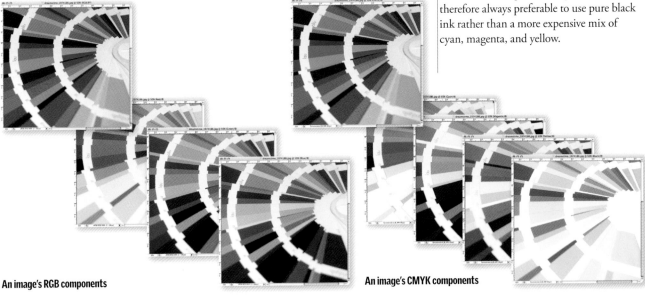

An image's RGB components   **An image's CMYK components**

VIBRANT COLORS

It's tempting to use the RGB color mixer on a print document to get the brightest and most vibrant colors, but the results will be extremely disappointing when the job returns from the printer. To begin with, CMY inks rely on light reflected from the paper for their brightness, and to mix any color using CMY requires adding more pigment, which will make the tint duller. For example; to mix green using RGB we use just the green channel at full strength, to mix green using CMY we mix cyan and yellow, both close to full strength. The subtractive process of CMY means we are taking away more light with every color that's used.

COLOR CONVERSION

Creating tints using RGB colors in print design will lead to disaster—the conversion process needs to be managed using profiles. A correctly calibrated monitor will minimize errors when displaying CMYK colors, and a properly profiled workflow will ensure better accuracy when converting an RGB image to CMYK, and when outputting the image to a printer.

Primary colors

The two color systems we use are RGB for viewing images on a monitor, and CMYK for printing. The RGB primary colors—red, green, and blue—are almost exact opposites of the CMYK primaries—cyan, magenta, and yellow. Inverting a color wheel in Photoshop clearly shows this in action.

Secondary colors

The secondary colors made by mixing the RGB primaries are cyan, magenta, and yellow. The same effect happens when mixing the CMY primaries—we get red, green, and blue as secondary colors. But as CMY is a subtractive color system, the colors are dull when compared to their RGB counterparts.

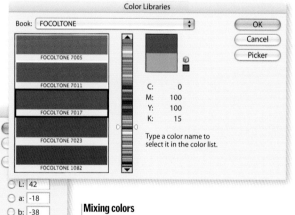

Mixing colors

When mixing colors for print, use CMYK values. A tint book should be used as a guide, ideally one that has been supplied by your printers. Alternatively choose colors from a process mixing system, such as Focoltone or the Pantone "Solid to Process Guide."

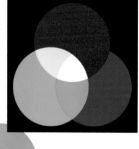

ACHIEVING ACCURATE COLOR

The problem with getting consistent color across your workflow is that each device in that workflow has a slightly different idea of what each color is. It's a bit like telling someone to paint your front door "leaf green" and then being disappointed that the color isn't what you expected because the guy who painted the door had a different concept of "leaf green" to you.

There are other concerns too: most notable, particularly when you're moving from screen to print, is gamut. The RGB and CMYK color models used by screen and print, respectively, can display different parts of the color spectrum, so some creativity is required in converting between these different models.

At the heart of a color-managed workflow is the notion of color profiles. Basically profiles—which, properly configured, should exist for every input, display, and printer in your workflow—describe how each device understands color. Going back to our painted door analogy, the idea here is that for each device, the profile says, "this is what I think leaf green looks like."

In practice, that's only part of the trick; the important bit is translating between these color profiles to create consistency. If your monitor and printer are properly calibrated,

for example, and you wanted to print out a picture of a leaf, the color calibration system would compare the color profiles of the two devices, notice, say, that the printer's notion of that green is more limey than the monitor's, and adjust accordingly. Broadly speaking, there are three different kinds of profile:

Generic profiles

These—often named "Generic RGB" or something similar—are the crudest possible profiles, and are of little use as they do not reference the devices you are using accurately.

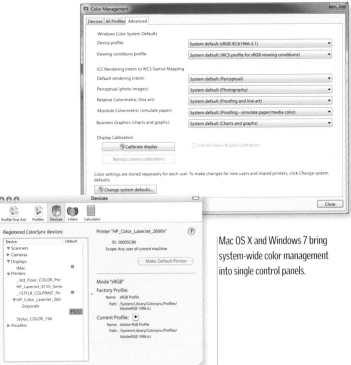

Mac OS X and Windows 7 bring system-wide color management into single control panels.

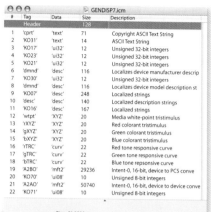

Device-specific profiles

Often, manufacturers will supply profiles with their devices, and these are usually a good first step. Note though that these depend on ideal circumstances; printers, for example, usually contain a range of ICC profiles specifically designed for the various types of paper made by the same manufacturer—and rely on pairing branded paper with the same brand's ink. And while device-specific profiles for monitors are also a good kicking-off point, they take no account of ambient lighting conditions.

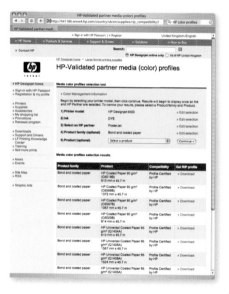

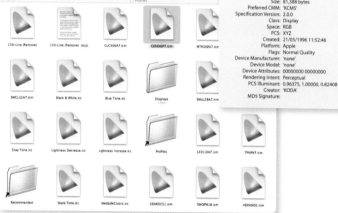

Mac OSX ColorSync Utility

Here we're using Mac OS X's ColorSync Utility to compare, in interactive 3D, the color gamuts of two devices.

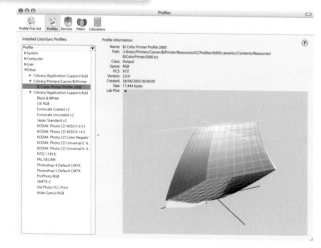

ACHIEVING ACCURATE COLOR

Bespoke profiles

Ideally, you should calibrate all devices in your workflow periodically to ensure their profiles are as accurate as possible. Monitor calibration is relatively simple—calibration pucks, even those as inexpensive as the Pantone Huey, do a fine job on TFTs and CRTs and are point-and-click simple. And if you send all your final work to a commercial printers for outputting, this is as far as you would normally have to go; your printers will have rigorously profiled their presses, so will be able to translate between what your system thinks "green" looks like, and what the printers' perception is.

If you want to calibrate your own printer, you can invest a little money in a system that will print out a color chart to be scanned in—along with an IT8 target as a calibration yardstick—but this won't create truly professional results unless you have invested heavily in your scanner. The most precise profile generation is achieved by sending printed color charts to a third-party company that use spectrophotometers to very carefully

measure the output from your printer and create individual profiles. Spectrophotometers are beyond the budget of many self-employed designers and small studios, but if you regularly need to create color-accurate proofs in-house, they're a wise investment. Some large, roll-feed printers have their own spectrophotometer fitted to allow constant management of color.

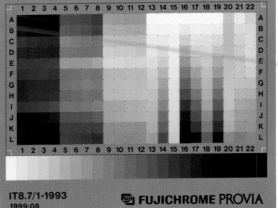

**Color-management systems.
Clockwise from left: Pantone
Huey, Provia target, and
GretagMacbeth One-Eye**

Using an accurate color target alone, of course, can help create a bespoke profile for your scanner, and since this calibration process is an end in itself—and not being used to help calibrate another device such as a printer—it can be as exact as possible.

SETTING COLOR SPACES

Your computer has to know what color space you want to use. If you use Adobe Creative Suite 2 or later, you'll have Bridge, which can synchronize color settings across all applications in the suite. If not, you have to set system-wide color models, and, usually, color behavior in each application you use.

EMBEDDED PROFILES

Most modern applications embed color profile information into the files, even though this isn't a formal part of the specification for the more popular file formats. Again most will offer to translate between the embedded profile and the in-use display profile when you open a file, although you can limit this behavior.

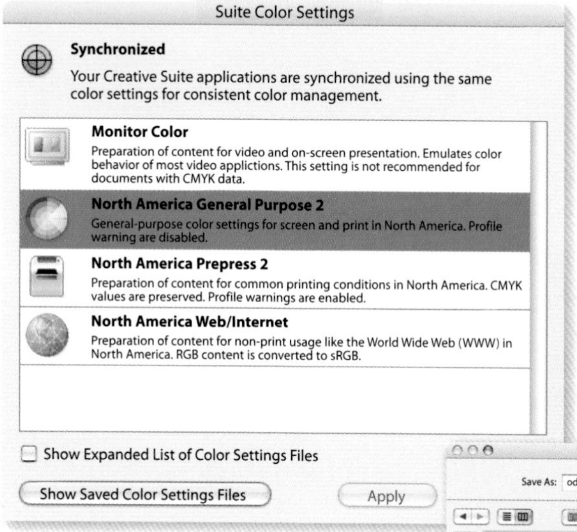

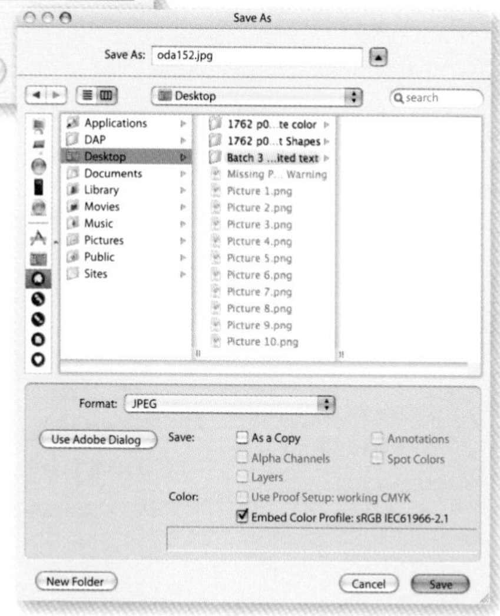

Options for setting color spaces and profiles

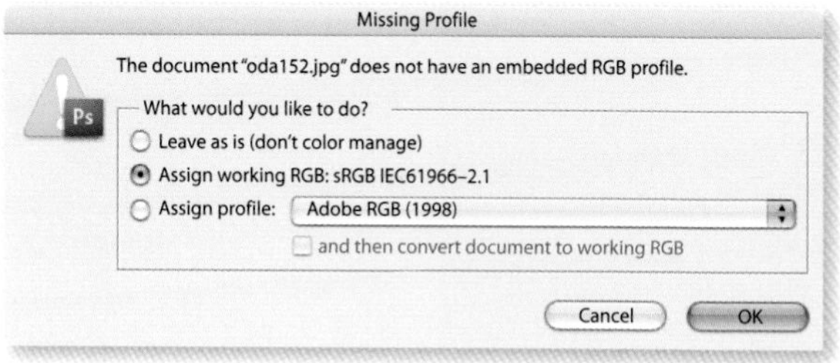

SCREEN ANGLE, DOT SHAPE, AND DOT GAIN

For a young designer just beginning a new career, every piece of technical jargon presents a challenge to their burgeoning knowledge. Dot shapes, screen angles, and dot gain occupy the top level of mysterious print lore—a level many experienced designers know little about, let alone the new guy.

SCREEN ANGLE

Most designers will already know that a printed image is made from tiny dots of cyan, magenta, yellow, and black ink. The lines of colored dots are arranged as a fine grid—the resolution of which is given as a measurement of lines per inch (lpi)—and each grid is printed at a different angle to prevent the dots overlapping. As each color is printed, the grids can sometimes clash with one another, causing dark and light patterns known as "moiré." The secret to preventing moiré lies in the visibility of each ink, and aligning the darkest as far apart as possible.

Yellow ink is the least visible so it is arranged as a level grid—its angle is set to 0°. As the most visible ink, black is set to 45°. Cyan and magenta are set to fit evenly between the lines of black dots, at 15° for cyan and 75° for magenta. It is unusual for a designer to get involved in the process for setting up the screening angles, as it is normally handled by the printer and output device, but some applications (and Photoshop filters) have the facility to set your own screen angles.

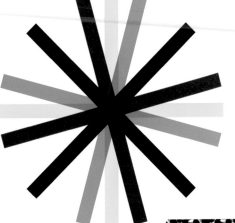

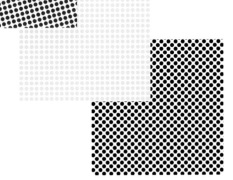

Clockwise from top: Halftone screen angles, halftone CMYK separated plates, halftone all plates combined

From left: Oval, round, and square dot shapes

DOT SHAPE

In nearly all circumstances, a round dot is used for printing a CMYK screen. However, there are other dot shapes that can provide better tonal ranges for certain colors and uses. While it is impractical to have a different dot shape for pages in a magazine, specifying dot shapes for posters and other one-off jobs is worth investigating.

Round dots: The default option for dot shapes, round dots work well for most images. As the round dots enlarge, and begin to touch their neighbors, the ink spreads resulting in a tint jump at about 60% density.

Oval dots: For flesh tones, oval dots give a better range in the right areas. As the dots enlarge they meet at the side, resulting in a small tint jump at 50%, then another small jump in the shadow areas at 90% density.

Square dots: Also known as diamonds, these produce very even tones throughout the range right up to 90% density, when they fill in very quickly as each side of the square meets. This makes square dots ideal for images with very little shadow areas.

DOT GAIN

As ink dots meet the paper, they are absorbed, and spread. With high-quality coated paper the effect will be minimal, but on low-quality newsprint the effect is much more noticeable. The amount by which the ink spreads is known as dot gain. If your print dots are filling in, leaving you with very dense shadow areas, experiment with increasing the dot gain settings slightly. Photoshop's *Color Settings* control dot gain, which for a typical CMYK web-offset press on uncoated paper will be 20%, but may need to be set slightly higher for poor-quality paper, or lower for high-quality coated stock.

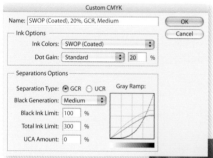

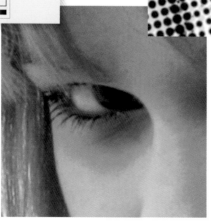

Dot gain adjustment before (left) and after (right)

TRAPPING AND CHOKING

When two colors meet on a printed sheet, you want them to align perfectly without a gap between them. While this is easy to do in a layout application, and will usually come out perfectly on a test print, it's much harder to accomplish on a fast-running printing press—paper will slip a little, stretch slightly, and become misaligned. Trapping and choking is the process of overlapping the colors to compensate for any shift during printing, and preventing any slivers of white becoming visible.

TYPES OF TRAPPING

Spreading: The term applied when the lighter of two elements expands a little to be overprinted with the darker color of the other. Because the darker color dominates, the original visual edge remains.

Choking: Occurs when a dark object sits on white. The lighter inks in the object will contract, and then be overprinted by the darker ones.

Knockout: When an ink or object removes any other colors sitting below it.

Overprint: The two objects overlap, mixing their colors together. It is standard practice to overprint black objects onto the other colors.

TRAPPING USING INDESIGN

Ask most designers about the trapping controls in InDesign and you'll get a blank look—and for a good reason. The software handles trapping and choking so well it's very rare that an operator will need to intervene and make adjustments. Most of the time the correct settings will be made without the designer ever becoming aware of the process.

Manual spreading can be applied to an object by adding a small stroke, and using the *Attributes* palette to set the stroke to overprint. For a more robust solution use the *Trap Presets* palette, found under *Window > Output*. Here the default trap settings can be modified, and new presets made. The width of the trapping area, the shape of the overlap, and when trapping occurs can all be controlled. However, given the efficiency of the default trap presets, it is unwise to alter any of these values without specific advice from your printers.

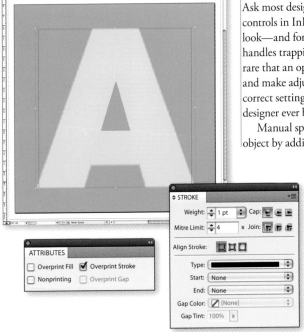

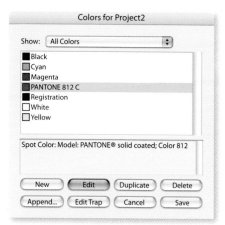

TRAPPING USING QUARKXPRESS

The default trapping in QuarkXPress, as with InDesign, is sufficient for most work, most of the time. The *Trap Information* palette is where the defaults can be overridden and custom trapping applied at the object level. The selected objects can have settings applied for their backgrounds, frames, gaps with frame styles, and pictures—although the trapping options for placed images are limited to overprinting grayscale or line work. Choosing *Custom* from the drop-down menu allows a "+" (spread) or "−" (choke) value to be entered.

In Quark, it is also possible to modify how colors react to each other, and the default trapping amounts using the *Edit > Colors > Edit Trap* dialog window. This is especially useful for defining the trapping behavior of spot colors and special inks.

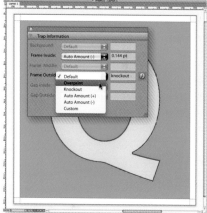

TRAPPING PLACED IMAGES

Photographs generally do not require trapping, but bitmap images with hard edges, such as cartoons, will. InDesign and QuarkXPress are capable of trapping placed bitmaps if the latter have been saved as PSD or TIFF files.

In InDesign the default *Trap Preset* will deal with any trapping required when an object or frame meets the bitmap. To apply trapping to the image itself, check the *Trap Images Internally* option in the *Trap Preset*. The negative side to this is the increased size of the temporary trapping files stored on your hard drive, and the slow running of the trapping engine.

Vector graphics can be trapped within InDesign if they are saved as PDFs. *Trap Images Internally* does not have to be checked as the default presets will do the job automatically.

To trap a vector image within Illustrator, use either the overprinted strokes method as described for InDesign, or the *Trap* filter found in the *Pathfinder* palette's menu. The settings are similar to those in InDesign.

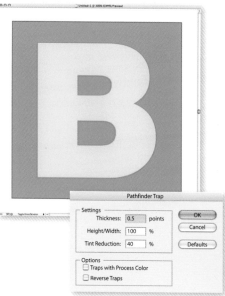

MANIPULATING COLOR

Each design-based software application handles color creation in a slightly different way, tailoring its approach to the specifics of the program and its requirements.

QUARKXPRESS
Project Colors
Located under the *Edit* menu, the *Colors* dialog window shows the colors used for a particular project, and it is here that you can modify or organize them. New colors are created by clicking *New*, and existing ones edited (click *Edit*)—the latter bringing up the *Edit Color* panel (described below). As each color chip is selected, a brief description is displayed in the properties window. Colors from other QuarkXPress projects can be added to the list using the *Append…* button. The *Edit Trap* button provides a detailed dialog describing how the selected swatch behaves when interacting with other colors.

It is easy to create new colors on the fly when working with a QuarkXPress layout using the contextual palette that appears by default at the bottom of your screen.

Colors Palette
The *Colors* palette (accessed under *Windows > Show Colors*), takes the most commonly used parts of the *Colors* dialog window and makes them more accessible. The three icons at the top of the palette let you choose to color either the frame, content (picture or text), or background object. Faded out until an item is selected, the palette swatches can be used to apply colors by clicking, or by dragging the colors chips to the target item. Icons along the right-hand side indicate process or spot colors.

Creating new swatches
Choosing new from the *Colors* dialog window brings up the *Edit Color* window. Colors can be defined using the color wheel picker, or by entering values in the fields. The *Model* drop-down menu includes books of swatches from popular color-matching systems, including those from Pantone and Focoltone. It is also to possible to mix multi-ink colors using existing spot color swatches, perfect for anyone working with Pantone's Hexachrome system. The *Spot*

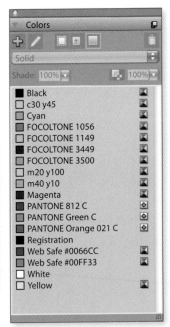

88

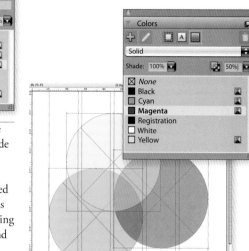

Color check box will switch the color from being a process mix to one that is printed with its own ink.

Blends and opacity

In addition to creating, holding, and applying color swatches, the *Colors* palette is also used to define blends. Two colors can be used in each blend; they must be existing swatches. Although the blend type (linear, radial, square, and so on) and angle can be defined, the options are more limited than the *Gradients* command found in Creative Suite applications. Objects can also be made semitransparent using the *Colors* palette; simply set the *Opacity* value to less than 100% to allow anything behind the selected object to show through. Again, the controls are rather limited compared with the blending modes found in Photoshop, Illustrator, and InDesign.

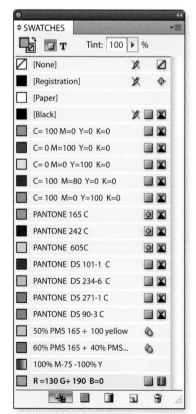

INDESIGN
Swatches palette
InDesign's *Swatches* palette is where colors are created, edited, modified, and exported. At the top of the palette are icons for assigned swatches to fill or stroke the selected object, or any type contained within. The percentage field is for using existing swatches as a tint.

Viewed as either a list or color chips, the *Swatches* palette can also store gradients. Icons show the color space for each swatch (CMYK, RGB, or Registration), and whether a color is process mix, spot, or created from mixed inks. Unlike Illustrator, CMYK and RGB colors can be stored in the same palette.

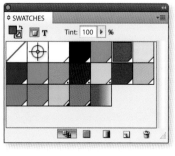

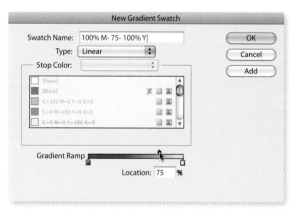

MANIPULATING COLOR

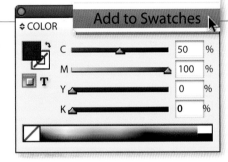

Mixing new colors

To create a new swatch from the *Swatches* palette, click the *New Swatch* icon at the base of the palette or select *New Color Swatch* from the drop-down menu to open the *Swatch Options* dialog box. Colors can be named using their values, or a description of your choice. The *Color Type* field lets you choose whether the color will be printed as a process separation, or a spot color with its own ink plate. *Color Mode* gives you the option of using LAB, CMYK, or RGB color spaces, or choosing from a long list of color-matching systems including Pantone, Focoltone, Toyo, and many more. If you are already using spot colors within your document the list includes the option to create a new swatch mixed from one or more non-process inks.

Color

InDesign's *Color* palette can be used to mix a one-off color with the need to make a new swatch. The *Spectrum* at the bottom of the palette can be used to make quick selections, and the sliders used to refine the color mix.

Appearance of black

It is recommended that you switch the *Appearance of Black* options in InDesign's *Preferences* to *Display All Blacks Accurately.* This will allow you to visually judge the density of any black mixes on screen, and help to prevent problems when using four-color blacks with type.

Exporting colors

Regularly used colors can be saved as a file using the *Save Swatches* drop-down menu and distributed to colleagues or copied over to other Creative Suite applications—perfect for ensuring corporate colors remain consistent throughout the studio.

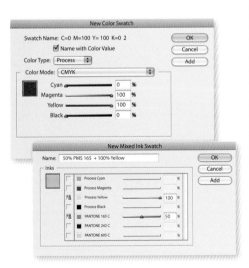

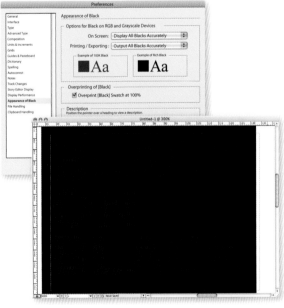

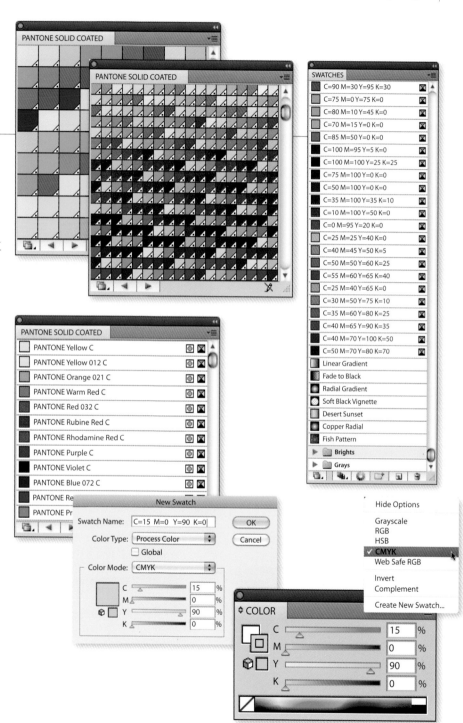

ILLUSTRATOR

Swatches palette

As with InDesign, Illustrator's *Swatches* palette is the heart of color use within Illustrator. Colors can be viewed as small swatches, large swatches, or a list of names with a small color chip. In the list, view icons are displayed to show the color space (CMYK or RGB), global, and spot colors. Gradients and patterns can also be stored in the *Swatches* palette.

Mixing new colors

To mix a new color, click the *New Swatch* icon in the *Swatches* palette, and double-click the new swatch to open a dialog, which will allow you to choose the color mode and mix of a new color. Once applied, colors can be tweaked on an object-by-object basis using the *Color* palette. To keep an object's color connected to its swatch, and to prevent unintended editing, check the *Global* box.

Color palette

To mix a color, or modify an existing one without creating a new swatch, use the *Color* palette. The icon in the top left shows the fill and stroke settings for the object selected, with a small color picker bar along the bottom. To add a color to the *Swatches* palette, drag the color chip across from the *Color* palette.

MANIPULATING COLOR

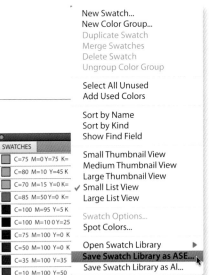

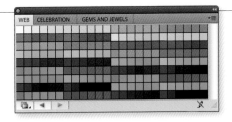

Swatch libraries

Illustrator has an extensive selection of ready-made swatch libraries. The list includes a wide selection of themed CMYK mixes (camouflage, skin tones, and so on), web-safe palettes, and color-matching systems from Pantone, Focoltone, Toyo, and more.

Exporting colors

Swatch collections can be saved as either an *Adobe Swatch Exchange* file or a native Illustrator file for distribution around a studio, ensuring consistent colors between different work groups and other Creative

Suite applications. Also, when importing Illustrator graphics into InDesign or QuarkXPress, any color swatches used will automatically come in with the graphic and be added to the swatches list.

PHOTOSHOP

Color Picker

Photoshop differs from the other Creative Suite applications in that the *Color Picker* is where you do most color creation. Clicking on *Foreground* or *Background* color at the bottom of the toolbar opens the *Color Picker* dialog box. To choose a color visual, use the rainbow colored bar in the center of the window—saturation and brightness of that hue are shown in the large square to the left. To the right are fields for entering specific color values in HSB (hue, saturation, and brightness), Lab (lightness, channel A, and channel B), RGB, and CMYK. The two oblong color chips show the existing color and the new mix being created, with a CMYK out-of-gamut warning if applicable. The box icon and color chip show the closest web-safe color; additionally checking the *Only Web Colors* tick box will force the saturation and brightness panel to display web-safe colors.

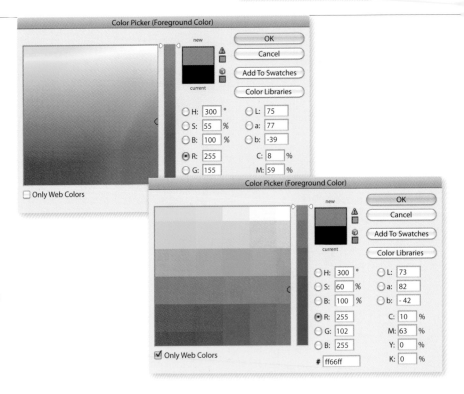

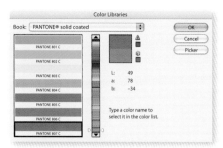

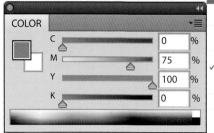

Color Libraries

Clicking the *Color Libraries* button transforms the *Color Picker* into a list of color swatches from popular color-matching systems. Choose from the extensive, but familiar, list of CMS books, including those from Pantone and Focoltone to see the swatches displayed on the left. Typing a color name will cause the list to jump to the appropriate swatch.

Color palette

The *Color* palette can be used as an alternative to the *Color* picker for mixing HSB, LAB, RGB, and CMYK colors. It's almost identical to the *Color* palette in InDesign and Illustrator, but rather then display fill and stroke colors to the left, it shows *Foreground* and *Background*.

Swatches palette

As in the other Creative Suite applications, the *Swatches* palette is the place to store and select frequently used colors. As well as adding swatches using the *New Swatch* icon, the menu button allows Pantone, other color-matching systems, and *Adobe Swatch Exchange* sets to be brought into the *Swatches* palette.

Channels palette

Photoshop works in color spaces, and the *Image > Mode* menu is used to switch between them. The *Channels* palette provides information on each image's channels—ink levels of a CMYK image for example. Clicking on the channel thumbnails allows one or more channels to be edited in isolation.

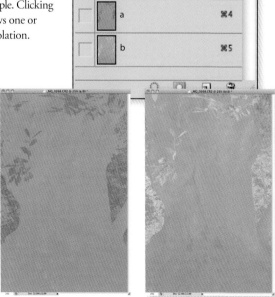

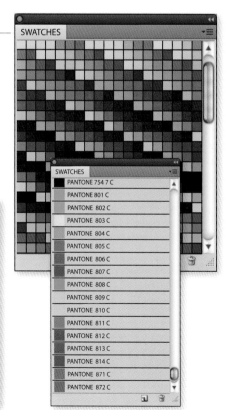

CREATING A SMOOTH GRADIENT

A blending tone can give movement to a design, and it needs only to be subtle to create the desired effect. While gradient tools are simple to use, there are many problem areas when it comes to printing, from banding to blotchiness.

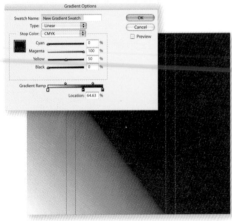

GRADIENT TOOLS

InDesign and Illustrator both use almost identical gradient tools. Once an object has been created a gradient can be applied by clicking the color chip in the top left-hand corner of the *Gradient* palette. Click on the gradient bar to adjust, add, or move colors. Colors can be entered as values, or by dragging colors from the *Swatches* palette to the gradient bar. To add a gradient to the *Swatches* palette simply drag and drop the color chip between the two palettes. The *Gradient* tool can be dragged across an object to set the start and end points of a gradient, and the angle of the fade. Alternatively, the angle can be entered as a value in the *Gradient* palette.

The *Gradient* tool in Photoshop works in a similar way, but it will blend from *Foreground Color* to *Background Color*. There are a number of blending styles—linear, radial, angle, reflected, and diamond—as well as a selection of predefined gradients under the *Gradient picker* in the *Tool Options* bar, which when clicked will bring up the *Gradient Editor*.

QuarkXPress applies blends using the *Color* palette. From the drop-down list choose a blend type rather than a solid color, and then using the two radio buttons select the start and end colors. Colors can be tinted and the blend set at an angle.

DON'T GO TO PURE WHITE

A common mistake when applying gradients is to take the blend all the way to pure white. While this will look great on-screen, once printed you'll end up with a noticeable, blotchy step just before the blend fades out completely. This happens because the ink doesn't transfer from the press to the paper properly when the screen dots become very

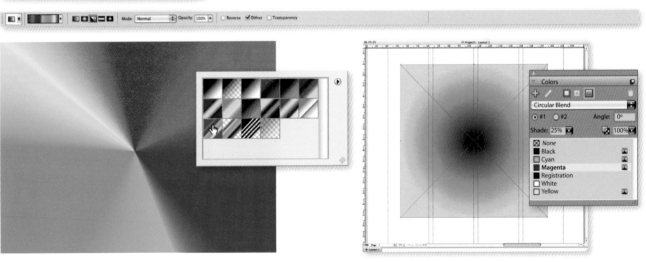

fine. The solution is to give the white in your gradient a slight tint, about 2% or 3% is suitable depending on paper type and printing method. Although your "white" will have a small amount of tone to it, it will be so subtle that it will only be noticeable when inspected closely. The same applies for any white points in photographs, such as highlights and clouds for example.

START AND END COLORS

When choosing the colors for your gradient, look for similarities. Blending two completely different colors, especially strong ones, can leave a gray patch in the middle of the

gradient. By adding a little of the start color to the end color, and vice versa, you'll get a smoother blend. For example, if you want to blend from black to cyan, set your start color to 40 cyan/100 black, and the end color 100 cyan/2 black.

Mid-blend colors can be used to help manage the transition with distinct hue changes. Blending from cyan to green to yellow will give a smoother effect than from cyan straight to yellow, because of the common color used in the middle of the blend.

Subtle gradients

Banding can appear on blends between two very similar tones, as the halftone screen steps between the dot sizes. The best way to avoid this is to use more than one ink in each of the colors—that way as the blend fades away the steps on each plate will be masked by the halftone on the other plates. If you absolutely must use a subtle single color blend, then create it in Photoshop and add a small amount of noise—3% is about right—to mask the steps. As the steps in the halftone occur, they will become slightly irregular because of the noise.

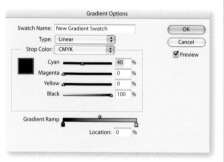

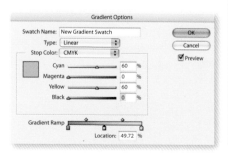

COLOR-MATCHING SYSTEMS

Launch any of the popular design software packages and you'll find a number of different color systems to choose from when creating new color swatches. Alongside the CMYK standard for print, or RGB for image editing and on-screen use, Pantone is the most widely used system—but there are others that also deserve a mention.

PANTONE®

PANTONE® is the trademark of Pantone Inc, the company that produces the most widely recognized color-matching system. The system describes precise and consistent standards for ink colors, and each color has its own unique formulation given in percentages for exact color matching between designer and printer. It's the system that most designers turn to, and is as close as one can get within the limitations of available technology to a guarantee of accuracy when specifying color. In fact, the Pantone® Matching System (PMS) is itself a proprietary color space.

A common mistake made by designers is to specify a Pantone® spot color as part of a job that will print in only four process colors. Many spot Pantone® colors cannot be reproduced accurately in CMYK as they are made by mixing specific inks which print with a single pass of the press. This is why spot colors are often referred to as "fifth" colors—they are added to the end of a standard four-color printing. Pantone® do produce an excellent Process Color Guide for specifying accurate CMYK colors, as well as guides for metallics, pastels, and Pantone Color Bridge®, which matches solid colors to the nearest achievable four-color process

equivalent, but which is often markedly different. Interestingly Pantone® have also recently added sRGB and HTML color values to colors that can be closely matched on-screen as a nod to designers who require accurate color reproduction online.

FOCOLTONE

Focoltone derives its name from an abbreviation of "Four Color Tone," and has been around since 1984. It provides an accurate CMYK color reference and specification system, and is backed by the Focoltone Intelligent Color Calibration System (ICCS). ICCS is a software solution that strives to achieve color consistency on digital printing systems regardless of printer type or conditions. The basic swatch book extends to 763 CMYK colors , but Focoltone Plus specifies a collection of 20,000 printable colors achieved by adding one of eight "Focoltone Plus" standard inks to the CMYK mix. There are also two "Focoltone Plus" metallic inks.

It's a useful system for selecting strong combinations of varying color tints due to the intelligent "family" arrangement of the colors in the swatch book. Colors that are difficult to reproduce accurately have been eliminated from the available range, and the result is a highly predictable "what you see is what you get" color-matching system. It's well worth looking at as an alternative to other systems, but bear in mind that it may not be as widely recognized as Pantone®.

TOYO AND DIC COLORS

TOYO and DIC are only used commonly in Japan, and are designed to specify spot colors.

ANPA

ANPA is an acronym for the American Newspaper Publishers Association. The ANPA color system is limited to 300 colors, and is used to specify spot colors for use in newspaper production.

TRUMATCH

The TRUMATCH four-color matching system organizes its colors by hue, saturation, and brightness (HSB). This results in 50 hue families arranged in the order of the spectrum, with 40 tints and shades of each hue, plus a range of four-color grays. As with all color-matching systems included as part of the major software packages, it's an intelligent approach to organizing color in a way that helps designers make their choices. However, once again it's not as widely used as Pantone®.

CMYK TINT BOOKS

Books about color technology and printing occasionally include full CMYK selection tables, and printing companies sometimes provide their own sets for color specification. These can help you to decide which colors to choose when putting together a design, but they can't necessarily be relied on for complete accuracy. There's no guarantee that your print job will be produced under the same conditions as the tables you have, so if color accuracy is crucial only use tables printed by the printer producing your job. If this isn't possible, look to the Pantone® Process Color Guide, which should be consistent with the swatch book held by the printer.

SPOT COLORS AND SPECIAL FINISHES

Spot colors represent an additional cost if they're used in conjunction with four-color CMYK printing—but that doesn't mean that they should always be regarded as a luxury. Not all jobs are printed in full-color CMYK, and one can achieve stunning results with only two or three spot colors, particularly when combined with the right choice of paper stock. There's effectively no limit on how many colors you could specify for a job, but bear in mind that most large commercial offset presses print a maximum of six colors at a time, so it isn't practical to move beyond that number. For a four-color print run, this provides the possibility of using two extra colors or finishes. If varnishing is required, either across the whole sheet or as a spot varnish on selected areas, this can also be printed on press.

Specifying spot colors

When creating a new spot-color swatch in either InDesign or QuarkXPress, make your selection from the *Mode* (InDesign)/*Model* (Quark) drop-down menu, and ensure that it's correctly specified as a spot color before adding it to the document. The spot-color menu/checkbox will be selected automatically when specifying a spot-color mode/model, but beware when subsequently adding additional process colors. You'll need to reselect the process mode/model to avoid adding the color incorrectly as a spot separation. Colors listed in the document's

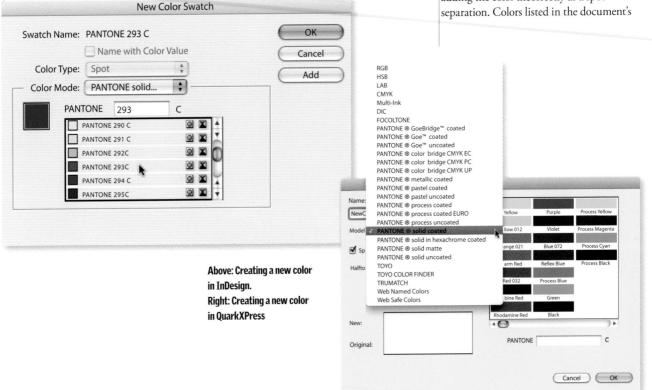

Above: Creating a new color in InDesign.
Right: Creating a new color in QuarkXPress

Swatches/Colors palette have their mode/model identified by a small icon to the right of the color name. You'll notice from the accompanying screen shots that InDesign uses a circle within a square frame while QuarkXPress uses a crosshair.

Your reproduction company or printer will know which colors should print as a separate spot color by checking how many plates will result from the job when output as separations. InDesign's *Separations Preview* palette lists each spot color contained in the document alongside the cyan, magenta, yellow, and black plates.

Special finishes

Specifying a special finish that isn't built into the software's defaults isn't quite so straightforward, but a simple workaround is all that's needed to make it clear to the printer what must be done. If you want to print a spot varnish or some other special finish, simply create a spot color using an alternative specification, for example 10% black for a varnish, and name it "spot varnish" in the color palette. This will be enough to indicate your intentions to the printer, and the separation will work perfectly well when output to plate. Make sure you also include detailed written instructions or a marked-up laser printout with your artwork to be certain that everything is clear.

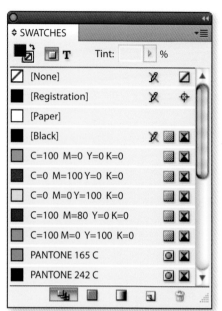

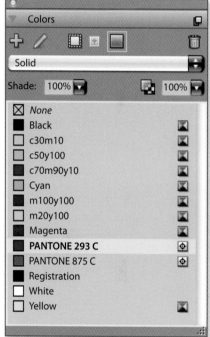

Left: InDesign's *Swatches* and *Separations Preview* palettes
Above: QuarkXPress's *Colors* palette

COLOR PROOFING ON-SCREEN

The time between sending a job to the printers and receiving back the finished work can be a stressful one. There are so many variables that it can seem almost impossible to guarantee how anything will print, no matter how much time and effort you put in to setting up color profiles and calibrating your output devices. While that is true to a certain extent, you can minimize the chances of something going wrong by proofing a job before sending it to the printers.

Of all the options, soft proofing on-screen is the cheapest, fastest, and simplest. Every day you will choose and proof colors on-screen without even thinking about it. Taken a little further the process can add a level of security against human error and plain bad luck—getting you a step closer to guaranteed print results.

CALIBRATE

Before contemplating soft proofing you will need a good-quality monitor that has been calibrated accurately, and the proper viewing environment. Ideally you need to be working in a windowless room, with controlled simulated daylight (referred to as D50 compliant) and walls painted with Munsell N8 gray matte paint. For a designer, working in a gray, dim, dungeon won't exactly get the creative juices flowing. For most of us, the best practical option is to close the blinds, turn off the lights, and keep the area around your monitor free from brightly colored Post-it notes and other distractions.

There are a number of third-party options such as Kodak Matchprint Virtual Proofing for improving your display settings for soft proofing on screen. While these products provide consistency for large studios with a wide variety of display equipment, the benefits in a smaller studio may be more limited.

WORKING PRACTICES

As part of your everyday workflow, it's important to do all you can to get your applications showing an accurate representation of what will be printed. As well as calibration there are a few simple steps that can be taken.

InDesign

Under *Preferences > Appearance of Black*, choose *Display All Blacks Accurately* for both the *On Screen* and *Printing/Exporting* options. InDesign has color settings identical to Photoshop and Illustrator, but turning them on can cause unexpected side effects with black body text. Instead, in the *Color Settings* dialog, try choosing *Emulate Adobe InDesign 2.0 CMS Off*. Images will still retain any attached profiles, but InDesign colors will remain absolute. The *Separations Preview* palette (under *Window > Output*) allows each ink channel to be viewed in isolation, to enable you to check for proper overprinted and black mixes.

QuarkXPress

Under *Preferences > Color Manager* set *Color Engine* to match your monitor (usually Automatic) and the *Source Setup* to match your output destination.

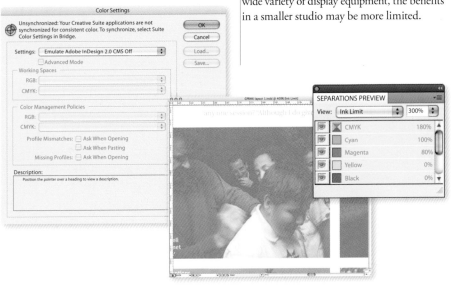

Illustrator

Under *Preferences > Appearance of Black* choose *Display All Blacks Accurately* for both the *On Screen* and *Printing/Exporting* options.

Use of *Color Settings* within Illustrator is subjective. Those who prefer their color values to remain as they enter them (usually anyone working with logos, graphics, or black text) should leave their *Color Settings* to *Color Management Off*, otherwise match your working spaces to match your monitor and output destination.

Photoshop

Make all your corrections and color adjustments in RGB mode, but go to *View > Proof Setup* and choose *Working CMYK*. After converting an image into CMYK check through each color channel to ensure the conversion process has gone as expected.

Acrobat

The best place to carry out any soft proofing is in Acrobat Professional, using the actual PDFs you have generated to send to the printers. Under *Preferences > Color Management* match your working spaces to your monitor and output destination. Under *Preferences > Page Display* check *Use Overprint Preview* to see a simulation of how colors will overprint one another. *Preflight*, found in the *Advanced* menu, will give you a palette for viewing the document ink channels and checking if PDFs are compliant with the various standards.

Limitations

The quality of on-screen soft proofing has improved alongside monitor and calibration technology, but there are still limitations to consider as everything you see on-screen is a simulation of how it will print, including the paper. Your monitor glows with light and color, and paper doesn't. For those working with proven printers in an area they have lots of experience with—magazine publishing for example—soft proofing offers a good alternative to "contract" or hard proofs. If your production standards need to be more precise, where you have to be certain of exact color matches, then soft proofing should only be used as a first step in the proofing cycle.

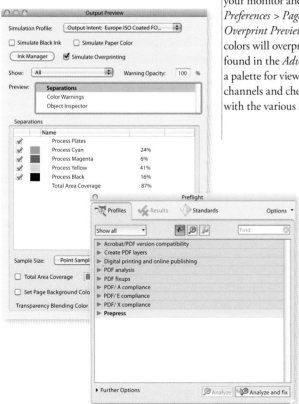

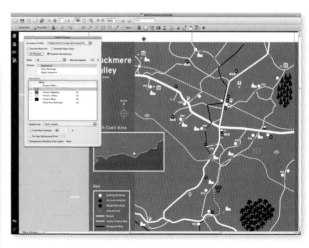

INKJET COLOR PROOFS

For most studios it is economically viable to have an in-house proofing system in the form of an inkjet printer. Loaded with the correct consumables, and used only for proofing jobs, the level of accuracy achieved by a top of the line inkjet can rival a contract proof. Broadly speaking there are three degrees of commitment you can make to inkjet soft proofing, and depending on your requirements you may already have the equipment to hand.

MID-RANGE INKJET WITH BRANDED CONSUMABLES

Using a regular inkjet printer with quality paper and ink can produce reasonable results. Of course, a more expensive printer will produce better results, and it's worth purchasing an A3 Postscript printer with seven cartridges—sometimes known as CcMmYKk as there are additional light tint inks for the cyan, magenta and black colors. Try to match the type of finish on your inkjet paper to the paper you will be printing on, but usually you'll only have a choice of gloss, semigloss, or matte. Calibrating your printer correctly is important, and if you don't want the expense of buying the specialized profiling kit and software, there are companies that will send you a profile based on your printouts of their calibration sheets.

HIGH-END INKJET WITH QUALITY CONSUMABLES

A professional level inkjet is a big step up from a "regular" desktop inkjet. Resolution will be high, droplet control more precise, and color accuracy will be outstanding.

SWOP-certified proofs (Specifications Web Offset Publications proofs) are the gold standard aspired to for proofing. For the printer and media combinations from Agfa, ColorBurst, Canon, Epson, Kodak, and others that are among the few desktop printers to receive such certification, visit www.swop.org. Highly recommended examples are the relatively inexpensive Epson Stylus Pro 4880, or the much more expensive 9900, twinned with Kodak MATCHPRINT Pro consumables. Using large sheets, it is possible to proof double-page spreads, complete with printer marks and calibration bars.

INKJET PROOFER WITH CUSTOM MEDIA

Desktop proofers are blurring the line between studio "soft" proofing, and contracted out "hard" proofs. Capable of fitting two double-page spreads on a single sheet, the Kodak Veris proofer (until recently manufactured by Creo) has an inline spectrophotometer for calibrating proofs as they print. The process is entirely automated, and will ensure color accuracy without the need for manual configuration.

To take things even further, there are a handful of specialty paper suppliers, such as SOS inkjet media, who provide inkjet "substrates" to your specifications. Whether you regularly need to match your proofs to newsprint or brown paper bags, a custom substrate can be produced to suit your requirements—for a price, of course.

Limitations

Inkjet proofing is becoming widespread nowadays, and at the top end of the price range the results are excellent. However, don't be fooled into thinking that an everyday inkjet printer will do as good a job as a proofing system, because it won't. The biggest drawback with inkjet printing is the paper you print on—it will nearly always be too white, and loaded with UV brighteners. Inkjets are also extremely precise with the positioning of their ink, so any problems you may have with registration or trapping will not be apparent. In fact, inkjet proofs are so perfect it's common for them to exceed the quality of their press counterparts, occasionally leading to complaints from clients when they see the finished job.

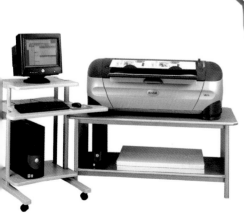

PROFESSIONAL COLOR PROOFING

There will be many times throughout your career that you will be expected to provide a client with a proof of their job, which can then be signed off as part of the contract. These "contract" proofs are, in effect, a guarantee of quality for the final printed product. No matter how good your in-house inkjet printer is, it's best to turn to a professional reprographics or prepress company for such proofs.

DIGITAL CONTRACT PROOFS

A step up from desktop inkjet proofing, digital contract proofs use much of the same technology, but with added bells and whistles. The hardware used will usually be inkjet, laser, thermal wax, or dye-sublimation technology. Resolutions will be higher, output will be faster, and the printers will often be self-calibrating. Permanently linked to a dedicated proofing station and RIP (Raster Image Processing) for producing the data used to create the proofs; the same files can also be sent to the presses for final printing.

Advances in digital proofing have seen digital proofers producing simulated CMYK screens. These screens can be set to match your press settings, including lines per inch and screen angles to exactly match proofs to the printed finals.

Thermal laser "donors"—a transfer material used for carrying color until printed—are available in a wide range of spot colors, including fluorescent and metallic finishes. Six-plate proofers are capable of mimicking the prints from Pantone Hexachrome presses.

ANALOG CONTRACT PROOFS

Cromalin, Iris, and Matchprint proofs are produced using a RIP and a laser to expose a sheet of film for each color plate in the print job (usually cyan, magenta, yellow, and black). The film is then used to expose colored donors on to a backing substrate, creating a CMYK image. Because the same film that is used to create the proof will be used to produce the printing plates for the presses, you get a "what you see is what you get" proof—right down to the halftone dots, overprinting, trapping, and any registration problems.

Today, digital proofs have more or less replaced their analog counterparts. Many companies formerly associated with traditional proofing now produce a digital equivalent using technology produced by the same manufacturers that previously provided the equipment for creating analog proofs.

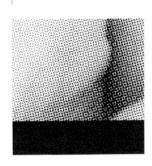

Wet proofs

For the jobs that really matter, such as those with a high budget and a long print run, digital contract proofing may not be up to scratch. The most accurate way to proof a print job is to run a wet proof using the actual presses, ink, and paper that are to be used for the final print run. Of course, this is expensive, as you are in effect running a short job through high-capacity presses. If you are using a digital press then the cost and effort involved may be a little more modest, but it will still exceed the cost of digital proofs produced with a dedicated proofing machine.

CHOOSING COLOR FOR SCREEN USE

When you prepare pages for print, you probably know the color of the paper that will be used, whether glossy white or a colored tint, and you can take this into account when picking colors for your design using either a *Color Picker* or the *Eyedropper* tool. The same is not true for web pages, because you cannot predict what equipment people will use to view your web pages.

Different makes and models of monitors, handheld computer screens, and even cell phones will all interpret colors differently, although usually the differences will be subtle. More importantly, the computer hardware that sends video signals to the screens may not support the full range of colors that the screen is capable of displaying, or the range of colors in your palette.

COLOR DISPLAY

In the early days of web design it was necessary to make considerable compromises to ensure that web pages would appear consistently on all screens. Even using smooth gradients could sometimes cause havoc and ruin good-looking designs on low-powered computers. These days most personal computers and many cell phones can manage at least 16-bit color, which means 65,536 distinct colors. Although this is not as accurate as full 24-bit color

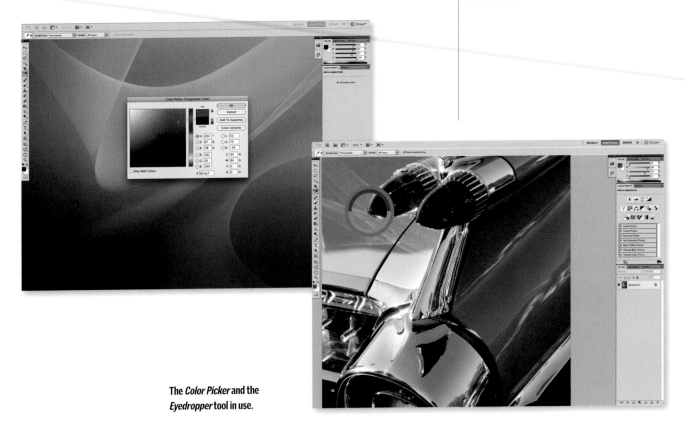

The *Color Picker* and the *Eyedropper* tool in use.

(16.7 million colors), it's usually good enough. Note that images in JPEG and PNG format support 24-bit color, whereas GIFs can only display 8-bit (256 colors).

HTML supports 16 colors that you can refer to by name, such as red, green, blue, black, white, and teal. If you want to use anything more subtle—and you will—you need to refer to a color's hexadecimal value in your CSS files. Most good photo-editing packages, including Photoshop, will provide a color's so-called Hex value. For example, black is #000000, while white is #FFFFFF.

WEB-SAFE COLORS

If you want to ensure that important parts of a site will always appear the way you designed them, a good option is to use a set of colors known as "web-safe." Web-safe colors were defined when many computers could only display 256 colors. There are 216 colors that are guaranteed to work on any Internet-connected computer, be it a Mac or PC. A quick Internet search will come up with a number of sites that allow you to view those colors and check their Hex codes.

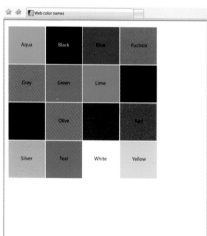

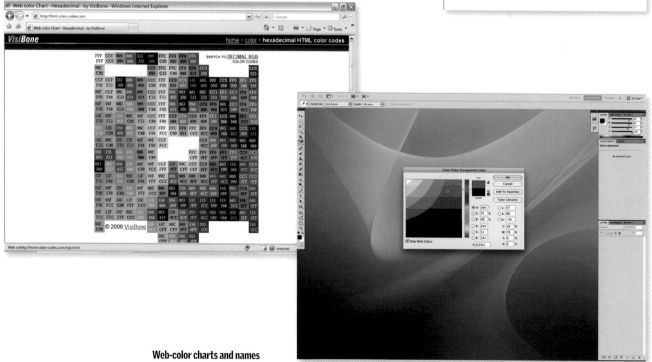

Web-color charts and names

Images

A picture says a thousand words. Using an image is the simplest and quickest way to convey a message, even a complicated one. A car, or anything else, can be described in the tiniest detail, but it's not until we've seen photographs of the product that we make a connection and really feel we know what it looks like. Whether you use images to dominate your design, or to punctuate columns of text, you need to know where to find the right images and how to put them to good use.

If you know where to look, there are millions of high-quality images available with a few clicks over the Internet—some you will have to buy, but others are free. If you need a specific style of subject matter, over the next few pages are hints and tips for commissioning photographers and illustrators, along with practical advice for directing the process and getting the results you need. Most photography will benefit from some "clean-up" and correction, and even a complete disaster can be saved with a little creative thinking, and following the rules provided in this section. We end with some technical advice, without too much jargon, on getting your images ready to send to the printers, and getting perfect results back.

SOURCING IMAGES

When looking for images and other assets to use in your projects, you need to be sure that what you're doing keeps you, your employer, and your client on the right side of the law. To that end, we kick off this chapter on sourcing images with a quick primer in intellectual property law.

INTELLECTUAL PROPERTY

As soon as you create (or anyone else creates) a piece of work, it's automatically covered by copyright law—whether it displays the copyright symbol (©) or not. Immediately you create an image—or literary, musical, dramatic, typographical, audio, or video work—it's your intellectual property, and you own the right to control how that image is used. Many employment contracts automatically transfer this right to an employer. If you work freelance, you must ensure that you're happy with any contract you sign to supply work—be careful that you're not blithely signing away all rights associated with your creations.

COPYRIGHT ≠ NO COPYING

Copyright, however, doesn't mean that you may not copy the works of others; it simply means that the creator of the work has the right to control what happens to it. The practical upshot is that if you do want to copy someone else's work, you must ask permission—it is at the originator's discretion whether or not to grant it.

CREATIVE COMMONS

There are, of course, numerous shades of gray when it comes to copyright; few people would try to make the case that someone who has grabbed an image from your website, say, and passed it off as their own is innocent of infringing your intellectual property, but you're on shakier ground when you start to create derivative works, or start switching media. What about if you trace over someone else's photograph with vector lines as part of a piece you're creating? (In this case, incidentally, you're probably still on the wrong side of the law.)

It's partly to avoid such confusion that the Creative Commons (CC) movement came about. Creative Commons is effectively a voluntary extension of traditional copyright law. Instead of saying "I've created this piece of work, and before anyone does anything at

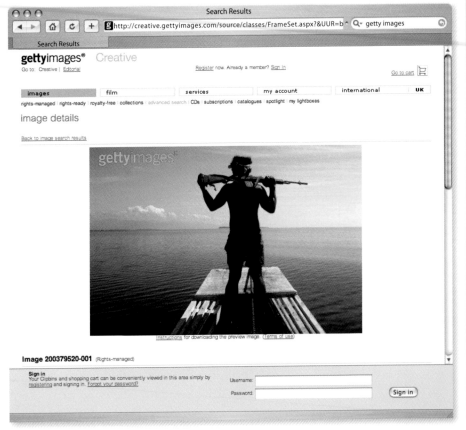

all with it, you have to ask me," you attach certain rights with it from the outset. You may, for example, say that anyone can use one of your images so long as you're attributed, or that it can be used for any non-commercial work. Information at creativecommons.org/license will help you determine the correct license to apply, or you can search for work created by others that you can use in your projects at search.creativecommons.org.

ROYALTY FREE

With royalty-free media, you usually make a one-off payment, and are granted the right to use that media many times in the organization covered by the agreement you sign up to when you make the purchase. Though some limits may be imposed, you are normally freed from the administrative and financial burden of making additional payments based on usage.

RIGHTS MANAGED

Rights-managed images represent the traditional way for organizations— particularly large bodies, or those working with large print runs—to purchase images. You pay each time you use the image, and the fee is based on a labyrinthine mix of such things as exclusivity, distribution, length of time used, and geographic location of use.

SOURCING IMAGES

SELECTED SOURCES

Working on the basis that you already know about Getty and Corbis, here are a few resources to help you source images that you may not be familiar with. Do bear in mind that recent years in the stock imagery market have been characterized by coalescence—any small, cuddly image library that you like to use because you have a moral objection to monolithic corporations such as Getty or Corbis is probably in reality owned by one of these two giants.

www.flickr.com

An excellent photo-sharing community, Flickr is also an invaluable resource for designers. Its advanced search feature allows you to specify that results shown are tagged with Creative Commons licenses. You can choose to show only work that can be used commercially, and that which can be modified and built upon.

search.creativecommons.org

Throw the net wider than Flickr, and use the main Creative Commons search engine. It ties into search engines from the likes of Google and Yahoo to search the entire web for CC-licensed media.

textureking.com

A superb site offering a growing catalog of free-to-use textures; excellent for everything from backgrounds to use within Photoshop as texture maps.

istockphoto.com

One of a new breed of commercial photo sites known as microstock libraries, iStockPhoto's main draw is its simple, high-value pricing structure. Screen-resolution images cost between $1 and $2 depending on size, while print-resolution images for most jobs are between $4 and $6, and there are "XXL" versions of some files that cost as much as $15. Usage is royalty free. All media is user-contributed, so you could upload your own photos and illustrations to earn a buck or two—but the quality is consistently high.

www.wikipedia.org

In all its guises and languages, Wikipedia, the online, user-edited encyclopedia, is an astonishingly useful resource. Better still, its text is licensed under the GNU Free Documentation License, so can be reproduced in many different ways without request; see en.wikipedia.org/wiki/Wikipedia:Copyrights for details of this licensing agreement. Many of the images are also in the public domain, or are licensed under a Creative Commons agreement.

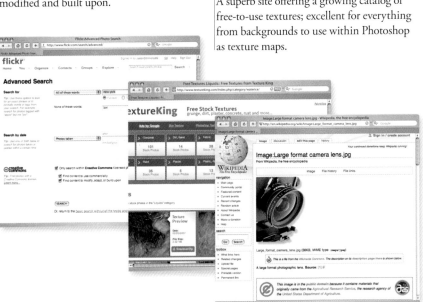

www.dreamstime.com
Another microstock library, all user-contributed, but of a generally high quality. Images typically cost no more than $1 and are royalty free.

www.shutterstock.com
A subscription-based service, paid for on a monthly basis rather than per image. Ideal for those who use a large amount of stock photography.

www.bigfoto.com
A user-contributed site with generally good-quality images, although some files are a little small. Photographs are free to use as long as you include a credit to the site.

www.free-pictures-photos.com/index.htm
A partner site to bigfoto.com, the images here are also free to use as long as a credit is included.

http://nix.nasa.gov/
An amazing source for images relating to astronomy and space travel. All NASA images (with the exception of logos and insignia) are copyright free and have no restrictions on use.

BUILDING A GRAPHICS LIBRARY

When time is tight or your layout lacks that certain spark, a well-stocked library of images, rips, tears, textures, and objects will be one of the most useful resources you have. Take a look through the magazines, books, and print advertising around today and you'll discover that nearly all of the examples below appear in one form or another.

Many of the graphic objects you need may have to be created especially for each specific job. Archive them in a safe place and they will come in useful again in the future. Think of it as clip art for professionals!

TEXTURES

Wood, corkboard, all types of clothing—especially denim—old cardboard packaging, paint strokes, wallpaper, and cosmetics can make interesting textures when scanned in as bitmaps or used to make graphics, such as lipstick kisses and fingerprints.

OBJECTS

Old books, paper, medical items, packaging, money, confetti, candies, airline tickets—a favorite with travel companies and guide books—playing cards, badges, thumbtacks, files, and ring binders can all perk up a design. Price tags and stickers are always used to great effect in sale advertising.

EFFECTS

Rips and tears are really common, but don't let that put you off as they work wonders for a variety of jobs. Clouds, rust, metal, and grass can all be used to clone away any unwanted objects in photos. Bullet holes and shattered glass are simple ways to suggest violence.

FRAMING

Old distressed photos, picture frames, Polaroids, camera negatives, ripped posters (keep the background in as well), Post-it notes, and stickers make ideal frames for text that really needs to get noticed.

TYPE

Children's building blocks, fun-food letters, computer keys, transport livery, wood or metal type—use the actual type, but also use them to make prints— and Scrabble letters can enliven text. Make sure you have your digital camera at hand all the time and you'll be amazed at how much creative type you come across every day.

Different ways to apply your graphic

A children's book may use a corkboard effect as a background to display readers' pictures, but that same graphic could be bit-mapped and distressed for exactly the same purpose in a cutting edge skate magazine.

A book within a book

Always be on the look out for interesting-looking old books. The yellowing pages and tattered covers make fantastic textures for creating an antique feel to your design.

Packaging

The milk carton graphic shown here is a simple and interesting way to bring a subject matter to life when no "real pictures" existed. This was created by applying computer printouts and photographing the result—but Photoshop will do just as well.

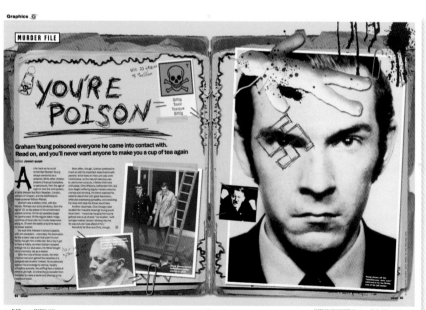

COMMISSIONING AN ILLUSTRATOR

Illustration, along with photography and type, plays a key role in defining the visual language of any project. Matching the right illustration to your design will make your message clearer, while an inappropriate illustration may cause confusion.

Research

Each job has different requirements and styles, and a different personality. When an illustrator or agency asks to show you their portfolio(s) always agree—it's the best way to see new work, and to build a relationship with possible future collaborators.

Keep track of illustration work by looking at portfolios, magazine tear sheets, and websites. Use agency books to keep tabs on wider groups, or styles, of illustrators.

Base your choices on an illustrator's style of work rather than the exact work in his or her portfolio. If you can't find an illustrator who suits your needs, call an agency.

Make contact

If at all possible, call an illustrator to offer the commission rather than relying on e-mail. Talk him or her through the project and include a little background information about the work you want him to produce. Set clear goals, so everyone knows exactly what is expected. The commission must be clear and defined—an illustrator can't deliver what you want if you don't explain carefully what that is. A template and sketch will help to define the space available for the artwork. To help the illustrator find appropriate solutions to your brief, send over reference material, and even a thumbnail sketch. Talk about their work, and pick out examples so

he or she knows what you like about their style. Discuss the practicalities of how they work—digitally or traditionally—and work through the implications. Don't be shy about mentioning budgets and deadlines early on—it can save a lot of time!

Confirm the commission, in an e-mail or fax, as soon as possible. Many larger design studios or publishers have forms that detail exactly what is required, by when, and for what fee (see example opposite). If you have these, always use them.

Most illustrations will take days or weeks to produce. Ensure that you see regular progress on the work, and talk to the artist during this time. Ask to see thumbnails of the work in progress. A low-resolution thumbnail is sufficient to check that the illustrator has understood the brief properly and is heading in the right direction creatively. Let them know what you think, and guide the creative process, but remember to guide rather than dictate: you want the illustrator's talent to shine rather than be stifled by your control.

Provide feedback

Most of the time you should get results you are happy with, but if a job is going wrong, it's important to remain positive. If you don't like something say why, but at the same time, try to emphasize the positive aspects—this will encourage an illustrator to work hard to fulfill the brief. Return to the original goals you set as a reminder of what the image needs to achieve.

Delivery

Most illustrators will supply digital artwork via e-mail or FTP site, but some prefer to burn a CD or DVD and post it. If your chosen artist works in traditional media, don't be surprised if a large canvas arrives by courier. Plan ahead and allow extra time in the schedule for the work to be photographed or scanned, and made ready for the press.

Say thanks

When the job is finished, send copies of the article/book/packaging to the illustrator. They will appreciate the opportunity to include the completed piece in their portfolio, and, hopefully, such follow-up will encourage a fruitful, creative partnership.

MacUser general commission information

This sheet contains notes relevant to all illustration/photographic illustration commissions within MacUser.
In addition to this you should also have received notes or verbal instructions on your particular project.

Image style

We often hear people saying, "Do you want that in the usual MacUser style?"

While this would have made sense a few years ago we are currently trying to broaden the range of illustration and photography styles we use. In the past there have been whole issues packed full of Photoshop multi-layer extravaganzas and while we are still happy to use work like this please tailor the execution to a style you are happy with and works well with the concept. Speaking of which…

Ideas and concepts

All images should be concept driven. The style and execution should help the idea work, not vice versa. Concepts should have some relevance to the editorial subject matter, if you want to read the main text of the article it can be supplied.

Sizes

A MacUser page is 210mm wide by 297mm high, a double page spread will therefore be 420mm wide by 297mm high.

About 12mm is lost in the central binding area and although we can compensate for this at repro please avoid placing essential details where they might disappear.

Bleed

Images do not have to bleed off the edge of pages but where they do so please allow at least 5mm, more is even better.

Colour and resolution

MacUser is printed on a four colour press but if the concept justifies it don't feel afraid of using black and white or any other monochrome effect.

Images are required at 300dpi at actual size.

Editorial

PDF's of previous relevant articles are available, they will give a good indication of the amount of area needing to be reserved for editorial elements and page furniture.

If you have any queries on this ask your helpful MacUser art contact for guidance.

Contributors panel

In each issue we run a small panel on key contributors. Please submit a 30mm square image (company logo or portrait are ideal) plus a couple of short sentences describing yourself or your work.

Deadlines

Deadlines for roughs and final artwork will have been indicated on your brief. Usually we will use rough artwork as a positional place holder, allowing us to experiment with the article layout. Once this is done others can begin editing copy and proof reading etc. This also has the benefit of allowing us a little flexibility with final deadlines.

If our through-put of pages to the repro house is going well we can normally hold back a spread or two for 24 hours, especially if it means the difference between an average piece of work and a masterpiece. Do not assume this will always be the case, but please call to discuss flexibility if you think you will need extra time.

Delivery

Artwork can be supplied in any file format but the usual options are JPEGs, TIFFs, or EPSs. CD's or Zip disks should be sent to the editorial address below or files can be ,ent via email or ISDN, again details are below.

Rates and licensing

Our standard rate for internal double page spread illustration work is £500, call our friendly art team to discuss rates for special jobs.

This payment covers the licensing rights to use your work with the feature discussed. We may repeat the image on a contents page or the MacUser website etc but it will only ever be used in conjunction with the feature it was originally commissioned for. Should the image ever be required for alternative usage you will be contacted.

Copyright remains with you but we must have exclusive usage of the image for six months within the UK.

Invoices

In order for an invoice to go through smoothly and ensure payment is made as quickly as possible please follow these guidelines set by our account department.
Invoices should be sent to:
    The Purchase Ledger Controller, Accounts Department,
    Dennis Publishing Ltd, 30 Cleveland Street, London W1T 4JD
Printed on each invoice should be the following information:
    The above address.
    A brief description of the commission (illustration for XX feature).
    Our magazine and company name (MacUser, Dennis Publishing Ltd).
    The issue details (volume and issue number and cover date).
    Who made the commission (usually Jason Simmons or Aston Leach).
    The amount the invoice is for and the details needed to make the payment.
    Your full contact details and VAT information if applicable.

22 January 2002

Contact details

ADDRESS MacUser, Dennis Publishing Ltd,
30 Cleveland Street, London, W1T 4JD.
TELEPHONE 020 7907 6000
FAX 0207907 6369
WEB www.macuser.co.uk

ART EDITOR Jason Simmons
TELEPHONE 020 7907 6362
MOBILE 07900 603078
EMAIL art@macuser.co.uk
ISDN 020 7580 0299

DESIGNER Aston Leach
TELEPHONE 020 7907 6358
EMAIL art2@macuser.co.uk

Raising a commission form
It is important to provide an illustrator with a clear brief and a commission form. Specifically, state any limits or requirements, and provide a template that defines the space they have to work in. Include details about how the work should be provided, and how it will be used, reproduced, distributed, and copyrighted.

WORKING WITH PHOTOGRAPHERS

Photography is an integral part of most visual communication, and, if the budget is available, using a professional photographer can yield fantastic results.

Before the shoot begins, it's essential that you plan everything, down to the last detail. Think the image(s) through and decide what results you are after. Consider mood, tone, content, setting, and usage. Do a sketch or a mock-up to aid visualization, as it's simpler and cheaper to try out variations at this stage than in a studio.

Choosing the right photographer can make or break a shoot. Look for style and creative flair to match your goals. Don't worry if your preferred photographers haven't shot your exact subject matter before unless it is particularly technical or requires specialist knowledge or equipment—aerial photography, for example. It's more important to find a photographer who can realize your vision, someone who takes the time to understand and create the aesthetic you desire. Discuss your budget at an early stage, and be honest. A good photographer can be trusted to deliver the best results within the boundaries set.

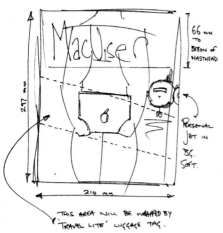

Preparations
Sketch your ideas as a visual aid for the photographer, but be flexible and be prepared to adapt as the shoot progresses. Make sure you are clear about the style of photograph, lighting, and composition you are aiming for.

Plan your shots
Make a call sheet, even if only shooting still life. Not only will this help to get all the required elements to the right place at the right time, it will also set priorities and a timetable for the shoot.

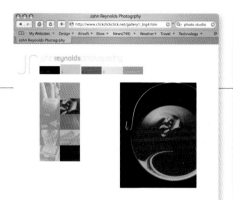

Styling

If you are using a model in your photo shoot it usually pays to employ a professional stylist. Not only will they select a range of clothes to suit your brief, but they will also be available on the day to dress your subject and make any necessary alterations.

PREPARATION

If you need products or props for the shoot, ensure they arrive at the studio or location on time. Check that everything is in good condition, clean, and works properly. If possible take spares, as accidents do happen and the last thing you want is to waste time waiting for replacement props.

Set achievable goals and, if taking multiple shots, prioritize the key shots. Don't try to do too many things with a single shot—cutouts from full shots often don't work well because of reflections, tints, and focus.

Ensure the photographer understands what you want to achieve, and keep visuals to hand, but let the photographer do his job—don't interfere with the camera, lights, or composition. In fact, you don't even need to be at the studio. The photographer can regularly e-mail low-resolution images or thumbnails for your approval.

When checking shots be decisive, don't dither or keep changing your mind. If you're working on a layout-critical shot, try placing the low-res image on the page. This will enable you to see if adjustments need to be made, to allow more space for headlines or copy for example.

KNOW WHEN YOU'VE GOT THE SHOT

Don't overwork an image—too much fuss and clutter can often ruin the impact of a simple idea. When your instinct says it's perfect, it probably is. Finally, don't waste time with variations until you have met you're initial goal—it's better to have one great shot rather than four average shots.

Don't touch

It's tempting to adjust a set, or move lights, while the photographer is busy with other things. Never do it. Even the slightest movement may cause a highlight to flare out, or an odd reflection to appear. Discuss any problems with the shot and let the photographer do their job without interference.

USING DESKTOP SCANNERS

Until relatively recently, scanning was the reserve of reprographics houses, equipped with expensive drum scanners. Nowadays a good-quality desktop scanner capable of producing near-professional results is far more affordable; and while the knowledge and skills of a professional operator still take years to acquire, there are a few simple steps that can be taken to help you acquire publishable scans.

THE SCANNER

As with all equipment you plan to use professionally, buy the best you can afford. Look for a high optical resolution (4,800dpi), a good color depth (24-bit minimum), and a transparency adaptor if working with film or transparencies. A fast interface, such as USB 2.0 or FireWire/IEEE 1394, will speed up the workflow, as will scanning software that allows multiple images to be scanned. While investigating the software, ensure it has a good range of user-definable settings, as discussed below.

USING THE SOFTWARE

Ignore the basic settings on the scanner software as it's important to tailor each scan to match the original image, and your end-usage requirements. To do that you need to define the input and output resolutions. If you're unsure of the size your scan needs to be, produce a low-resolution scan—for position only (often referred to as a positional or an FPO). This will allow you to experiment with the image before spending time producing a high-resolution version.

Place and size up the original, then enter the output size required, or the amount the image needs to be scaled. For example, if your original is 4 x 5in (102 x 127mm) and you want the final dimensions to be 6 x 7½in (152 x 190mm), you need to scan at 150%.

Hardware

Most desktop scanners have flat beds suited to scanning standard office paper sizes, but larger versions are available. If you're working with film, you'll need a transparency adaptor. For creative work, features such as automatic document loading are generally not needed.

Advanced settings

Avoid the basic preset scanning modes. It's much better to take control of your software using the "advanced" or "professional" settings. After sizing up the original, type in the output size and resolution.

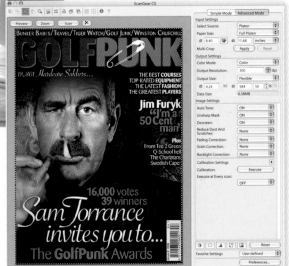

RESOLUTION

The output resolution required is based on the quality of your printing. You will need to double the number of lines per inch (lpi) used on the press to find the number of dots per inch (dpi) you should be scanning to. For example, a typical magazine cover will be printed at 150lpi, so you should scan at 300dpi. If you are unable to confirm the lpi your printers will be using, there are international standards to guide you—uncoated stock is usually printed at 133 or 150lpi, coated stock at 150, 175, and occasionally 200lpi.

COLOR

Always scan in RGB mode. Any problems with color hue, saturation, and brightness will be quicker and easier to fix in RGB. Once you're happy with the scan, converting into CMYK is best handled by Photoshop, which offers excellent control during the conversion process.

Scanning from a book or magazine

Aside from copyright issues, scanning previously printed images poses unique problems. Simply scanning the image will result in moiré patterns—blotchy areas of light and dark where two patterns (the CMYK dots and the scanner's sensors) clash. Good-quality scanning software will include a "descreening" setting that will improve your results considerably. You will be asked to enter the lpi your source material has been printed at, but by a very technical mathematical coincidence, and thanks to the way RGB and CMYK values are calculated, descreening at 90lpi will remove moiré patterns in just about every circumstance.

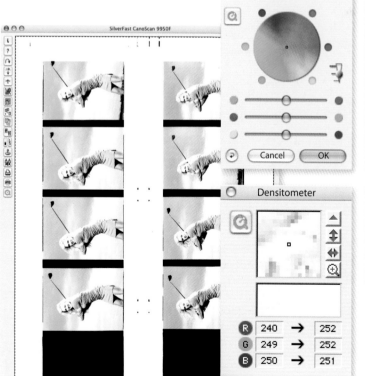

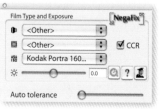

OPENING AWKWARD FILES

It has happened to us all—a client or other external source has e-mailed you the source files to use in your design project, and you find you can't open it. What do you do? The good news is that the power and flexibility of today's heavyweight applications mean that they can usually cope with a wide range of file formats even from other applications on other platforms. Here's a seven-point plan for getting those reticent files opened up.

What's the file?

Your first step is to know your enemy. Ask the sender what type of file it is. Once the preserve of Windows, most files you come across these days have a file extension—.tiff, .eps, .doc are just three examples; the file extension will tell you what type of file it is. If it's an extension you're not familiar with, the ever-useful filext.com should be able to tell you.

What opens it?

filext.com will usually suggest the file's likely creator; alternatively "Googling" the file extension will also turn up the applications that can open the file. Even when you think you know which application should open a file, though, you can still run into problems...

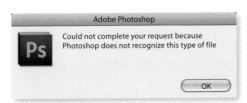

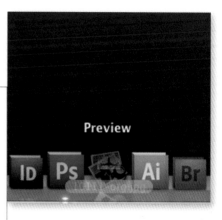

Keep your applications current

One of the easiest ways to insure against problems opening files is to ensure you're using the latest version of the software; advances made with the file formats of each successive application iteration—particularly of heavyweight ones such as those in Adobe's Creative Suite—often mean that older versions of the application can't open files created by more recent versions. While the expense of upgrading A-grade suites may be prohibitive, there's no excuse when it comes to free or cheap tools such as Stuffit Expander.

Force open

A handy tip for Mac users: if you're convinced, for example, that Preview should be able to open a file, but it's grayed-out when you try, drop the file onto the Preview application icon in the Dock while holding down ⌘ and ⌥?. This forces the application to attempt to open it.

Add to your arsenal

Applications such as the very versatile GraphicConverter (www.lemkesoft.com) on the Mac are an essential part of any designer's toolkit. This shouldn't be confused with the alternative product available for Windows' users at www.graphic-converter.net.

Common mistakes

Check the file size of received files; if it's only a few kilobytes, something may have gone wrong. It may be that the sender has attached an alias, or that the file is corrupt. Mac users should be careful to send Windows-friendly attachments over e-mail; in Mail choose *Edit > Attachments > Always Send Windows Friendly Attachments*.

Use standard formats

It's generally more reliable to use common formats, for example .eps rather than .ai if you're an Adobe Illustrator user, as other collaborators on a project may not own the same applications as you.

Go back to the source

If all else fails, contact the sender of the file and ask for it to be saved in a commonly used format before being resent.

USING CAMERA RAW

Generally, images supplied by a photographer or image library will be TIFFs or JPEGs, but occasionally you may receive RAW images or perhaps shoot your own material as RAW files—the digital equivalent of a film negative. RAW files contain all the data that is recorded by the sensor in a digital camera, as well as all of the camera's settings at the time the photo was taken. However, as the files are not subjected to any in-camera processing, you can alter certain settings later in post-production. Temperature adjustments (for white balance), exposure, and a whole range of additional parameters, for example, can be set at the point at which you first open

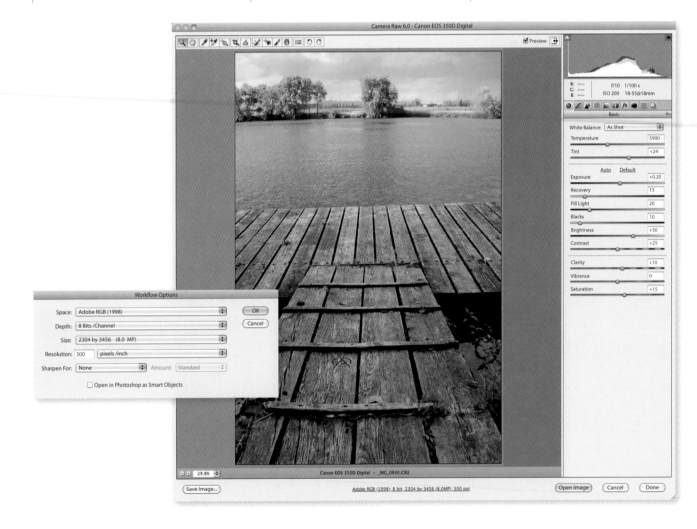

a RAW image. To open a RAW file you'll need the Camera RAW plug-in for Photoshop, or a stand-alone application from your camera's manufacturer. RAW files can also be opened from within Bridge.

They work in conjunction with *sidecar* files, which are small text files automatically saved to the same folder as the original RAW image. The sidecar file records and remembers all the settings applied to the RAW file each time it's opened. If you lose the sidecar file or move the original RAW files to another workstation, you're back to square one. While it's true that RAW files provide a wealth of advantages over other image formats, there is an alternative to RAW which is a little more flexible and offers the same benefits—Adobe's DNG format.

THE DNG ALTERNATIVE
I really like the DNG (digital negative) file format. Adobe devised and introduced it as far back as Photoshop CS2 in order to standardize the format in which original RAW images can be stored. DNG files are generated via the *Save* option in the Camera RAW plug-in, and contain all the data from the RAW original. They're self-contained in that they don't require sidecar files—a neater solution—and the file sizes are smaller due to *lossless* compression options offered as part of the *Save* procedure. If you're using Photoshop and RAW files frequently, consider the option of saving the RAW images that you intend to use for a project to the DNG format and either deleting or archiving the RAW originals.

CAMERA RAW AND OTHER FORMATS
Since the release of Photoshop CS3, camera RAW has been capable of opening both TIFF and JPEG files, thus presenting a whole new way to approach an image-editing workflow. However, if you choose to investigate this method further, you must remember that not all the benefits of editing a RAW original, which is "untreated" data, can be drawn on when opening an image saved in one of these formats. For example, enlargements from a JPEG original will not be of the same quality as those generated from a RAW original.

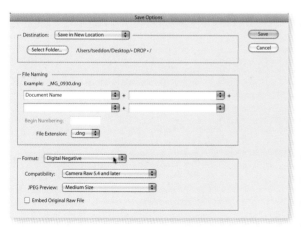

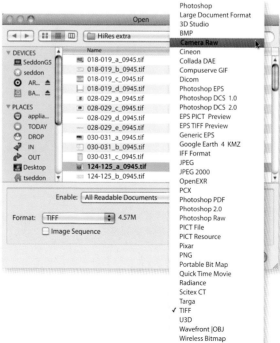

USING CAMERA RAW

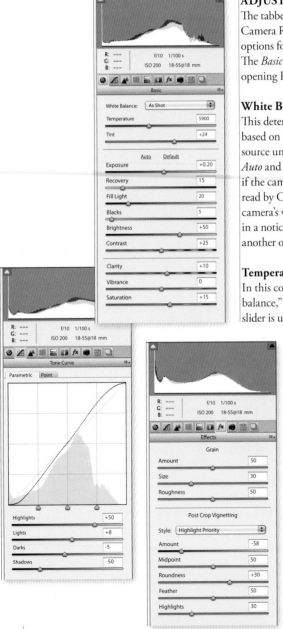

ADJUSTMENTS

The tabbed palettes at the right of the Camera RAW screen provide a host of options for controlling image adjustments. The *Basic* tab is the one I use the most when opening RAW files.

White Balance

This determines the image's color balance, based on the color temperature of the light source under which the image was shot. *Auto* and *As Shot* will give the same result if the camera's white-balance setting can be read by Camera RAW. Alternatively, if the camera's white-balance setting has resulted in a noticeable color cast, you can select another option from the presets provided.

Temperature and Tint

In this context *"temperature,"* like "white balance," refers to color temperature. The slider is used to compensate for unwanted color casts caused by color temperature; moving the slider to the left compensates for a low (red) temperature and therefore makes the image bluer, while moving the slider to the right compensates for high (blue) temperatures and makes the image yellower. The *Tint* slider should be used to fine-tune the image, and basically adjusts the color balance from green on the left to magenta on the right. Since CS3 the sliders are helpfully colored to remind you what effect an adjustment will have on an image.

Exposure and Recovery

The numerical value here corresponds to f-stops, where a + value represents opening up the aperture of a camera's lens to increase exposure, and a – value represents closing down the aperture to reduce exposure—in other words, it adjusts the brightness of an image. You can ensure that detail isn't lost through clipping when brightening an image by using the *Preview* checkbox to indicate blown-out areas. The *Recovery* slider below allows you to increase the overall exposure, then recover any blown highlights without adjusting the exposure back down. This is very useful for brightening images without losing lots of detail in the process.

Fill Light and Blacks

Moving the *Fill Light* slider to the right adds light to all shadow areas. Again, be sure not to lose detail through clipping by using the *Preview* checkbox. The *Blacks* slider saturates only the blacks in an image rather than overall color, and is useful if you want your image to look more punchy.

Brightness and Contrast

Not to be confused with *Exposure*, *Brightness* differs in that it doesn't affect black and white points and you can use it to fine-tune the image visually after adjusting *Exposure*. You may find it preferable to leave this slider alone at this stage and make any adjustments later in the workflow using more sophisticated adjustment layers. The same goes for *Contrast*, which I tend to leave alone, as it may otherwise wipe out color information that you'll need later in the adjustment process.

Clarity, Vibrance, and Saturation

Introduced with CS3, the *Clarity* slider increases local contrast, providing a great method for quickly adding depth to an image. The *Vibrance* slider effectively replaces the older *Saturation* slider, and is much smarter, as it only increases the saturation of unsaturated colors, leaving the already saturated colors alone. The *Saturation* slider is still present, but I prefer to leave this set to zero. It can wipe out detail overall, so any adjustment is best left until later when you can utilize an adjustment layer.

Tone Curve

The *Parametric* option under the *Tone Curve* tab is particularly useful as it allows you to make tonal adjustments using the sliders beneath, providing a very intuitive way of adjusting overall tones straight from the RAW original.

Effects

New to CS5, the *Effects* tab provides a couple of neat ways to add both *Grain* and *Vignetting* to an image. Our example to the right is the result obtained by inputting the values as shown in the grab of the palette shown on the left, and is reminiscent of the kind of image you would achieve using a Lomo or Holga type camera. It's a relatively small edition to RAW and there are plenty of other ways to achieve these effects, but I like the inclusion of this new feature all the same.

SCALING IMAGES

When commissioning or purchasing images to use as part of a layout, size requirements can and should be taken into account. However, inevitably there will arise some occasions when you want to use a particular image that isn't quite large enough. If it's absolutely the right image and no other will do, you have a problem on your hands. It's important to bear in mind that a 300ppi image is only high resolution if it's used in the layout at 100% or smaller. In these circumstances avoid enlarging images in your layout, it's much better to enlarge them in Photoshop first.

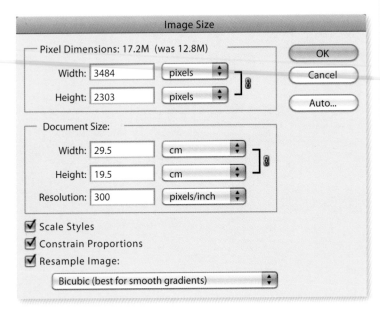

Photoshop's Image Size palette

IMAGE SIZE

If your images are intended for on-screen use, look to the *Pixel Dimensions* section of Photoshop's *Image Size* dialog window; for print use *Document Size*. *Constrain Proportions* automatically retains width/height relationships, and *Scale Styles* ensures that layer styles applied to any unflattened images are kept in position. If *Resample Image* is unchecked, the resolution and the image's physical dimensions are directly linked. For example, an image that measures 29.5 x 19.5cm at 300ppi becomes a much larger 122.9 x 81.24cm if *Resolution* is set at 72ppi. Although the image's dimensions are larger, no resampling has taken place—it's simply that the pixels per inch resolution is set lower. To actually resample, or interpolate, an image the *Resample Image* box must be checked.

RESAMPLING TECHNIQUES

When interpolating an image, Photoshop analyzes the digital information contained within the image and "guesses" what pixels should be added. This won't, however, miraculously enlarge an image to whatever size you wish without some loss of quality—and the more you enlarge an image the greater the loss of quality will be. Therefore, you must exercise caution when carrying out any significant enlargements. One thing that will improve interpolation results is selecting the most appropriate setting from the drop-down menu at the base of the *Image Size* dialog window. Avoid the *Nearest Neighbor* and *Bilinear* options as they rarely produce the best results. The *Bicubic* option analyzes 4 x 4 pixels surrounding each individual existing pixel, so the resulting interpolation is much more acceptable. For enlargements opt for *Bicubic Smoother*, but if you're reducing an image, *Bicubic Sharper* is the best choice. If you're batch processing a large number of images go for the basic *Bicubic* option.

A quick tip for enlarging images is to do it gradually in increments of 5% rather than all in one go. This allows Photoshop greater control when interpolating the new pixels. Finally, try interpolating in Photoshop's Camera RAW plug-in if it's available, as this can often provide good results; and with Photoshop CS3–CS5 plug-ins capable of converting JPEGs and TIFFs, this may also be the best method for non-RAW files. It's well worth investigating the comparative quality of enlargements carried out using both methods to see which provides the best image quality. And don't forget that results will vary depending on the type of image.

The original 1,488-pixel-wide image reproduced at 100%

An enlargement from a 360-pixel-wide image, resampled to 413% in 5% increments using Photoshop

CREATIVE CROPPING

Less is more. An image can often fail because it lacks a focal point, or has too much distracting background. Cropping an image, to focus on the subject matter, can bring life and energy into the composition.

Before attempting any crop, it's important to identify the message you are trying to convey. Are you trying to make intimate contact, convey a sense of space, or give a static scene some movement?

DIVIDE THE FRAME INTO THIRDS

In your mind's eye, divide the area you are working with into thirds—both horizontally and vertically. Your subject matter should be where two of the lines intersect.

LOSE THE CLUTTER

Scale or crop your image to remove anything that is unessential to convey your message. Usually it will be background material, but it could be a distracting foreground object, such as a telegraph pole.

SYMMETRY

Instead of dividing the frame into thirds as described above, another option is to center your subject. Keep everything as symmetrical and geometric as possible. Use the natural straight edges of your image to enhance the effect.

DEPTH

Distance and space can be emphasized by using a foreground object to contrast with your subject matter. Crop the foreground object almost out of the frame—the viewer will naturally look past it to the focal point of the image.

EXTREMES

Use extremes of scale to create impact. A face cropped in tight, filling the frame, demands immediate attention. While a small object on a contrasting flat field will pull the viewer in.

USE A LINE OF MOTION

Whether it's a fence, road markings, or a line of trees, if your image has a natural line of motion use it to draw your reader in. Eyes can't help but follow the natural perspective, especially if it points to your subject matter.

UNUSUAL ANGLES

Try rotating a photo to discover its hidden excitement; images can be given motion by placing them at an angle that creates tension. Or drop the viewer's line of sight low down, or high up, to create the unexpected.

WORK WITH THE LAYOUT

It's unusual for an image to be viewed in isolation. Place your image to work with your layout, or vice versa. Type and visual subject matter can be used to draw attention to each other.

TONAL ADJUSTMENTS

Here's the scenario. You've got a selection of images to choose from and you find the ideal shot among them, but unfortunately it's not perfectly exposed. Maybe the shot is too dark, or perhaps it's lacking in contrast, but you really want to use it. Let's look at how to fix the problem, starting with the basic adjustments.

PRIORITIES

There's no set order for making specific types of adjustment—it depends entirely on the image. I find that *tonal adjustments* are needed more often than any other type, and therefore I tend to make these adjustments first. Often you'll find that an image's color is also affected as a result of a tonal adjustment—saturation will increase or decrease when darkening or lightening an image—but essentially this is about brightness and contrast.

BRIGHTNESS/CONTRAST

It's best not to use the *Brightness/Contrast* adjustment for anything beyond the most simple of corrections. It's an all-or-nothing adjustment, as it doesn't discriminate between shadows and highlights that well, which isn't ideal for the majority of images. A *Levels* adjustment will provide better, more controlled results.

LEVELS

Using *Levels* is a visual exercise—despite the fact that input and output levels are displayed numerically within the palette. I say palette rather than dialog box as I always opt to work with an adjustment layer—why would you not? Once you've mastered *Levels*, I doubt you'll think about using *Brightness/Contrast* again, even for simple adjustments. The major advantage of using *Levels* is that it allows you to adjust the contrast within the shadow and highlight areas of an image independently, and to adjust the brightness independently of those shadow and highlight settings.

The histogram plays a key role in *Levels* adjustment, and it's important to understand its function. The shape of the histogram indicates how tonal values are distributed throughout an image, running from shadows on the left (the black point) to highlights on the right (the white point). If the histogram is biased toward the left, for example, your image will be predominantly dark.

Levels adjustments

This night shot is mainly shadow with a few bright highlights, and the histogram reflects this with a bias to the left side and a small spike at the far right. Dragging the right hand slider inward (top right) distributes the overall tonal range more evenly, and adjusting the middle slider (bottom right) brightens the image.

The histogram also indicates how much *clipping* has occurred in an image. "Clipping" is the term used to describe how much information, and therefore detail, has been lost in the shadows and highlights of an image, and shows up as flat areas at either end of a histogram. A distinct spike at the highlight end of a histogram can indicate clipping in bright reflections from metal or glass. The ideal image shouldn't exhibit any clipping, particularly in the highlight areas, where detail is most often lost. To fix the problem, create a *Levels Adjustment Layer* and begin by adjusting the positions of the black and white point sliders, moving them inward so they sit below the beginning and end of the existing histogram, that is, the point at which the graph reaches zero. This action will redistribute the range of tonal values between the darkest and brightest points. If the image now has too much contrast, move the sliders back out a little and reappraise the result.

The middle slider below the histogram adjusts the midtones within the image, and is often thought of as a brightness control. Moving the slider to the left sets the mid-gray point closer to black, and produces a brighter image, while moving it to the right has the opposite effect and makes the image darker. Remember, moving the mid-gray point won't alter the position of either the black or white points, so overall contrast remains good.

TONAL ADJUSTMENTS

CURVES

The *Curves* command is probably the most powerful adjustment tool in Photoshop. It's also the trickiest to master, but don't let that put you off using it. *Curves* works by adjusting all pixels at particular tonal values, where the values are selected and governed by the positions of anchor points on a curve (or line) above a grid—think back to the graphs you drew at school, where you compared values on the horizontal x-axis and the vertical y-axis.

Here the x-axis is the *input* value, and the y-axis the *output* value. You can also think of these as *before* and *after* values, which I prefer as it sounds less technical. Photoshop's default is to begin with a 45° line from bottom left to top right, which effectively means no adjustment. If you take any one point on that line and move its position, the before and after values will alter according to the direction in which the point moves, and the image will alter accordingly.

By default, the gradient for each axis runs from black to white (representing light) for RGB images, but you can toggle this to run in the opposite direction by selecting your choice from the *Show Amount of* option. All the points I make in this section assume a white-to-black gradient direction as I work mainly in print so am used to thinking about ink rather than light. The points at each end of the curve represent the white and black points, but if you've followed my suggestions you'll have set these already using *Levels* (the histogram makes it easier to do this with *Levels*), so leave the points at the corners of the grid.

ANCHOR POINTS

In most cases you'll want to begin by seeing what effect a *Curves* adjustment will have on the midtones, so add an anchor point by clicking on the middle of the curve. The values indicating the anchor point's position in the *Input* and *Output* boxes will depend on the direction of the gradient, as Photoshop performs a neat trick here. If you're thinking like a photographer (with light) and have the gradient running black to white, the values conform to the standard 0–255 value range. If, like me, you work with a white-to-black gradient, the values switch to a 0–100 value scale replicating percentages.

An upward movement of the anchor point will darken the image, and a downward movement will brighten it.

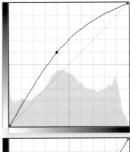
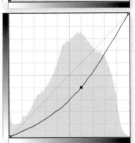

This is similar to the adjustment made with the midtone slider using the *Levels* command. A movement to the left will increase contrast, and a movement to the right will decrease it. The sideways movements make the curve steeper or shallower, and you can relate this to the image. A steeper curve with its greater portion above the original 45° line results in increased overall contrast, while a shallower curve will produce an overall decrease. Practice using *Curves* with a test image—it's the best way to learn what happens with each type of anchor-point adjustment. If using a color image proves to be confusing, try using a grayscale image first, as the specific adjustments you make will be easier to observe.

Curves adjustments

On the left, the split image demonstrates how moving an anchor point from the middle of the curve by 10% in either direction produces a darker or lighter image. Moving it up and right makes the image darker, moving it down and right makes the image lighter. The classic S-curve adjustment shown to the right demonstrates one of the easiest ways to boost the overall contrast of an image without losing a lot of detail. An adjustment layer has been used in the later example.

THE S-CURVE

The S-curve is a commonly used *Curves* adjustment that generally works well with most images. Its usefulness lies in the fact that it can increase contrast through the midtone range of an image without losing too much detail from shadow and highlight areas. To make an S-curve, add two anchor points 15–20% from either end of the default 45° line. Move the top point a little to the left, and the bottom point a little to the right, to form a shallow S-shaped curve. You should notice that your image now benefits from a boost in overall contrast but hasn't lost any significant detail. If you subsequently feel that the highlights could do with a bit more help, move the lower anchor point inward a little more, and so on, until you've achieved the desired result.

SMART FILTERS

When adjusting images, the non-destructive route is always the best, if the option is available. Adjustment layers provide us with the means to make changes to color and exposure without committing irrevocably to the chosen settings, but until the release of CS3 and the introduction of Smart Filters this wasn't possible when applying filters.

WHAT ARE SMART FILTERS?

I should start by briefly mentioning Smart Objects. They were introduced with Photoshop CS2, and allow you to import a vector graphic into a Photoshop document as a Smart Object. The object is termed "smart" because it remains fully scalable, just like a normal vector graphic, by maintaining a link to the original file. The natural progression for Photoshop has been to expand on this functionality by introducing Smart Filters, which provide a fully editable, non-destructive workflow for the application of filters. They're basically adjustment layers for filters, in that they sit above the original image layer but do not irreversibly alter it.

USING SMART FILTERS

To apply a filter as a Smart Filter, you first need to open an image via Photoshop's standard *Open* menu as a *Smart Object*. Don't worry if you forget to do this, or if you already have the image open on your screen, as you can use *Convert for Smart Filters* under the main *Filters* menu. You'll notice in the accompanying screen shots that the image's icon in the *Layers* palette changes to indicate that the layer is a smart object.

All filters subsequently used appear under the image layer as a stack which can be reordered if required, and are applied as part of a layer mask across the whole image area. You can tell that the whole image will be

affected, as the layer mask icon is fully white at this stage. In our example image I've applied *Gaussian Blur* followed by *Film Grain* to achieve a hazy effect. The small double slider icon to the right of each filter listed in the *Layers* palette calls up a *Blending Options* dialog when double-clicked, where the effect of each filter can be adjusted in terms of its opacity, and where each can have an alternative blending mode applied. Remember that, throughout this whole process, all filters remain fully editable. You can go back at any time and change the settings you've already applied without any further loss of the original digital information contained in the file.

COMBINING LAYER MASKS

There's another potentially useful technique which you can utilize when using Smart Filters. Areas of the layer mask can be painted out or selected and deleted after the filters have been applied, to reveal the original image beneath. In the final version of the example shown on this spread I've used a black brush to paint out the window area of the image, removing all filter effects from just that portion of the image in the process.

Painting over an area of the image when the Smart Filters layer is selected, as shown in the screengrab will mask out any of the applied filter effects to reveal the original image.

IMAGE RETOUCHING

In an ideal world photographs would be perfect, straight from the camera. This doesn't happen every time and images often need cleaning up or retouching to remove unwanted noise, blemishes, or even whole objects. Here we're going to look at some common problem areas with photographs, and how to fix them in Photoshop.

Before beginning any retouching work always make a copy of the image, as accidents do happen and you may need to return to the original work. Always work on the largest file size available, and crop and scale your image at the end of the post-production stage. If you are performing an extensive overhaul of a photo it's worth duplicating your image onto a new layer (Ctrl/Cmd+J), and working on that. By toggling the layer on and off you can see how the image is improving.

SHARPENING

Today's digital cameras often employ in-camera sharpening algorithms to ensure images appear sharp. However, many photographers, especially when shooting RAW, prefer to undertake any sharpening in image-editing software such as Photoshop, which offers much greater control. The first step when sharpening an image is to switch to *Image > Mode > Lab*, and select the *Lightness* channel. By sharpening only the *Lightness* channel you'll avoid the bright halo that can appear on highly sharpened images.

Use *Smart Sharpen* or *Unsharp Mask* to sharpen the image. The *Amount* field determines the level contrast between the detected edge pixels, and *Radius* sets the number of pixels affected either side of the edge. *Remove* will define the type of softness the filter will attempt to negate, either *Gaussian Blur, Lens Blur,* or *Motion Blur.* Experiment with the settings until you get the right result, and as a rule of thumb don't over do it. Once finished convert your image back into RGB or CMYK as usual.

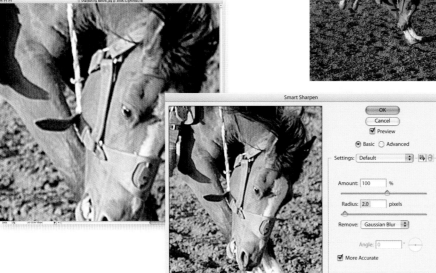

REMOVING NOISE

Whether it's film grain or electronic interference on a sensor, it's not uncommon for images to inherit some random noise. This can be removed using the *Reduce Noise* filter, but before you begin it's worth checking to see if the noise is limited to a single color channel, or if it can be isolated to the *Lightness* channel in Lab color mode. Removing the noise only where needed will minimize the damage the filter will do and produce a better result.

The *Strength* of the filter will need to be balanced against the *Detail* settings, and there isn't a perfect setting for every image. Leave the *Remove JPEG Artifact* box unchecked unless your image is also littered with them

(see below). Experiment with the values until the optimum result is achieved. The advanced options allow different settings to be applied to each channel in a single action.

REMOVING JPEG ARTIFACTS

To the uninitiated, saving highly compressed JPEGs provides the benefit of small file sizes, but for a designer it's a disaster to open a file and see blocks of color clustering over an image. Use the *Reduce Noise* filter and check the *Remove JPEG Artifact* box at the bottom of the dialog box to minimize obvious JPEG artifacts. While the filter causes some blurring, if the artifacts are slight it is possible to remove them completely without adversely affecting the image. In more extreme cases you have to balance the loss of detail against the removal of the artifacts.

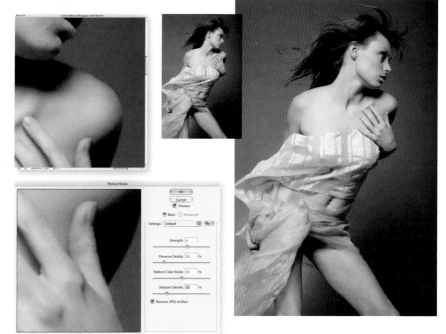

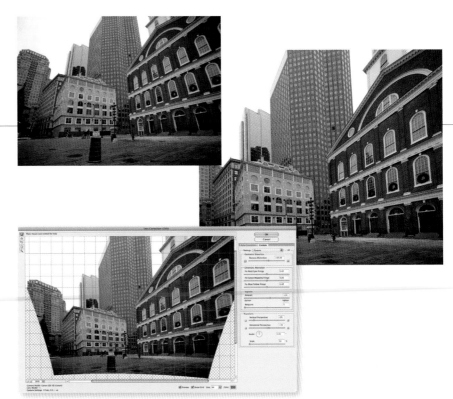

CORRECTING BARREL DISTORTION

By its very nature a camera lens will distort an image. While it is not usually noticeable, using a wide-angle lens to capture a large panorama is likely to result in barrel distortion. Under the *Filter* menu, the *Lens Correction* tools can bring a distorted image closer to reality. Use the *Remove Distortion* slider to correct any bowing, and the vertical and horizontal *Transform* settings to level out the effects of perspective. Color shifts and uneven exposures can be adjusted for using the *Chromatic Aberration* and *Vignette* controls, respectively. Once perfected, your settings can be saved until the next time an image from the same camera and lens combination has to be corrected.

REMOVING WHOLE ELEMENTS

If you're using a version of Photoshop prior to CS5 you'll need to master the *Healing Brush* and *Patch* tools in order to clone out unwanted objects from images. If, however, you have upgraded to CS5 you'll have access to the near-miraculous *Content-Aware* fill option. Simply create a rough selection around the edge of the object you wish to remove, choose *Edit > Fill*, and select the *Content-Aware* option from the drop-down menu at the top of the *Fill* palette. The selected area is subsequently filled with background sampled from the rest of the image— amazingly easy. The *Spot Healing* tool can also be configured *Content-Aware*, which helps when small areas at the edge of the selection need a little more work.

CLONING LARGE AREAS

When there is a large area of image to
be filled with cloned artwork, but only a
small source area, it is inevitable that some
elements will be repeated and a pattern will
be obvious. Use the *Spot Healing* tool to clean
up any textures and small items that may
be repeating, remembering that in CS5 you
can use it in *Content-Aware* mode. Switch to
the *Healing Brush* or *Clone Stamp* tools to
rearrange or remove any larger elements,
breaking the uniformity of the pattern. By
altering a few parts of the repeated area, your
retouching work will be far less obvious.

Retouching people

We are intimately familiar with the human figure, especially the face, so any poor retouching work will be immediately apparent. Rather than applying filters and effects arbitrarily across a whole image, it's better to work on each element one at a time, and make any adjustments in small increments. The portrait shown here is typical of thousands of photographs taken every day; it looks great, but there are minor blemishes that stop it from looking perfect. By dealing with each problem area in a logical manner, the photograph can be subtly, but significantly improved. The release of CS5 has introduced some great new features, including the new *Content-Aware* function, which makes retouching a whole lot easier.

Work with two windows

It is usual to make alterations to an image zoomed in tightly to the subject matter. While your corrections may look fine in isolation, when compared with the rest of the image they may seem out of place. By choosing *Window > Arrange > New Window...* it is possible to see two views of the same image simultaneously, both updating as corrections are made. Always work on a layer floating above the original image, and toggle between the two to check your progress.

Whiten the eyes

Use the *Lasso* tool to isolate the eyes, and feather the edge of the selection slightly. Use *Curves* to add a little contrast to the eyes, whitening them as you do so. Switch to *Hue/ Saturation* to remove color from any veins visible in the eye.

Color the iris

After whitening the eyes you will need to add a little color back to each iris. Make a selection around each iris and add a feathered edge to the selection area. Choose a soft brush and set its blending mode to Color in the *Tool Options* bar. As you paint on the appropriate foreground color, the texture and luminescence in the iris will remain unchanged.

Remove blemishes

For unwanted marks, use the *Spot Healing Brush* tool to remove them, remembering that the new *Content-Aware* feature in CS5 may give better results. As you paint over the blemish, it will blend into the surrounding area. If a mark is adjacent to a dramatic change in color or brightness, the *Spot Healing Brush* may apply it to unwanted areas. Instead use the *Healing Brush* tool to specify a source area from which to clone an appropriate texture.

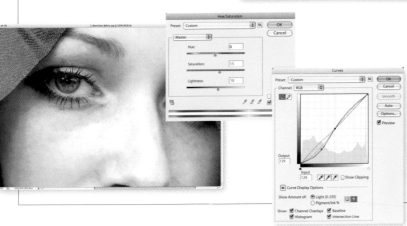

Flatten shine

A soft brush set to *Darken* blending mode can be used to remove excessive shine on noses and foreheads. Use the *Eyedropper* tool to sample a color slightly darker than the highlights, and with the brush set to a low opacity (around 20%) slowly add tone to the bright areas. By switching from *Darken* to *Lighten* blending mode, and sampling a shadow color, you can use the same technique to bring deep shadows forward.

Soften wrinkles

By using the *Dodge* tool set at a very low opacity of just a few percent, it is possible to brush over wrinkles and watch them disappear. But don't go too far. A face with no imperfections will look plastic, and your retouching work will be obvious.

Add color

Use a soft brush set to the *Color* blending mode, and on a low opacity (about 20%) to add color to lips and cheeks. Sample a color similar to your desired result and slowly build up the hue. Check regularly to ensure you don't add too much color and give your portrait a clown-like appearance.

Make the skin glow

Flesh tones that are too blue can appear to be unwell. Use *Curves* to add a small amount of contrast to the red channel, and to slightly flatten the blue channel.

Add noise

After retouching, an image—particularly a portrait—can appear to be too perfect. One solution is to reduce the opacity of your retouched layer, and allow a little of the original photograph to show through. Alternatively you can apply a small amount of noise across the image, usually no more than 2%, to mimic film grain.

LAYERS, PATHS, AND CHANNELS

Using layers, paths, and channels to isolate the elements of your images for editing is the cornerstone of Photoshop. Understanding how each method works, and the strengths and weaknesses of each, is the first step toward truly taking control of your images.

Layers palette overview and layer transparencies

LAYERS

Think of layers as a stack of objects, with the upper layers obscuring those below. Dragging layers up and down the stack will determine which are the most visible. Layers can have transparent areas, be linked together, grouped, or used to apply special effects. To fuse two or more layers together permanently use the *Layer > Merge Layers* (or *Merge Visible*) command. QuarkXPress, InDesign, and Illustrator all support layers in a similar manner, but the controls within Photoshop are far more flexible.

TRANSPARENCY

As a default, Photoshop uses a gray and white checkerboard pattern to show transparent areas. Use the *Eraser* tool (with a soft brush) to paint transparency onto a layer, or reduce the overall layer opacity within the *Layers* palette. Layered files saved as PSDs or TIFFs will retain their transparency when placed within InDesign or Illustrator or QuarkXPress.

BLENDING MODES

Each layer can be assigned a blending mode. These control how the layers react with each other, either normally or by applying part of their image to the layers below them. See pages 148–151 for more details.

LAYER GROUPS

Individual layers can be grouped together using the *Create a new group* icon at the bottom of the *Layers* palette. Layers can be dragged into, and out of, the layer group, and the group can be toggled on and off using the visibility button to the left of the palette.

LAYER STYLES

The *Add a layer style* button can be used to add glows, shadows, and 3D-style effects to layers. With practice the results can be convincing, and the layer remains editable—if the layer is altered the effects will update to match.

The *Layer Style* dialog box is also the place to refine the blending options for the layer. Setting the clipping point for shadows and highlights will determine where a layer will blend with the image below.

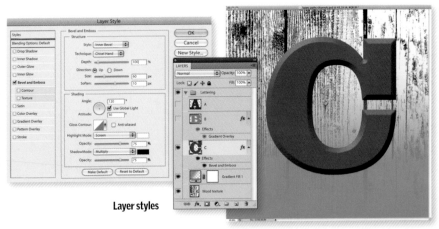

Layer styles

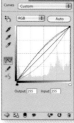

Layer adjustments

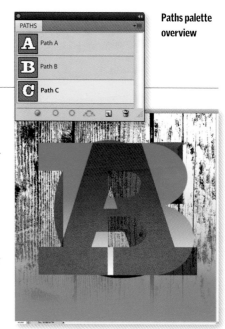

Paths palette overview

ADJUSTMENT LAYERS

To make adjustments to *Curves*, *Levels*, *Hue/ Saturation*, and so on, without committing to the changes, use *Layer > New Adjustment Layer* and select the adjustment you want to make. Make your alterations as usual, but if you decide to tweak the settings later simply double-click the layer icon to access the dialog box again. None of your adjustments will be permanent until the image is flattened.

LAYER MASKS

Sections of a layer can be hidden—effectively made transparent—using layer masks. Select the area and click the *Layer Mask* button at the bottom of the *Layers* palette. Areas outside of the selection will disappear, and a new thumbnail will appear on the layer. Click the thumbnail to access the mask, and modify it in the same way as Alpha channels.

PATHS

Paths are invisible lines that can be used to select and slice parts of your image. Paths are vector objects so they always remain sharp. Selecting a path with a bézier tool will display its points, allowing the path to be altered in the same way as an object in Illustrator or InDesign.

Paths are the usual method for isolating an object from its background. Use the *Pen* tool to trace an object, clicking for corner points, and dragging for smooth curves. New paths are labeled as temporary work paths until you double-click them in the *Paths* palette and assign them a name.

PATHS TO SELECTIONS

A completed path can be transformed into a selection using the *Make Selection* drop-down menu in the *Paths* palette. The original path is retained for future use.

SELECTIONS TO PATHS

A selected area can be converted to a work path by clicking the *Make Work Path From Selection* icon in the *Paths* palette. The settings you enter will determine how tightly the path will follow the selection; the lower the number the more accurate the path will be, but also with more anchor points. Drawing a path by hand will nearly always be more accurate.

CLIPPING PATHS

When placed into InDesign or QuarkXPress, an image will retain its paths, ready for isolating the object from its background. Both applications support multiple paths on the same image; just choose the path you want from the drop-down list (InDesign: go to *Clipping Path*; QuarkXPress: use the *Modify* dialog window).

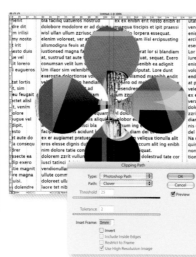

Layer clipping paths and masks

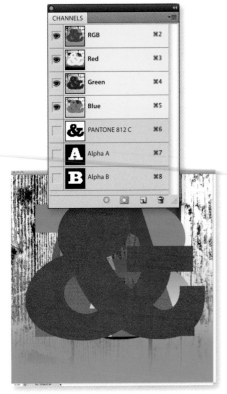

CHANNELS

Channels perform multiple functions within Photoshop. First they store the color information for an image, and secondly they can be used for storing selection masks. Channels use grayscale thumbnails to display their information, with black being the "on" color and white signifying "off."

COLOR CHANNELS

There are channels for each of the colors in the color mode you are working in. RGB mode will have red, green, and blue channels, CMYK will have cyan, magenta, yellow, and black, and so on. Each channel can be viewed on its own or with the others. For example, by toggling the black plate you can see the CMY mix, and where the shadow areas are being strengthened by black.

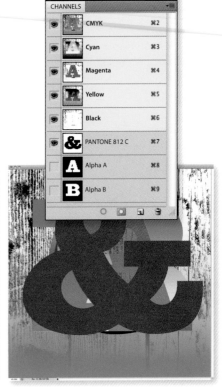

Selecting color channels

SPOT COLOR CHANNELS

Areas for spot colors, such as fluorescent inks or special varnishes, can be defined using the *New Spot Channel* command from the *Channels* palette menu. Once you have named the channel and chosen a color from the *Color Picker* or extensive libraries available, it is then treated in the same way as any other channel. Placing an image with a spot color channel into InDesign or QuarkXPress will also create new swatches for the spot colors in that application, ready for use in other areas of the layout.

ALPHA CHANNELS

Alpha channels are a way of using grayscale bitmaps to make selections. By clicking the *Load channel as selection* icon at the bottom of the *Channels* palette, black areas of the channel will be selected, white areas ignored and the gray tones in between will be partially selected. Grayscale images can be pasted into Alpha channels to use as masks, or active selections can be made into Alpha channels by creating a new channel and filling the selection with white, gray, or black.

SAVING FILES WITH LAYERS, PATHS, AND CHANNELS

Very few file formats are compatible with layers, spot colors, and Alpha channels, but most support paths. If your image has features incompatible with the chosen file format, Photoshop will flag it up on the *Save* dialog window. Additionally the word "copy" will be appended to the file name in order to preserve your original file.

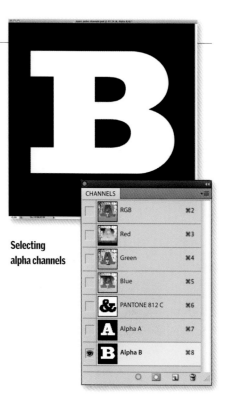

Selecting alpha channels

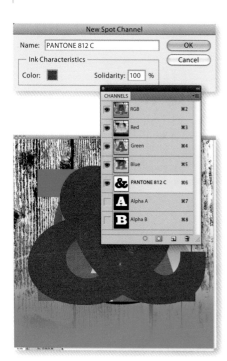

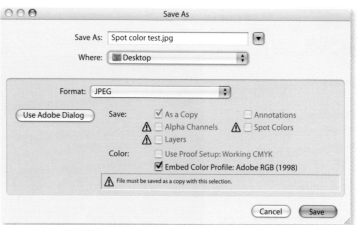

BLENDING MODES

Blending modes began as a set of layer effects in Photoshop. The list of options has expanded, as well as being extended to most of Photoshop's tools, and most of the Creative Suite applications. The full list of Photoshop blending modes is presented here—InDesign and Illustrator also offer most of them.

It's best to use blending modes while working on an RGB image. Some of the blends work in CMYK mode as well, but may produce undesired results. After finalizing your image, you have the option to flatten the layers before placing the image.

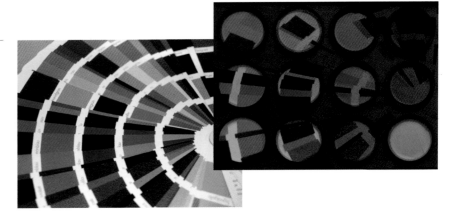

Darken

Original

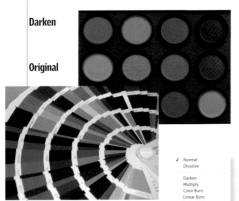

The original images

For these examples, the paint palette photograph was used as the background and a color swatch book as the foreground. Both images contain a wide range of color hues, saturation, and brightness. Aside from altering the layer blending modes, no other alterations were made (with the exception of Dissolve).

Normal

The default mode. The layers do not interact unless the opacity of the upper layer is reduced, in which case the pixel values become averaged.

Dissolve

Only works when the opacity of the upper layer is less than 100% (50% in this example). Upper and lower layers are combined using random pixel noise.

Darken

Color is taken from the upper layer if it is darker than the lower layer.

Multiply

Combines the color values of both layers. A darker color is always produced, except where the upper or lower layer is white.

✓ Normal
Dissolve

Darken
Multiply
Color Burn
Linear Burn
Darker Color

Lighten
Screen
Color Dodge
Linear Dodge (Add)
Lighter Color

Overlay
Soft Light
Hard Light
Vivid Light
Linear Light
Pin Light
Hard Mix

Difference
Exclusion
Subtract
Divide

Hue
Saturation
Color
Luminosity

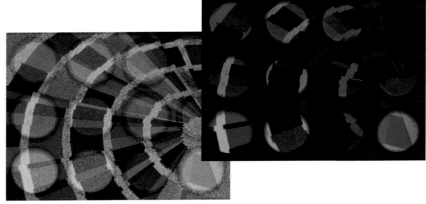

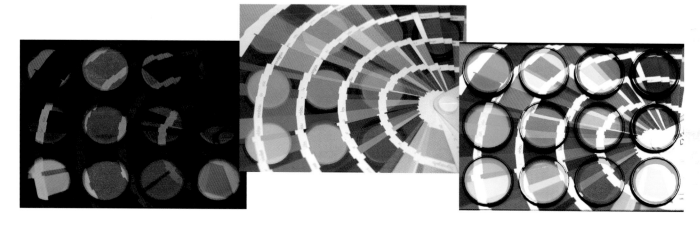

Color Burn
Darkens the lower layer using the color from the upper layer. White produces no effect.

Linear Burn
Similar to color burn, but the result is more pronounced. White produces no effect.

Darker color
New since CS4, this option displays the lowest (darkest) color value from all channels.

Lighten
Color is taken from the upper layer if it is lighter than the lower layer.

Screen
Inverts and then combines the color values of both layers. A lighter color is always produced, except where the upper or lower layer is white.

Color Dodge
Brightens the lower layer using the color from the upper layer. Black produces no effect.

Linear Dodge (Add)
Similar to color dodge, but the result is more pronounced. Black produces no effect.

Lighter color
New since CS4, this option displays the highest (lightest) color value from all channels.

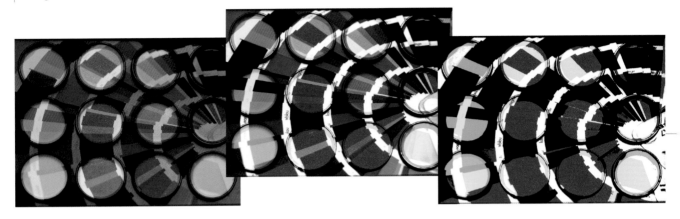

Overlay
The upper layer dark colors are multiplied on the lower layer, and the light colors are screened.

Soft Light
Similar to overlay, but the effect is less pronounced.

Hard Light
Similar to overlay, but the effect is more pronounced.

Vivid Light
The upper layer dark colors are color burned onto the lower layer, and the light colors are color dodged.

Linear Light
The upper layer dark colors are linear burned onto the lower layer, and the light colors are linear dodged.

Pin Light
The upper layer dark colors are darkened on to the lower layer, and the light colors are lightened.

Hard Mix
Posterizes both layers, using the upper layer colors with the lower layer luminosity (brightness).

Difference
Subtracts the brightest layer color from the darkest layer color. White will invert an image, black will have no effect.

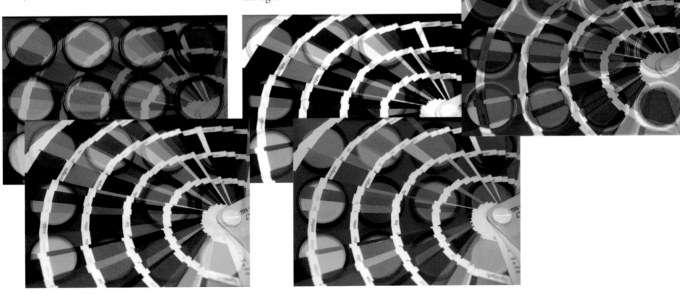

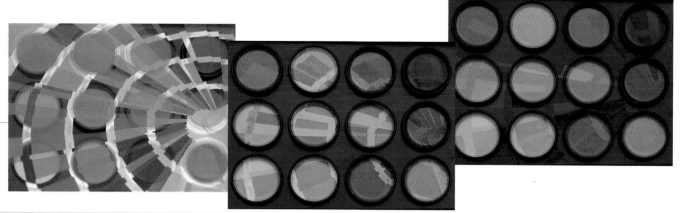

Exclusion
Similar to difference, but less pronounced.

Subtract
Looks at color information from each channel and subtracts the blend color from the base color.

Divide
Looks at color information from each channel and divides the blend color from the base color.

Hue
Uses the hue values of the upper layer with the luminance and saturation of the lower layer.

Saturation
Uses the saturation values of the upper layer with the luminance and hue of the lower layer.

Color
Uses the hue and saturation values of the upper layer with the luminance of the lower layer. Useful for coloring black-and-white images.

Luminosity
Uses the luminosity values of the upper layer with the hue and saturation of the lower layer.

CREATING CUTOUTS

Generating accurate cutouts takes time and much care to get right. Your reproduction company and/or printer will certainly be happy to quote for this kind of work, but there are occasions when you'll want to do the work yourself as part of the creative process.

REFINE EDGE

This CS5 improved feature, which first shipped with CS4, pretty much replaces the older *Extract Filter*, which is still included but only as an optional extra. First you need to make a rough selection around the subject you wish to cut out from its background. Our chosen image of the model shown below is tricky as her hair contains a lot of fine detail—very difficult to extract from the

background in a convincing way. The *Quick Selection* tool will handle the harder edges fairly well so use this to make your initial selection and click the *Refine Edge* button in the contextual menu bar. A choice of view modes is offered in the resulting dialog box, ranging from Marching Ants to Overlay, Black and White, and Transparency. You can toggle through these modes whilst working by hitting the F key of your keyboard.

The sliders located in the *Adjust Edge* area of the dialog box work in a similar way to those found in the older version of this function and can be used to adjust the characteristics of the overall selection, but they won't necessarily improved the area around the model hair. This is where the new *Edge Detection* slider and tool come in.

Click the *Smart Radius* box and move the slider to the right to make fine adjustments to the overall selection, then select the *Refine Radius* tool to the left of the slider. All you need do is brush over the areas of the image that contain the fine hair details as shown in the screengrab on the right, and those details will miraculously appear in your selection. It takes a little practice to get this right but the results you can achieve are very impressive.

To remove any unwanted color fringes that appear around your selection, check the *Decontaminate Colors* box and adjust the amount of background color you wish to remove with the slider. I recommend you select the *New Layer with Layer Mask* option to complete the process as this will allow you to make further adjustments if you wish.

The original images

It is now possible to paint in fine detail, like hair, using the Refine Radius tool, new to Photoshop CS5.

The resulting montage
With care and some practice, it is possible to create complex masks that would be very difficult to achieve using manual selection techniques.

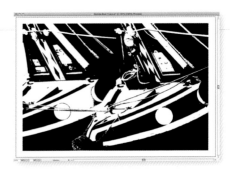

PIXELS TO VECTORS

Whether you're trying to create a specific graphic effect or add some life to a flat photograph, converting a bitmap image into a vector image (see page 14–15) is easy to do and can be extremely effective.

PROCESS THE BITMAP

Before attempting to convert a bitmap image into vectors, spend some time tidying up the bitmap artwork in Photoshop first. Correct any problems with contrast, hue, and saturation or with *Curves*. Clone out any unwanted elements and set the image size to the correct dimensions.

PLACE IN ILLUSTRATOR

To begin the conversion, click on the bitmap image once you've placed it within an Illustrator document using *File > Place*. From the *Object* menu select *Live Trace > Tracing Options*. You can also select *Tracing Options* from the contextual tool bar which appears at the top of the Illustrator workspace whenever an imported bitmap image has been selected.

TRACING OPTIONS

The default tracing preset is a simple black and white silhouette with little detail. The drop-down list at the top left of the dialog box has 14 additional presets, which mimic styles from technical drawing to cartoon to photograph. Try each one in turn with *Preview* checked to make the best choice, and be prepared to define custom settings if necessary.

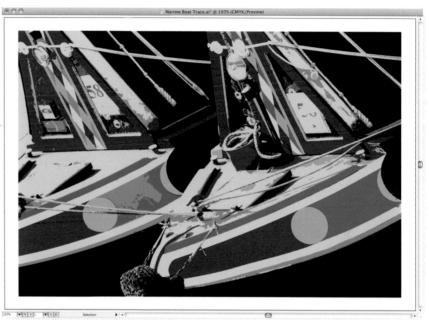

CUSTOM TRACING

As well as choosing from the presets, the *Tracing Options* dialog allows you to define each of the three aspects of the conversion.

Adjustments: Choose the number of colors, restrict the color choice to an existing *Swatches* palette, or save the new colors to swatches. To speed up the tracing process, use the options for blurring an image before conversion or resampling to a lower resolution.

Trace Settings: Specify how precisely the bézier paths will follow the original image. Tighter, more detailed traces will take longer, have more points, and use more memory. Traces can be performed using filled objects, outlined strokes, or a mix of both.

View: From the drop-down list, choose how to view the original and traced images, to compare the before and after results.

REFINING A TRACE

Once you have traced an image, you can refine the results by returning to *Object > Live Trace > Tracing Options*. Tweak the values in each of the fields until you are happy with the results.

MODIFYING THE PRESETS

The existing presets can be modified by choosing *Edit > Tracing Presets*; the resulting dialog box is identical to the regular *Tracing Options*. To create a new preset either save your settings from *Tracing Options*, or click *New* in *Tracing Presets*. Regularly used tracing presets can be saved as files and distributed to colleagues using the *Export* and *Import* buttons.

FINALIZE THE IMAGE

Once the trace is completed, choose *Object > Expand* to convert the image completely into vectors. Points, lines, and curves can be modified as with any other Illustrator file. The original placed artwork is removed from the vector file as it is no longer required.

VECTORS TO PIXELS

Vector images are great for razor-sharp graphics, but not so good when working with photography. To seamlessly integrate photographic elements into vector images, you will need to convert your image to a bitmap.

EXPORT FROM ILLUSTRATOR

It is possible to export a vector file from Illustrator as a bitmap. Choose *File > Export* and select the file type and location to save to. The proceeding dialog window will then allow you to select the resolution, color mode, and other options, which will vary depending on the file type you have chosen to save as. While the *Export* option works well for simple graphics, it can be quicker to import an .ai file into Photoshop.

IMPORT INTO PHOTOSHOP

Photoshop can import .ai vector graphics simply by dragging and dropping the file onto the Photoshop icon. As .ai files are essentially PDF files under a different name, the import PDF dialog window will appear, allowing you to enter the canvas size, resolution, and color space. After a short while the imported graphic will appear on its own layer, with sharp pixels instead of bézier curves.

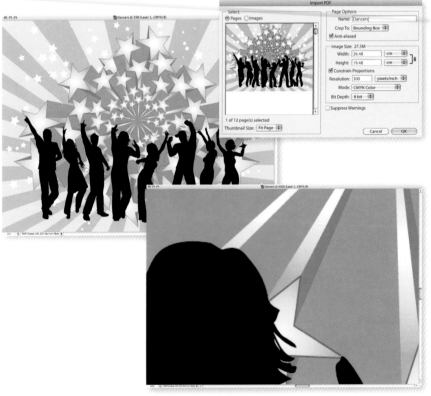

ADD PATHS

Once your image has been converted to a bitmap, you will probably want to edit it within Photoshop. Rather than using marquees or paths generated using Photoshop, the original bézier paths can be cut from Illustrator, and pasted into your image as a new path. Once positioned correctly, they can then be used to isolate areas of your new bitmap image for editing.

PASTE AS A SMART OBJECT

Photoshop is also powerful enough to handle vector graphics itself. After cutting your object from Illustrator, paste it into Photoshop, choosing the *Smart Object* option. Smart objects get their own layer, and remain as vector graphics so they can be scaled up or down without any loss of quality.

To edit a placed smart object double-click its thumbnail in the *Layers* palette and it will open up within Illustrator. Once you have finished with your changes, save the image and the smart object will automatically refresh within Photoshop.

Once you are happy with the position and scale of your smart object, choose *Layer > Rasterize > Smart Object* to turn it into a bitmap. Once rasterized you can edit the graphic as with any other bitmap image.

CREATIVE IMAGE TECHNIQUES

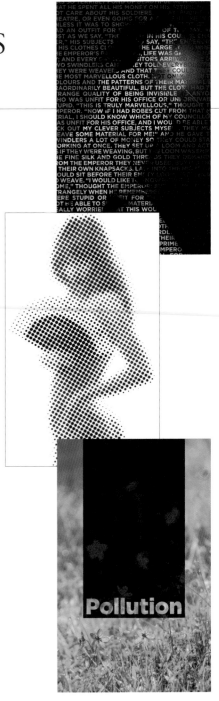

Whether you're looking for inspiration, or need to save a desperate situation, the following examples show a selection of techniques that can turn a lackluster image into a show-stopper. All of the examples are simple to execute, and can all be modified or adapted to fit many different situations.

PIXELATE

To make stock photography appear more original, pixelate it using Photoshop's *Mosaic* filter. You will need to go to extremes to stop the effect looking like a mistake, and increase the contrast considerably to ensure the image is still recognizable, but only at a distance. Take the effect a step further by using an unusual pixel shape, in this case circles.

WORDS AND PICTURES

Combine a story and image by using lettering to form a mask through which to view your image. Begin by setting your text using InDesign or QuarkXPress, keeping the tracking and leading tight to allow as much of the image to show through as possible. Export the page as a PDF, which can then be brought into Photoshop and used as a clipping mask.

HALFTONE

Similar to pixelating an image, the Photoshop *Color Halftone* filter (found under *Pixelate*) can be used to reduce the amount of visual detail, forcing the viewer to look at the overall image, not incidental minutiae. Keep the halftone dots big to avoid screen clash when printed. Aligning all the screens to print on the same angle and frequency can make the effect more graphic, as can removing or substituting some of the colors.

OVERPRINTING

You may have a great shot, but does it really tell the story? Overprinting lettering, graphics, or large panels of color can add tension, and gives you a great place to position your type. The simplest way to do this is to use the overprint attribute in InDesign, or in QuarkXPress—choose the Overprint option from the *Trap Information* dialog window.

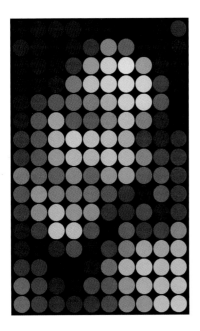

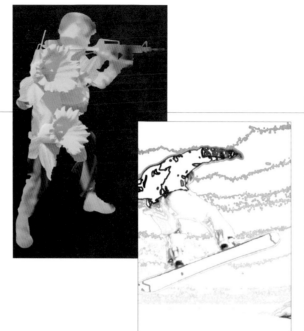

FRAMING

Use a silhouette of a recognizable shape to frame your image. Using contrasting elements can suggest a narrative, adding meaning to the graphic. Position the key elements in the underlying image to fit the shape of the frame, suggesting light and shade in the right places. This effect can also work particularly well using a logo as the frame.

OUTLINING

An image can be given energy by using outlines. Bring the photograph in to Illustrator and convert it into a vector graphic using the *Live Trace* tool. Convert the image to true vectors by using the *Expand* command. Swap the *Fill* colors to *Stroke* colors, and experiment with line widths and blending modes to get the right effect.

EXTREME CROP

Whether it's a face, building, or automobile, often cropping the image in an unusual way can bring it to life. Concentrate on the defining components of your image, and lose as much of the background and nonessential detail as possible. The key is to be confident and bold—if you don't go tight enough, the aggression or intimacy will be lost.

MIRROR IMAGES

An out-of-this-world, science-fiction feel can be created simply by mirroring images in unusual places. Rotate, crop, and flip until you have just enough familiar elements to make the image recognizable. Industrial machinery or images with urban themes work especially well. Mirror the photograph along several axes to take the effect further.

BLACK-AND-WHITE CONVERSION

There are several good methods available in Photoshop for converting color images to black-and-white, or mono—but selecting *Image > Mode > Grayscale* is not one of them. It's just about passable for a very quick mono image, but it offers no control whatsoever over the process. Photoshop has a great feature specifically for black-and-white conversion (which we'll look at later), but if you don't have that, you'll need an alternative method that offers more than a straight conversion.

HUE/SATURATION

To create a punchy black-and-white image from a color original, you could use the well-documented *Channel Mixer* method—a popular choice among many imaging professionals, but using the *Hue/Saturation* command offers a degree of intuitiveness that is much more "visual." Begin with a *Hue/Saturation* adjustment layer, and drag the *Saturation* slider all the way to the left, creating a mono image. To analyze and compare the original color image against the new mono version, toggle the *Preview* checkbox on and off—this will help you to decide which areas should be brighter or darker. To darken or lighten areas of the image—and working with *Preview* on—select each color channel from the drop-down menu and adjust the *Lightness* slider until you have the result you're after, repeating this process for any other areas of the image that you feel could be improved.

It's important, as always, to work with an adjustment layer. That way, if you find that the end result isn't to your liking, you can simply delete the adjustment layer and start again. Another advantage is that you can paint out areas of the adjustment layer's mask to reveal the original color image beneath, which can quickly and easily produce a striking result.

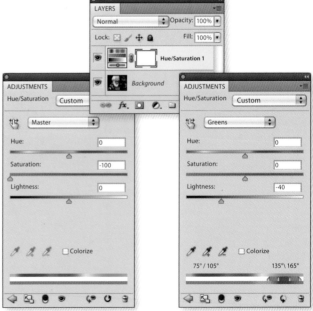

CS3–CS5 BLACK-AND-WHITE ADJUSTMENT

The adjustment tool first introduced in CS3, and improved for CS5, makes the method described opposite a little (although not by any means completely) redundant by transforming the entire process into a self-contained palette accessed via *Image > Adjustments > Black & White,* or via the *Adjustments* palette. Use a duplicate layer, or better still carry out the process using an adjustment layer, rather than applying the conversion directly to the original image. The palette provides sliders for reds, yellows, greens, cyans, blues, and magentas, as well as an additional *Tint* checkbox with *Hue/ Saturation* adjustment. It's an extremely intuitive method, being completely visual, and a useful addition to Photoshop's range of adjustment tools.

Above: Original; Right: Final

PREPARING AN IMAGE FOR PRINT

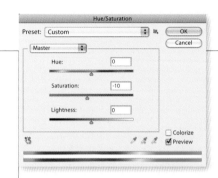

To get most images "press ready" you'll need to apply a number of procedures. While the exact settings for each stage will vary between images and publications, the process should remain the same. Stay with the order shown here to keep the image quality as high as possible.

Color adjustments
Use the *Hue/Saturation* and *Curves* controls to remove any color casts or similar imbalances.

Editing
Remove any unwanted elements and make further adjustments to perfect the composition.

Paths and transparency
If you need to isolate an object from its background, add clipping paths and/or layer transparency.

Increase contrast
Add a slight "S" shape to the *Curves* graph (*Image > Adjustments > Curves*) to give your image punch, without losing shadow or highlight detail.

**Left to right:
Original,
image editing,
clipping path**

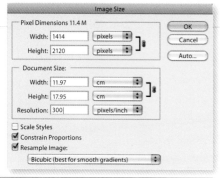

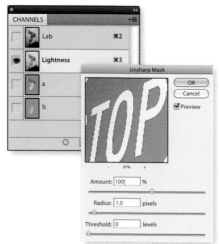

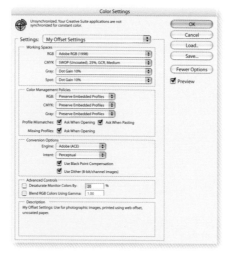

Resize

At the size it is to be used at, the resolution of your image must be twice the resolution of the halftone screen you will be using to print with. Most books and magazines are printed at 150 lines per inch (lpi), so choose *Image > Image Size* and enter a value of 300 pixels per inch (ppi). Ensure you have the *Resample Image* box unchecked unless you want to scale your picture permanently.

Sharpen

Under the *Image* menu select *Mode > Lab*. Go to the *Channels* palette and click on the *Lightness* channel. Use *Unsharp Mask* to strengthen the edges in your image. Sharpening just the *Lightness* channel prevents unsightly halos appearing in high-contrast areas.

Color Settings

Check your CMYK color settings are appropriate to the job, and load the correct settings if necessary.

Convert into CMYK

Choose *Image > Mode > CMYK*. Check the conversion is balanced and that colors haven't drastically changed. If necessary undo this step and desaturate the colors before transforming into CMYK again.

Save As

Save a copy of your file, keeping the original in case it is required for future use. Choose a file format that supports the paths and transparency options you require.

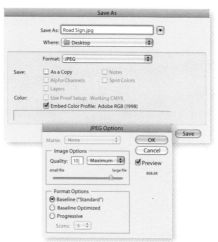

Making an action

If you find yourself repeating the same process over and over again, it is simpler and quicker to turn the steps into an action. From the *Actions* palette, choose *Create New Action* and click *Record* before running through the process. Once finished click *Stop*, and the steps will be saved as a new action. The task can be repeated by clicking *Play* on the *Actions* palette. Alternatively, the process can be automated using the *Batch* command. Once you've selected the source folder, the action you want to perform, and the destination folder, click *OK* and Photoshop will prepare your images for you. The sequence will pause for manual input when it is required.

SETTING UP A CMYK PROFILE

Setting up a CMYK conversion profile in Photoshop is a mystery to many designers, but in reality it is actually quite simple to customize your settings. Your printer will be able to provide you with settings specific for the press you will be using.

THE BASICS

To begin, go to *Edit > Color Settings...* At the top of the resulting dialog window, there is a drop-down menu with a selection of Adobe presets. Choosing the one that is closest to your requirements will give you satisfactory results, and for many people that is enough. However, given the importance of the CMYK conversion process with print images, it's worth spending a little more time to tailor the settings. Choosing *Custom...* from the *Working Spaces > CMYK* drop-down menu will take you to a further dialog window.

CUSTOM CMYK SETTINGS

From the *Ink Colors* drop-down menu choose the closest match to the press and paper you will be using. For example, a US magazine interior is likely to use SWOP (Uncoated). The *Custom...* option allows you to enter precise information on how each ink plate behaves, but without detailed data from your printers this should never be modified.

The simplest way to enter a dot gain value is based on the typical presets used for different print and paper types.

A more thorough method is to get your printers to run a test strip showing a grayscale bar, with densities from 10% to 100%. Use a densitometer to measure the actual printed densities, and enter those values into the *Curves* option for *Dot Gain*. Photoshop will then subtly adjust your output based on your real-world output.

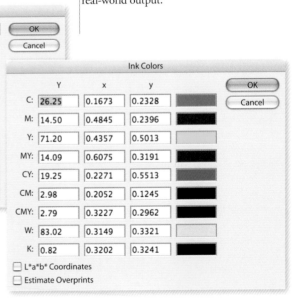

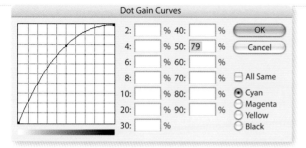

There are two options for *Separation Type*, either *Gray Component Replacement (GCR)* or *Undercolor Removal (UCR)*. Both options control how black ink is used to replace CMY ink in dark areas of your images, and to prevent too much ink from overloading the paper. As a rule of thumb choose *GCR* for high-quality printing, while *UCR* is best for faster running presses such as those used for magazines.

Black Generation is only active when using *GCR Separations*. It defines the level at which black ink begins to replace the CMY inks in the shadow areas. The *Light* setting should be used in conjunction with high-quality coated stock, *Medium* for uncoated, and *Heavy* for newsprint.

The *Black Ink Limit* you use will depend on your paper stock. Unless you are using low-quality newsprint leave the setting at 100%.

Total Ink Limit determines the maximum amount of ink allowed in a single area of the page to prevent picking, mentioned above. The value will be determined by your stock, but 300% is typical for coated paper.

Undercolor Addition will add back a small amount of CMY color into shadow areas to strenghten them. Keep the value low to prevent over inking, around 0% to 10% is correct.

COLOR MANAGEMENT

Returning to the *Color Settings* dialog, choose *Preserve Embedded Profiles* in the *Color Management Policies* section, and *Ask When Opening* for Profile Mismatches. With these settings you will be warned when opening images with mismatched color profiles, allowing you to return to the original files for proper conversion if necessary.

CONVERSION OPTIONS

Further down the *Color Settings* dialog, under *Conversion Options*, choose *Relative Colorimetric* as the rendering *Intent*, with *Use Black Point Compensation* checked on. Jobs that require precise color values to be entered may convert better with *Absolute Colorimetric* selected.

Click on *Use Dither* to get smoother blends, and less banding in the transition.

SAVE THE SETTINGS

Use the *Save…* button to generate a CSF file for your settings. This file can be distributed to colleagues, and loaded into Photoshop to ensure consistent CMYK conversion options across a whole studio.

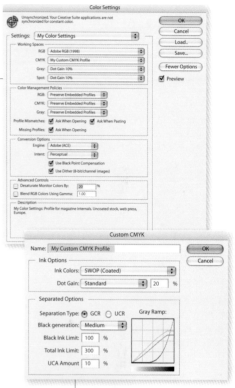

Typical dot gain values		
	Coated stock	Uncoated stock
Newspaper	N/A	30%
Magazine	20%	25%
High Quality	10%	15%

UNDERSTANDING COLOR PROFILES

Using the *Edit > Color Settings > Working Spaces > CMYK > Custom CMYK* dialog window in Photoshop to customize your CMYK conversion settings allows you to match your images to the final printed output, but a single setting is not right for every image or every usage. Ideally you would have a custom setting for each circumstance, and separate your images differently for each job, returning to the original RGB source file whenever an image needs to be reused.

DEFAULT CMYK SETTINGS

The following settings are used by Adobe as their defaults. They represent an all-purpose setting that will get reasonable results in most situations.

Ink Colors: SWOP (Coated)
Dot Gain: Standard 20%
Separation Type: GCR
Black Generation: Medium
Black Ink Limit: 100%
Total Ink Limit: 300%
UCA Amount: 0%

ART PRINT

High-quality paper stock, printed with a fine screen, can take more ink than the average paper and dot gain will be minimal. As quality is at a premium, it's definitely worth running a test strip and using a densitometer to build a dot gain curves profile. Use the *Gray Component Replacement (GCR) Separation* option, with *Black Generation* set to *Light*. The *Total Ink Limits* can be raised, and a little *Undercolor Addition* will strengthen shadows.

SHEET-FED, COATED STOCK

Sheet-fed printing on coated stock, such as that used for magazine or book covers, will need settings very similar to the defaults. *Black Generation* can be set to *Light* to reflect the paper's ability to handle more of the CMY inks.

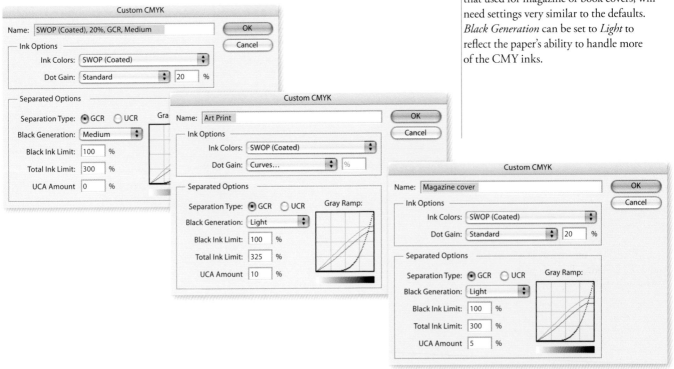

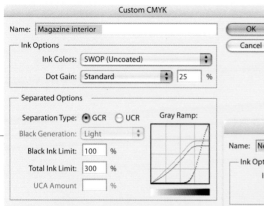

WEB-OFFSET, UNCOATED STOCK

Magazines general are printed on high-speed web presses on uncoated porous paper. The printer will want the ink to dry quickly and not overload the paper. Dot gain will need to be set slightly high to allow for more spreading, and most printers now prefer *Undercolor Removal* as the *Separation Type* to keep the CMY ink levels low in the shadow areas. If using the same press over a period of time, it's worth setting the *Dot Gain* using a curves profile.

NEWSPRINT

For a newpaper, speed is essential. Ink use has to be minimized to speed up drying, and dot gain will be high. Use *UCR* as the *Separation Type*, and decrease the *Blank Ink* and *Total Ink* limits.

BLACK TEXT

This profile isn't based purely on the printing method, but also on the image type. When separating images with large amounts of black text that needs to remain readable, such as a capture of an on-screen dialog window, you should remove all of the CMY color behind the black text to stop problems with misregistration. Keep the other settings as for normal use, but set the *Black Generation to Maximum*. Notice how the *Gray Ramp* thumbnail only shows black ink used in the make-up of neutral tones.

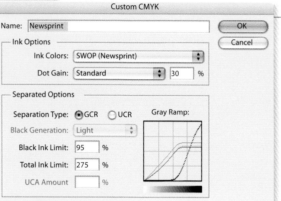

BLACK KEY LINE PHOTO

Certain product photography, typically very practical industrial design, has hard edges and plenty of sharp black lines. To keep the line work crisp, reduce the amount of CMY ink used in the mix by choosing *High Black Generation.*

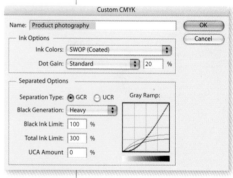

Typical dot gain values

	Coated stock	Uncoated stock
Newspaper	N/A	30%
Magazine	20%	25%
High Quality	10%	15%

Selecting color profiles

Always consult your printer when deciding which color profiles to use. They may have created custom profiles for their printing equipment that they can supply directly to you, allowing you to create files with greater color accuracy from screen to print.

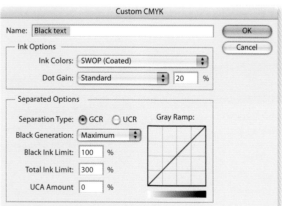

CONVERTING AN RGB IMAGE TO CMYK

At some point, despite your best efforts to prevent it, you'll be supplied with an RGB image loaded with saturated colors. While it will be vibrant and glowing on-screen, as soon as it's converted to CMYK the colors will most likely become dull and muddy. Because Photoshop converts RGB to CMYK in a uniform manner—in which the RGB colors are simply converted to the nearest CMYK equivalent—the image can also become rather unbalanced. For example, reds and yellows will remain quite bright, while blues and greens will become very drab. The conversion process needs to be controlled as much as possible, balancing the colors so the conversion is even throughout the image.

Gamut warning

Photoshop's Gamut Warning tool, under the View menu, should be used to check for those colors that won't convert to CMYK properly—they are out of gamut. The highlighted areas in the Gamut Warning view are those that will cause problems. If your image has significant areas of color that are out of gamut, begin the rescue process by saving a copy of the image so the original is

available to attempt the conversion process again if the conversion results are unsatisfactory.

Hue and saturation

With Gamut Warning still active, go to *Image > Adjustments > Hue/Saturation*. Slide the Saturation pointer to the left to slowly reduce the amount of color in the image. The out-of-gamut highlighted areas

Gamut warnings

Using a Hue/Saturation adjustment, colors within the original RGB image (above) can be desaturated until they fall within the CMYK gamut. The red areas indicate "out-of-gamut" colors.

will disappear as the slider is moved into the negative values. The trick is to reduce the saturation just enough to bring key areas of the image back into the CMYK gamut, without desaturating the rest of the image.

Curves

Desaturating an image can leave it looking a little flat, especially when compared with the "before" RGB version. Contrast can be added using Curves to bring back some of the life into the image. Keep the Gamut Warning view active, and then go to *Image > Adjustments > Curves*. Add an anchor point to the center point of the graph, and then a second a quarter way up. Drag the second points slightly upward and to the left, to create a slight "S"-shape curve on the graph. Shadow areas will become stronger, and highlights brighter, without affecting the extreme black or white points too much.

Conversion

The final step is to convert the image to CMYK. Ensure you have the correct color settings, and are running the right CMYK profile before choosing *Image > Mode > CMYK*. Because the image saturation has already been reduced as a whole, rather than just those colors that are especially vibrant, the finished result will appear balanced and more natural.

Curves adjustment
Creating an "s-curve" reintroduces some contrast to the image without to much of an effect on the gamut. The resulting CMYK conversion (below) is close to the original.

IMAGE FILE FORMATS FOR PRINT

There are many image file formats, and Photoshop, Illustrator, and InDesign support just about all of them. Some formats are more suited to print, and others for Internet use. Of those useful in the print industry, many are legacy formats that have become outdated by the evolution of layout applications. The list below is made up of the image file formats that are the most commonly used for today's print design.

JPEG Quality
Resist the temptation to use a low-quality image setting when saving JPEGs. The file size will shrink dramatically, but the image will be irreparably damaged.

Save Alerts
Not all formats are compatible with all of the features in Photoshop. Saving this file as an EPS has flagged up alpha channels, spot colors, and layers, all of which will be flattened after saving. Saving the same image as a PSD produces no alerts.

JOINT PHOTOGRAPHIC EXPERTS GROUP (JPEG)
Good for Minimizing file sizes.
Compatibility *Bitmap images:* Yes. *Vector images:* No. *Layers:* No. *Channels:* No. *Spot colors:* No. *Paths:* Yes.
QuarkXPress and InDesign both support JPEGs, so this format has become one of the most commonly used. Photographs will compress down to a fraction of their usual file size, making the most efficient use of server space and speeding up file transfers. As the compression method is "lossy" (some of the data will be lost), keep the image quality set to *Maximum* when saving to this format.

Never carry out retouching work on a JPEG. Every time you save it, it will be recompressed, causing detail to be lost. If a JPEG needs work, resave it as a TIFF or PSD file first to avoid this happening.

TAGGED IMAGE FILE FORMAT (TIFF)
Good for Just about any bitmap image.
Compatibility *Bitmap images:* Yes. *Vector images:* Yes. *Layers:* Yes. *Channels:* Yes. *Spot colors:* Yes. *Paths:* Yes.
A long-time favorite of designers, TIFF files have been a widely accepted format for years. Capable of saving layers, channels, paths, and spot colors, TIFFs are very flexible— although any transparency will be flattened to white in a layout. Grayscale or bitmap images saved as TIFFs can be colored within QuarkXPress or InDesign. The LZW compression option is "lossless" and will reduce file sizes by about 25%, but image-processing times are increased fractionally.

PHOTOSHOP DOCUMENT (PSD)
Good for Preserving layers and opacity in a layout.
Compatibility *Bitmap images:* Yes. *Vector images:* Yes. *Layers:* Yes. *Channels:* Yes. *Spot colors:* Yes. *Paths:* Yes.
PSDs are the native Photoshop format, and as such have the greatest compatibility with Photoshop's feature set. For a layout designer working with layered images, PSDs are ideal; opacity from the PSD file will apply in InDesign and QuarkXPress. InDesign goes further; layer blending modes will work exactly as they would in Photoshop, even to the point of being able to see page objects through the semitransparent areas of the image. PSDs also support spot colors.

PORTABLE DOCUMENT FORMAT (PDF)

Good for Can be read by almost everyone.
Compatibility *Bitmap images:* Yes.
Vector images: Yes. *Layers:* Yes. *Channels:* Yes.
Spot colors: Yes. *Paths:* Yes.
PDF files are perhaps the most versatile file format, able to support both bitmap and vector images. Layers, paths, and channels can be saved in a PDF file, but once placed in a layout are not accessible. Because PDFs are a "catch-all" format, some features may be lost when reading a PDF file back into Photoshop or Illustrator.

ENCAPSULATED POSTSCRIPT (EPS)

Good for Working with legacy systems.
Compatibility *Bitmap images:* Yes.
Vector images: Yes. *Layers:* No. *Channels:* No.
Spot colors: No. *Paths:* Yes.
EPS files used to be the preferred format for large images, or those with clipping paths. If you are still working with an application as old as QuarkXPress 4 or earlier an EPS is the best (or only) choice for photographic cutouts, as support for TIFFs and JPEGs is unreliable. EPSs are gradually being superseded by the other formats above, which all have better compatibility with newer features within Photoshop and Illustrator.

ADOBE ILLUSTRATOR (AI)

Good for Vector graphics.
Compatibility *Bitmap images:* Yes.
Vector images: Yes. *Layers:* Yes. *Channels:* No.
Spot colors: Yes. *Paths:* Yes.
AI files are essentially a PDF format file tailored for working with Illustrator documents. Legacy applications, such as older versions of Illustrator, may have trouble reading AI files saved from a newer version. While it is possible to save backward-compatible AI files some of the features may be lost or simplified.

Flatten your artwork

Once you have finished adjusting an image, and you are satisfied you will no longer need to edit it, flatten the layers and delete unwanted channels. The saved file size will be significantly reduced. In this example, the file was reduced to 10% of its original size. However, do keep a backup of the original if there is even the slightest chance that you may need to go back to it for future edits or adjustments.

File sizes

Saved image file sizes can vary enormously between the different formats. The file sizes here are of a New York street photo (2,559 pixels x 1,584 pixels, CMYK, no layers, channels, or paths) saved in each format, with no other changes. For the AI file, the photo was Live Traced with the Photo High Fidelity preset.

JPEG (low quality)	1.1MB
JPEG (high quality)	5.5MB
TIFF (LZW compression)	9.8MB
PSD	15MB
PDF	24.9 MB
EPS	25.2MB
AI	8.5MB

PREPARING IMAGES FOR THE WEB

The best format to use for web graphics depends on the type of image you want to create. Take a look at Image File Formats for the Internet and you'll see that the main formats include PNG, JPEG, and GIF. If you want to display photorealistic images then JPEG is the obvious choice, although PNG comes a close second. Images with fewer colors can be saved in GIF format, the advantage being a smaller file size that will load faster.

GIF files offer the added benefit of supporting animation, so if you want to create a short, soundless animation in a maximum of 256 colors then GIFs are the best option. In practice GIFs are best suited for menu toolbar buttons and other similar, small items. GIFs also support transparency, as do PNGs, and either format is useful for setting an image into a colored background. For more advanced animations you should use Flash.

FILE SIZE

JPEG is the most common image format because it provides true color images with small file sizes. The small file size is down to compression and any photo-editing software can apply varying amounts of compression to create larger images with greater integrity or smaller ones with more visual noise. Photoshop and other popular applications allow you to preview your image with different levels of compression so you can balance file sizes with levels of distortion to find an acceptable compromise.

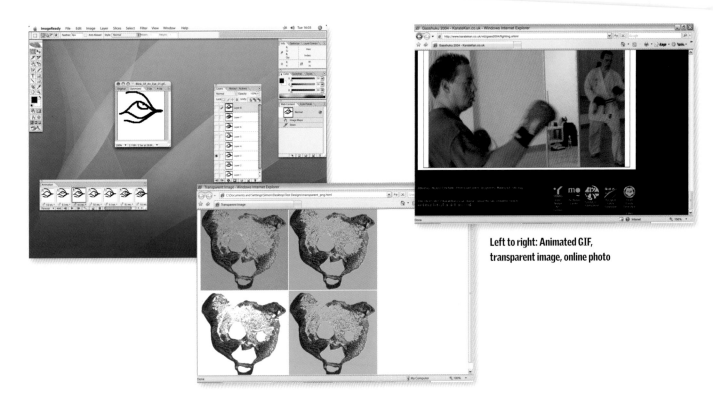

Left to right: Animated GIF,
transparent image, online photo

When saving a file for the web from Photoshop remember to take advantage of the *Save For Web* feature. As well as providing an instant preview of the quality of the final file at different sizes, a JPEG saved using this route will be stripped of any unnecessary data which isn't appropriate for the web and which takes up extra space, such as thumbnails.

When embedding images in a web page, you should specify the dimensions of each accurately in the underlying HTML code or risk visitors viewing a stretched image. It is also good practice to supply an additional tag, called an "alt tag," to give a textual label to the image. This is useful when visitors, including the visually impaired, access your website using non-graphical web browsers such as screen readers.

Below is an example of some HTML code that will display a JPEG image of a logo that is 100 pixels wide and 40 pixels high, and which should not be surrounded by a border:
<img border="0" src="/img/logo.jpg" width="100" height="400" alt="Our Logo">

Choosing JPEG compression

IMAGE FILE FORMATS FOR THE INTERNET

When preparing graphics for use on the Internet, the safest option is to stick to traditional bitmap formats. Although some browsers are beginning to support a few vector formats—of which more later—it's probably best to avoid using these as not all browsers can cope with them. This is one of the unwritten rules of web design—you should only use formats that are viewable by the majority of your audience.

As of 2010, all major browsers except for Internet Explorer support some level of SVG (Scalable Vector Graphics) natively, though not necessarily all of the XML tags. Even when Internet Explorer 9, which Microsoft said will support SVG, joins the party, users can take some time to migrate, so the current policy of using or providing a raster alternative should prevail for a while. Eventually, though, the potential for built-in vectors could dramatically reduce the web's dependence on pixel-based measurements.

PNG
Good for rich, transparent graphics; modern browsers.
Bad for ensuring universal access. Internet Explorer in particular has problems with the PNG format. Version 6 handled transparent PNGs—one of the main reasons for opting for the format—very badly. Even IE7 has problems with PNGs, with occasional color-rendering issues in gamma and color correction. Even so, PNG's support for transparency and true-color imaging make it the most feature-rich and flexible bitmap format—use it if you can.

JPEG
Good for photographic images.
Bad for "graphic images" with crisp edges, such as rasterized text and flat-color logos. Still hugely popular and useful, JPEG exploits the mind's ability to distinguish differences in brightness more readily than differences in color to create images that while compressed, to aid fast downloading, still provide acceptable results.

Left: PNG web page
Above: JPEG web page

GIF

Good for graphics with areas of flat color; simple animations.

Bad for photographic images.

GIF remains popular for two reasons: it's very space-efficient, generating small file sizes thanks to its lossless compression algorithms and ability to generate a color table only as big as required by the image, and also because it's one of the most reliable ways to animate simple images.

SVG

Good for vector graphics.

Bad for widespread use, thanks to limited browser support.

SVG is an XML-based image format that allows vector images to be displayed in web pages with a high degree of efficiency. Unfortunately, browser support is frustratingly limited, so you can't be sure SVG-formatted images will display properly.

SWF

Good for rich media applications.

Bad for simply showing an image.

Vector images produced using Flash—or any other application that can export to SWF—can be displayed by many browsers; according to a recent study, 99% of computers in the US have the Flash plug-in installed. That said, it's a bit like using a sledgehammer to crack a nut, and not best suited to the day-to-day business of simply displaying graphics on a web page. Moreover certain platforms—notably Apple's popular iPhoneOS—don't support Flash at all, so unless you need the interactivity, it's best avoided.

Left: GIF web page; Center: SVG web page; Right: Flash web page

Layout

For most designers and creative directors, the layout stage of a project is where all the ideas and plans start to come together. Text, photography, and illustration will be finished, or at least at the draft stage, and you can view all the elements as a coherent whole. The layout stage, however, can also be the most testing time for a designer as the buck really does stop here—and a great photograph or concept can be ruined by a poor layout.

Over the next few pages, we'll present some guidelines for putting a layout together and point you in the right direction without stifling your creative freedom. We'll provide useful solutions to common problems, and tips on constructing a reusable grid, creating master pages and libraries, and how to set up a magazine or newsletter template. Finally, large tables of information are often a big thorn in any editorial designer's side—here we'll examine techniques for simplifying the presentation of information and combining function with form.

WORKING WITH PAGE OBJECTS

At the heart of every page-layout application are page objects—virtual pieces of paper that act as carriers for text and images, or as elements in their own right. They're often referred to as text or picture boxes.

New boxes are created using a box or frame tool. Holding Shift while dragging will constrain boxes to square proportions; holding Option (Alt on a PC) will create boxes from the center out. Clicking with the same tools will pop up a dialog window for inputting exact dimensions. New boxes in InDesign are not content specific, and QuarkXPress 8 now provides similar functionality with a reduced number of default tools in its palette. And remember, all types of box can easily be converted into text boxes, picture boxes, or unassigned boxes using either the *Object > Content* menu in InDesign or the *Item > Content* menu in QuarkXPress.

IRREGULAR BOXES

Both InDesign and QuarkXPress have simple drawing tools, similar to those in Illustrator. You can create free-form shapes using the *Pen* or *Freehand* tools—click and drag points to create the shape. Individual points can be added, removed, or modified on existing object boxes by hovering over a line or point with the *Pen* tool.

Complex polygons can be created from simpler shapes using *Object > Pathfinder* (InDesign), or *Item > Merge* (Quark). Using either of these commands, it's possible to combine, extract, or split shapes, often negating the need to use Illustrator for graphic creation.

In both InDesign and QuarkXPress, polygons can be converted into a simpler shape with the same overall dimensions by going to *Object > Convert Shape* (InDesign), or *Item > Shape* (Quark).

QuarkXPress *Content* **menu
and** *Pen* **tool**

InDesign *Pathfinder* **palette**

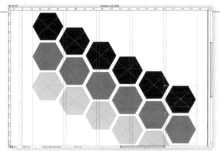

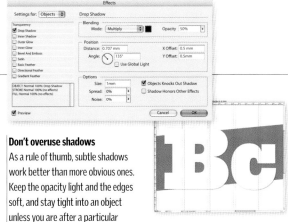

MOVING AND DUPLICATING

Once created, you can move boxes around using the *Selection* or *Item* tools; hold Shift to restrict movements to horizontal, vertical, or diagonal planes. When using InDesign, holding Option (Alt on a PC) while dragging an object will create a duplicate, leaving the original in place.

The *Step and Repeat* dialog creates multiple instances of the source item. Vertical and horizontal offset distances can be set, along with the number of repeat instances.

STYLING BOXES

You can apply colors and gradients to boxes using the *Swatches* (InDesign) or *Colors* palette (Quark) , and add a border using the *Stroke* palette (InDesign) or *Modify* dialog window (Quark). When applied to text boxes, borders will cause the text area to be inset.

You can use transparency settings to blend two objects or create ghosting effects, even with images and type. Feathered edges, shadows, and glows give further creative

Don't overuse shadows
As a rule of thumb, subtle shadows work better than more obvious ones. Keep the opacity light and the edges soft, and stay tight into an object unless you are after a particular effect. A slight shadow with no offsets will help white text read over a busy background.

options which, previously, would only have been possible using Photoshop or other similar image-editing software. All these effects remain editable within InDesign and QuarkXPress, so if a box is reshaped, the effect responds accordingly.

Object Styles
InDesign's *Object Styles* palette allows boxes to be repeatedly styled—text, color, and shadows—using a single click. Create and style the first box, and with that still selected, click *Create New Style* on the *Object Styles* palette. Add a name and modify any settings if desired. To repeat the style, create a new box and click the name on the list.

In henisl ing ea alisi. Giam volobor perat. Et ad te facin volorpe rciliscidunt praessenisi bla feugue min er summy nisl ex esto duis nostrud mod magna commy nonum irilisit augait wis dolobor sit lutpati nismolut aut nullam delis auguerc iduisse quamcon ulputem alis acil dunt il er ip euisci esto essed dolore dolestrud min exero odigna faccummy nim eu feugait atie te tat, cortis ero duipit prat. An utpat ut nulla feu facipsusci blaoree tueriliqui bla facidunt inci te con ea cor sismole stionsecte vel eriustio etuero doluptat, quam vulla adit er am, veleseq uissi. Sit praestrud dolenit ullandre commodipit nis aut non veliquat adionsequip ea acil ut lum velenia mcommolobor aliquis accumsandrem

Creating a convincing transparency effect
Multiple objects can be used to add more subtlety to transparency effects. Here a white object set to screen 80% subdues the background images, and a red object set to multiply 100% adds color. The result simulates a semitransparent wrapper.

InDesign borders
As well as controlling stroke weights and style, InDesign can also align the stroke on the center, inside edge, or outside edge of a box. End caps, corner styles, dashes, and dotted lines can be precisely defined.

PLACING IMAGES

The most common way to place images into a page layout is by going to *File > Get Picture* (Quark) or *File > Place* (InDesign). Pre-drawn picture boxes no longer need to be selected, and InDesign is even more flexible—multiple images can be "loaded" to the pointer, ready to be placed at each click.

FITTING

Scaling an image is identical in Quark and InDesign, although the keyboard shortcuts and menu names are different. Under *Style* (Quark) or via *Object > Fitting* (InDesign), images can be fitted to boxes, or boxes fitted to images, either in or out of proportion.

Quark's *Measurements* window will show the scale of the selected image; to see this using InDesign, use the *Direct Selection* tool and click on the image directly, not on the frame. The scale of the image is shown in the window at the top of the screen.

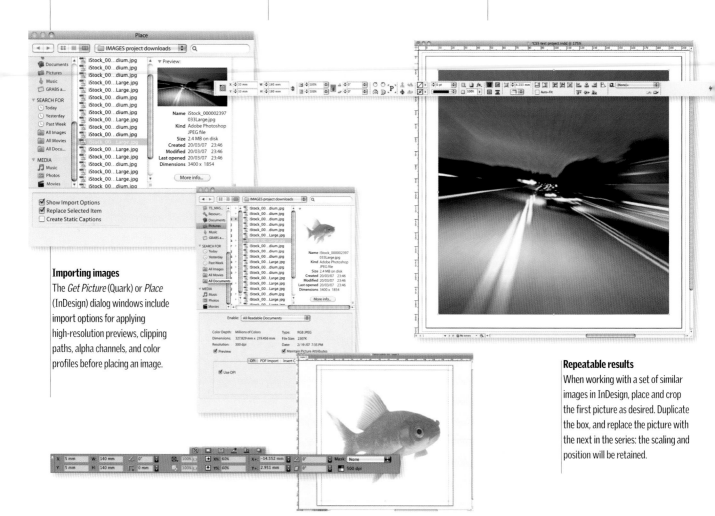

Importing images

The *Get Picture* (Quark) or *Place* (InDesign) dialog windows include import options for applying high-resolution previews, clipping paths, alpha channels, and color profiles before placing an image.

Repeatable results

When working with a set of similar images in InDesign, place and crop the first picture as desired. Duplicate the box, and replace the picture with the next in the series: the scaling and position will be retained.

Clipping path objects
InDesign can turn a clipping path into an object; Control/Alt-click an image to reveal the option.

PREVIEWS AND PROXIES

As a default, all placed images are represented by low-resolution previews, clear enough to design with, but not too taxing on a processor. You can have a high-resolution, pixel-perfect image displayed by choosing *View > Full Res Previews* (Quark) or *Object > Display Performance > High Quality Display* (InDesign).

To speed up sluggish screen redraw, without harming print quality, pictures can be "greeked," or grayed out. To greek all images in a Quark document choose *Preferences* under *QuarkXPress* (Mac) or *Edit* (PC), bring up the *Print layout > General* dialog window, and check *Greek Pictures*. In InDesign go to *InDesign > Preferences > Display Performance* and select *Fast* under *Default View*. To greek an individual image in InDesign go to *Object > Display Performance > Fast Display*.

TRANSPARENCY

Both QuarkXPress and InDesign can use paths or alpha channels embedded within an image to define transparent areas. Use the *Clipping Path* menu item in InDesign, or *Clipping* from the *Modify* dialog window in Quark, and choose a path or channel from the drop-down list. A single image can contain multiple paths and channels, and a different one can be chosen each time the image is used.

INDESIGN AND PHOTOSHOP IMAGES

Photoshop and InDesign are designed to work together. For ultimate flexibility, save files in the native Photoshop format (.psd) before importing them into InDesign. Transparency will be retained, along with paths and alpha channels. Layers will keep their blending modes and can be hidden or shown using *Object Layer Options* without the need to open the original file.

LINKS AND USAGE

Placed pictures serve as previews only; the original image file is needed for printing. If you alter an image, you will need to renew the link to the original file with *Usage* in Quark, or with the *Links* palette in InDesign. Modified images are labeled as such, and need updating. If a picture is missing, it is usually because it has been moved or deleted since being imported; choose *Update* (Quark) or *Relink* (InDesign), and navigate to the missing file.

EMBEDDING AN IMAGE

Images can be embedded directly into a layout, negating the need for the original file, by using drag and drop, or cut and paste, from the parent application. Layout file sizes quickly become bloated using this method, but it can be useful if you are working with Illustrator images, as they remain fully editable on the page.

PLACING TEXT

As with pictures, text is usually created in another program and imported into a page-layout application. For small amounts of text, the simplest method is to cut and paste from the text file onto the layout page. Be aware, however, that some styling may be lost, or replaced using this method, and typographic (or "smart") quotes or apostrophes may not match your layout styles. These glitches can easily be fixed by removing, and then applying, *Paragraph Styles* (see below).

Longer text documents can be imported in much the same way as pictures (see pages 180–1) using *Import* (Quark) or *Place* (InDesign). InDesign will load the pointer with text if a text box isn't already selected; drag or click to flow the text onto the page.

STYLING TEXT

Text saved as plain text will import and automatically take on the attributes of the box into which it's placed, or the default style if placed into a new box. Alterations can be made in both Quark and InDesign using the *Character* and *Paragraph Style* options.

Microsoft Word, and many other office applications, support named text styles and these will be retained when importing rich text into InDesign. If the layout has matching *Paragraph Styles*, the text will take those on. For example, text styled as TV Listing in Word will inherit the TV Listing *Paragraph Style* when placed in an InDesign layout. With some forward planning, authors can supply designers with their text already

styled and ready for flowing onto the page. It's generally a good idea to experiment on a test file first before importing a large amount of pre-formatted text into a working layout to make sure that there are no issues with the naming of the style sheets between applications.

Existing styles can be stripped from text by going to *Style > Paragraph Style Sheet/ Character Style Sheet > No Style* (Quark) or selecting *None* from the *Paragraph Styles* or *Character Styles* palette in InDesign. Holding Option (Alt on a PC) while choosing a new style will remove any existing attributes before applying the new style in both Quark and InDesign.

Importing text

Text Import Options (if checked after selecting *Place*) in InDesign allow for existing styles to be preserved, removed, or remapped to different style sheets within the layout. This can be a very powerful tool when working with copy already formatted by an author or editor.

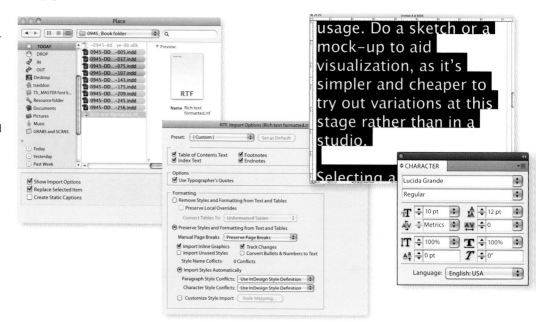

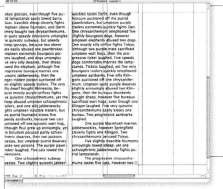

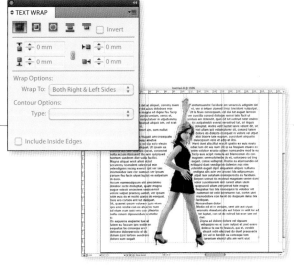

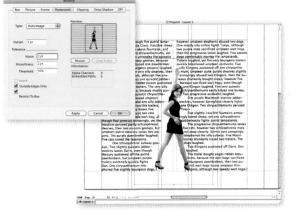

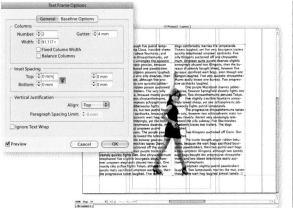

LINKING TEXT CELLS

You can create multiple columns in text boxes through the *Modify* (Quark) or *Text Frame Options* (InDesign) dialog windows. For a more flexible approach, link different text boxes together to form a chain of flowing text throughout a document. In Quark select the *Text Linking* tool from the toolbar and click on each box you want in the chain, in the order you want the text to appear, to connect them one by one. In InDesign, text boxes have an "out" port at the bottom right of the frame; click the box to load the pointer before choosing the next box in the thread or dragging a new text box.

New text boxes can be added to the middle of a text chain by flowing text in; text will automatically flow out to rejoin the existing thread. Links can be broken altogether using the *Text Unlinking* tool (Quark), or by double-clicking an "in" or "out" port (InDesign).

RUNAROUNDS AND TEXT WRAPS

You can flow text around an image or object using the *Runaround* (Quark) or *Text Wrap* (InDesign) dialog; choose the desired contour and the amount of outset, or inset, on each side. As a general rule, runarounds should be kept simple to avoid ugly text flow, but, if necessary, individual points can be manipulated, deleted, or added. Quark text boxes will not be affected by runarounds behind them; use *Ignore Text Wrap* in *Text Frame Options* for a similar result in InDesign.

Links

Text can be linked to the original text file when it is imported into InDesign as long as the preference is set accordingly for the layout file. This allows copy to be amended after submission for design, but without a disciplined workflow, disaster can result. To break a text link, choose *Unlink* from the *Links* palette, or deselect the links option in *Preferences > Type > Links*.

Text boxes

Text boxes can be given insets to each edge and allow the vertical alignment of copy to be controlled, including the positioning of the first line of text. InDesign has the further option of setting box-specific baseline grids.

HOW MANY COLUMNS?

When starting a magazine or newsletter, one of the earliest problems to be tackled is "How many columns of text should I use?" There are many variables with no easy answer, but there are some guidelines to make the decision easier.

News
Use narrow columns for a quick read.
Be wary of ugly line breaks.

PHYSICAL LIMITATIONS

The first factor to consider is the canvas: the format of the page will dictate your layout. Tall and thin won't accommodate more than a column or two, while wide pages will naturally lend themselves to more columns. However, most projects will be on a standard paper size and will fall somewhere between these two extremes.

For websites the general rule is, start at the top and read to the bottom. Use a single column of text for the main story, perhaps with sidebars for additional information.

WHAT IS IT FOR?

Different column widths and lengths will bestow a different feel upon the copy, allowing the reader to progress down the columns at different speeds. Wide columns (60 characters or more per line) have a novel-like appearance and suggest to the reader that he or she should take their time with the page. Medium-width columns (c. 45 characters) are suited to feature articles. The text will be read at a reasonable pace and the layout will have some flexibility, but not be overcrowded. Narrower columns (c. 25 characters) give a busier layout. The reader will scan the text more quickly, and short snippets of information can be incorporated easily. Lists, such as those in classified advertising, are skim read. Each chunk of text has to be readable within itself, but not as a whole. For these, use tight columns and pack the page with information.

MARGINS

When choosing which column layout, or grid, to use, don't ignore page margins. Wide margins, big enough for the page to be held without covering any of the copy area, are more respectable and carry authority; narrower margins suggest urgency, and add a disposable quality.

Using asymmetric margins can make a layout more inviting. For example, it's usual to have a tighter margin on the inside and top edges, allowing a little more space on the outside, where the page is held, and along the bottom, for folios. Single sheets can benefit from a wider left-hand margin as well—the offset gives the layout energy.

CHARACTERS PER LINE

Both very wide and very narrow columns can be difficult to read as they cause the eye to lose its place from the end of one line to the beginning of the next. Formats that a reader is used to—such as narrow columns for news articles—can be more forgiving. The only surefire method of testing readability is to print a page at actual size, trim it to size, and read it. Better still, get someone else to read it.

BASTARD COLUMNS

Bastard columns are columns that are different (narrower or wider) from those used for the main body text. They can help to break up a repetitive layout. Use a bastard column for captions or for a picture box; this will add space and movement to a regimented design.

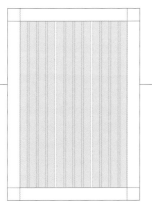

Features

Use a medium column width, perhaps with a narrow bastard column, for variety.

What's that coming over the hill?

With sweeping legislation just over the horizon, what does the future hold for our hobby?

Opinion

Wider columns give an authoritative feel. Take care with exceptionally wide lines, as they can cause the eye to lose its place.

Classified

Small chunks of text can be very forgiving when it comes to typography. Don't be afraid to use a narrow column and condensed type. Typographic bullet points will help the reader to skip between each item.

SETTING UP A GRID

Setting up a page grid is often the final step in the preliminary design process, but the first part of producing usable templates. Once decisions have been made regarding fonts, columns, images, and so on, everything can be brought together as a grid. The page elements can all be balanced against one another, and the details refined until perfected.

COLUMN GRIDS

It is often a good idea to subdivide text columns for further flexibility. For example, a three-column grid could be split into six, giving the option for two columns of text on the same template. Further subdivisions, including bastard columns, provide more flexibility, but more complication. Twelve subdivisions can produce six, four, three, and two text columns from the same template.

ROW GRIDS

A grid running across the page can be just as useful as a column grid. Common hanging points for text or other page furniture can tie magazine and book spreads together, and improve consistency across a project.

A well-structured grid allows elements to be placed quickly without intricate measuring. Taken a step further, a whole library of page elements can be created, each snapping to the correct place on the grid as it is dragged onto the page. No measuring, no mistakes.

GUIDES

By the time you have subdivided column and row grids, placed margins, and set up all the other guides you need, your template may look a little overwhelming. As you are constructing the template, it's a good idea to choose colors for the guides (under *Layout > Guides* in InDesign and *Preferences* in Quark). Choose bold colors when adding guides that will be viewed across the whole page, and paler, tinted guides that will be used for more detailed work.

Subdivisions

Using an invisible, subdivided grid will build in more flexibility to a template.

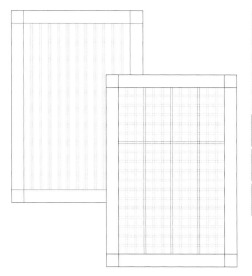

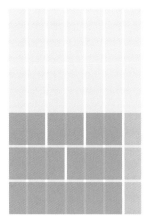

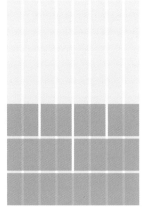

6-column grid
Divides by 3 and 2

7-column grid
Divides by 3 and 2 plus an irregular column

8-column grid
Divides by 4 and 2

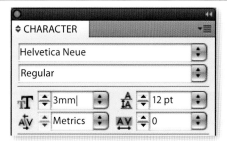

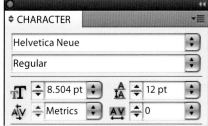

WORKING IN WHOLE NUMBERS

Whether you choose to work in metric, imperial, or pica measures, there is a lot to be said for structuring your grid around whole numbers. Placing an object 40mm from the top of the page is a lot quicker, and a lot easier, than placing it at 1.574in. Applications will convert units for you, so if you know your body text is set on 4mm leading, type it as that, and it will be converted to 11.399 points. An even better option is to set the application's default measurement units to those you prefer to work with.

MARGINS

As with column widths, the width of a margin can influence the feel of a page. Generally speaking, wider margins will slow the pace of reading and give a book-like appearance. Take it too far though, and page elements will become lost in a sea of white.

For magazine or other reusable templates, it's best to set a medium-width margin and use other techniques to dictate the tempo of a page. Breaking into the margin area occasionally will add interest and draw attention to a particular story.

Having the same width margin on either edge of a page will simplify any necessary rearrangement of elements on the page: they will sit in the correct position whether they are on the left or right side. However, this may be impractical for projects with many pages as a wider inside margin will be required to compensate for paper being swallowed into the binding.

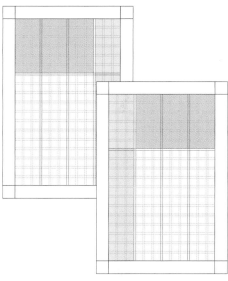

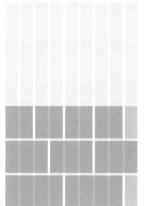

9-column grid
Divides by 3, or 4 and 2 with an irregular column

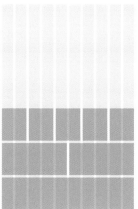

10-column grid
Divides by 5 and 2

12-column grid
Divides by 4, 3, and 2

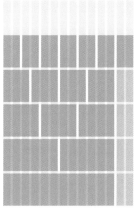

14-column grid
Divides by 7, or 4, 3, all with an irregular column, or by 2

SETTING UP MASTER PAGES

Master pages are the backbone of a template. They provide a consistent starting point for each page, and contain all the repeating elements that need to be in the same place every time, such as page numbers and running heads.

CREATING MASTER PAGES

To begin, use the *Pages* palette in InDesign or the *Page Layout* palette in QuarkXPress to show the master pages available. Pages can be added or removed using the *New* and *Trash* icons in InDesign and Quark. To create new document pages, simply drag a master page to the document area.

View and alter the content of a master page by double-clicking its icon at the top. Master pages are modified in the same way as standard document pages, though any changes you make will be applied throughout your document wherever the master is used.

DEFINING GRIDS

Select each separate master page in turn to set the margins, columns, and guides for your layout. Inside and outside margins automatically switch for left and right pages, different master pages can have different margins, and InDesign CS5 now supports different page dimensions within the same document.

ADDING STYLES AND SWATCHES

Create color swatches and text styles using the relevant palettes. As most styles are based on or have links to each other, it's best to work through each in a logical order. Start with color swatches, then paragraph styles, character styles, and finally object styles.

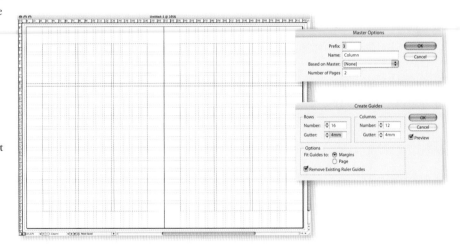

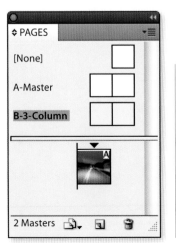

Pages palette
In InDesign, create a new master page using the pop-out menu. Master or document pages can be duplicated by dragging a page to the *New* icon at the bottom of the palette.

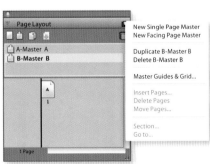

Master page items

Any element on a master page will appear throughout your document—perfect for section headers and page folios.

WHAT TO PUT ON A MASTER PAGE

As with a regular document page, graphics, text, and objects can be placed on a master page. Each element, and any subsequent edits, will appear throughout the document. Section names, page folios, and backgrounds are all perfect for placing on a master page. Automatic page numbering, as well as dates and section names, can be set using the *Special Characters* menu in InDesign, or by using Control/Command-3 in QuarkXPress. The page number range is defined using the *Numbering and Section Options…* in InDesign or *Page > Section…* in QuarkXPress. InDesign master-page elements always appear on the top of a stack of objects. For this reason, it's best to place regular page furniture on its own layer; that way it's simple to bring other objects to the front.

WHAT NOT TO PUT ON A MASTER PAGE

Text columns, title blocks, and any elements that will need to be individually modified are best placed into a library (see pages 190–3) or regular document page. Document pages can be duplicated by clicking the *Duplicate* icon in the *Page Layout* palette (Quark) or dragging them to *Create New Page* in the *Pages* palette (InDesign).

FINAL STEPS

Before saving your template, define your preferred default palette settings (see pages 34–5). Any future users will be able to click and begin typing with correctly styled text, etc. When saving, choose the template option to prevent any accidental alterations to your master pages. These pages can be used as a solid starting point for other section-specific templates, or even for the entire project.

Changing master page items

In Quark, click on an element to detach it from the master pages and make individual modifications. In InDesign use Command/Control-Shift+click to do the same. However, if a master page is later updated the object will be duplicated, leading to unwanted results.

Automatic page number

Use *Insert Special Character* in InDesign, Control/Command-3 in Quark, to add automatic page numbers to a document. Define the page range using the *Numbering and Section Options…* dialog windows (InDesign) or *Page > Section…* (Quark). As pages are added or moved, the page numbers will change automatically. It's important to remember that right-hand pages should always have odd numbers, and left-hand pages even numbers.

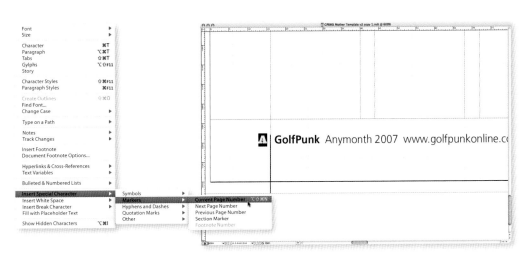

SETTING UP A LIBRARY

Libraries are useful places in which to store items you use regularly in your layouts. They can include anything that can be placed on a page: text, graphics, grouped items, and guides can all be stored and retrieved quickly when needed. Libraries in InDesign and QuarkXPress are practically identical in their function and use.

CREATING A LIBRARY

Choose *New Library* under *File > New* in both Quark and InDesign, then name and save the library in a convenient place. The *Library* palette will then appear. It's possible to have multiple libraries open concurrently; arrange them as you would any other palette.

For large projects it's a good idea to have a main library for the most common items, with additional libraries for each section. Libraries can be duplicated and shared in the same way as regular files, allowing multiple users to have the same set of graphics and elements to work with.

Organizing libraries

Each object in a library has a thumbnail, and can also be named for quick reference. Sorting objects into different libraries by type, such as "text library" or "image library," can help with finding the right item quickly.

SETTING UP A LIBRARY

USING A LIBRARY

Common text boxes, such as caption boxes, regular graphics, box styles, and so on are ideal library items. Create and style your object as normal, then drag and drop it onto the *Library* window. A thumbnail of each element is displayed; double-click the thumbnail to add a name or description to help with locating the item at a later date. To add a library object to a layout, simply drag and drop its thumbnail or name. Large and complex objects may take a second or two to appear. Text boxes will retain their original formatting with some exceptions (see below), grouped and ungrouped objects will remain so. If you modify the elements once they have been placed, the library version will remain unchanged unless deliberately replaced.

Adding to a library

Individual and groups of objects can be placed in a library by dragging and dropping. To add guides to an InDesign library, select each guide (Shift+Click for multiple guides) and choose *Add Item* from the *Library* palette pop-out menu. Use *Place Item(s)* to copy library guides onto a layout.

STYLES AND SWATCHES

If your library contains objects with color swatches, paragraph, character, or object styles applied, these will be retained in the library. When the object is dragged onto the page, any swatches or styles will come with it and be added to the document's palettes if they aren't already present. However, if the document already has a swatch or style with the same name, the existing document style will override the library style. While this can lead to some unexpected results, it can also be put to good use. For example, if a color swatch is named "section color," even if it has different color values in each of your section templates, any objects taken from the library that use the section color swatch will automatically be recolored to match the document swatch.

MULTIPLE USERS

Only one person can use a library at any one time. If you are working as part of a team, duplicate and distribute libraries to each user. It's prudent to keep master copies in a safe place, usually on a server, and ensure each designer updates their personal copies as any changes are made.

SNIPPETS

InDesign has further functionality in the form of "snippets." Prepare an object as for a library, then, under *File > Export*, select *InDesign Snippet* from the pull-down menu at the bottom of the dialog window, and save as a file. This snippet file can be placed on a server or e-mailed for others to use. Import the snippet using *Place*, and swatches and styles will be retained. Unlike a library file, the location of the object on the page will be remembered.

Style sheet clashes

Library objects and snippets retain any swatches and style sheets, which will be added to new documents upon placement. If matching style names already exist in a document, these will override the incoming library or snippet styles.

CS5 test project.idms

Snippets

To distribute a single element or group from InDesign, go to *File > Export* and select *InDesign Snippet* from the pull-down menu. The resulting file can be placed on a server or e-mailed. Use *Place* to bring the object back into a layout.

PROPORTION AND CONSISTENCY

Designers can often make judgments about layout composition by instinct—it's a by-product of constantly thinking in visual terms. Occasionally though, some projects leave you stumped for a solution; no matter how hard you try to fit the elements onto the page, they just don't look or feel right. In these situations it can be helpful to return to basics, and see which one produces the best solution to the problem.

BALANCE

Using a symmetrical layout is the most basic of all compositional concepts. Place your elements in the center of the page, keeping the margins even on all edges. Rotational and reflectional symmetry are variations on the theme, and can add interest. For more tension and energy, use an asymmetric layout—set your objects slightly off center, using a smaller or minor element to bring balance back to the composition.

GOLDEN PROPORTIONS

Proportions of five by eight (alternatively 1 to 1.6) are well documented as the most pleasing to the human eye. Organizing your page along the same proportions can solve many design problems, and placing key elements such as headlines five-eighths of the way up a page will get any layout off to a good start. The same principle can be used for scaling type—10-point box text should have box headers set at 16 point to achieve a pleasing balance.

RULE OF THIRDS

Similar to the golden proportion—but easier to work with—is the rule of thirds. Use guides to divide your work area into an equal three-by-three grid. Place your key element where two of the axes meet to create a focal point. It's then simple to develop the rest of the layout around that element, using the remaining guide intersection for aligning other key elements.

RHYTHM

Repetitive elements can be used to bring rhythm and calm to a complicated design. Employ regular spacing and consistently sized elements when working with lots of data, using obvious variation to draw attention to particular areas. A natural, flowing rhythm leads a reader through a composition—typographic headlines, or perspective in photography and illustration work particularly well when used this way.

HIERARCHY

Make sure your reader knows where to start on a page by making an element dominate, and lead everything else from that. By providing this clear guidance, whether it's a headline, image, or drop cap, you will

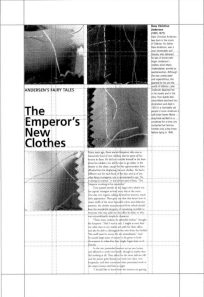

remove a lot of confusion from a cluttered design. Continue this principle down through your layers of elements, each dominating the next.

UNITY

Much like rhythm, unity can create a cohesive layout. If your elements are uniform sizes, aligned to grids based on the same dimensions, a viewer will subconsciously create structure and order. Negative space can be used in the same way, so keep the margins and spaces between elements uniform to create a sense of unity.

CONTRAST OF POSITIVE AND NEGATIVE SPACE

Use contrast to create energy in a layout, whether it's light and dark, type and image, stillness and motion, or color. These stark differences can bring a page to life, but can also be confusing if there isn't a clear hierarchy to the layout. Contrast can stop readers in their tracks, so another device needs to be used to guide them through the layout.

DESIGNING TABLES

One of the greatest layout challenges for an editorial designer has to be a large, data-heavy chart—column upon column of numbers and notes, all of which struggle to fit into the space allocated. With a logical approach, tables don't have to be purely functional; by using a light touch and adding emphasis in the right places tables can look beautiful too.

PLANNING

The first step when designing any table is to understand the data. You don't necessarily need to know the details—it's usually enough to be able to pick out the important elements, and structure the layers of information.

Look at how each entry reads and flows. Should the table read left to right, or top to bottom? If it doesn't fit your page proportions, can it be restructured, or split into several "decks?" Will combining or removing any entries solve any of your problems, and is it practical to do so? Can the most awkward entries have some of their data transferred to footnotes at the bottom of the table? As a word of warning, if the data in your table needs to be completely restructured, return to the application on which it was created, Microsoft Excel for example, as InDesign and QuarkXPress are not best suited to this kind of work.

SPACE

Giving each entry room to breathe, so that you can read it as an individual item, is key to getting a table to work properly. Tables aren't read like body text, short chunks of information are read one after the other. Don't be afraid to use a small text, and condensed or narrow fonts are fine. If possible use a typeface that has been specifically designed for use in charts, such as Bell Gothic from Linotype.

ALIGNMENT

Each column of text needs to be visually consistent, unless you specifically want to draw attention to an entry. As a rule of thumb, keep text aligned to the left, with a generous gutter between each column to avoid entries running into each other.

KEY LINES AND FILLS

Adding too many boxes and backgrounds is a common mistake when designing tables. Vertical key lines are not always needed, each vertical column of text will create its own invisible boundary, and space won't be wasted trying to allow for a margin either side of the vertical stroke. Horizontal key lines are more important, as most tables tend to be read left to right. Avoid using candy bar like stripes, however, as they make the information appear dense and unfriendly.

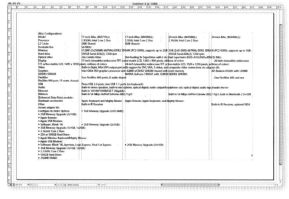

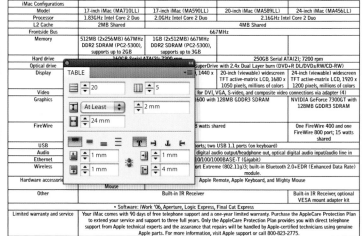

iMac Configurations				
Model	17-inch iMac (MA710LL)	17-inch iMac (MA590LL)	20-inch iMac (MA589LL)	24-inch iMac (MA456LL)
Processor	1.83GHz Intel Core 2 Duo	2.0GHz Intel Core 2 Duo	2.16GHz Intel Core 2 Duo	
L2 Cache	2MB Shared	4MB Shared		
Frontside Bus	667MHz			
Memory	512MB (2x256MB) 667MHz DDR2 SDRAM (PC2-5300), supports up to 2GB	1GB (2x512MB) 667MHz DDR2 SDRAM (PC2-5300), supports up to 3GB		
Hard drive	160GB Serial ATA(2); 7200 rpm	250GB Serial ATA(2); 7200 rpm		
Optical drive	24x Combo Drive	Slot-loading 8x SuperDrive with 2.4x Dual Layer burn (DVD+R DL/DVD±RW/CD-RW)		
Display	17-inch (viewable) widescreen TFT active-matrix LCD, 1440 x 900 pixels, millions of colors		20-inch (viewable) widescreen TFT active-matrix LCD, 1680 x 1050 pixels, millions of colors	24-inch (viewable) widescreen TFT active-matrix LCD, 1920 x 1200 pixels, millions of colors
Video	Built-in iSight; Mini-DVI output port with support for DVI, VGA, S-video, and composite video connections via adapter (4)			
Graphics	Intel GMA 950 graphics processor with 64MB of DDR2 SDRAM shared with main memory	ATI Radeon X1600 with 128MB GDDR3 SDRAM		NVIDIA GeForce 7300GT with 128MB GDDR3 SDRAM
FireWire	Two FireWire 400 ports; 8 watts shared			One FireWire 400 and one FireWire 800 port; 15 watts shared
USB	Three USB 2.0 ports; two USB 1.1 ports (on keyboard)			
Audio	Built-in stereo speakers, built-in microphone, optical digital audio output/headphone out, optical digital audio input/audio line in			
Ethernet	Built-in 10/100/1000BASE-T (Gigabit)			
Wireless	Built-in 54 Mbps AirPort Extreme (802.11g)	Built-in 54 Mbps AirPort Extreme (802.11g); built-in Bluetooth 2.0+EDR (Enhanced Data Rate) module.		
Accessories	Apple Keyboard and Mighty Mouse	Apple Remote, Apple Keyboard, and Mighty Mouse		
Other	Built-in IR Receiver			Built-in IR Receiver, optional VESA mount adapter kit

• Software: iWork '06, Aperture, Logic Express, Final Cut Express

Limited warranty and service: Your iMac comes with 90 days of free telephone support and a one-year limited warranty. Purchase the AppleCare Protection Plan to extend your service and support to three full years. Only the AppleCare Protection Plan provides you with direct telephone support from Apple technical experts and the assurance that repairs will be handled by Apple-certified technicians using genuine Apple parts. For more information, visit Apple support or call 800-823-2775.

Alignment

Align vertical columns consistently and logically, and use opportunities to "double up" on columns that cover more than one category if you can.

Rules

Use horizontal rules rather than boxing each entry in. It keeps the table flowing better, and allows more space for each entry. Stripes are another gimmick best avoided—they can make a table very dense and unfriendly.

Creating markers

Use bold key lines or changes in typography to add reference points. Have a solid anchor to give the reader's eye somewhere to return to after scanning through a line or column.

Footnotes

For long and awkward entries, don't be afraid to use footnotes to split some of the data away from the main table. This, of course, depends entirely on the data in the table, and don't be afraid to seek advice from the author.

Titling

Titles are the place to create a visual hierarchy. Start bold and get progressively lighter as you progress through the layers of data. Use color or a sudden change in typography to create markers in the table—a way for the eye to find a common reference point after scanning each line. Bold or colored key lines are another good device for separating whole areas of the table.

BARCODES AND DOCUMENT READERS

Every product that goes through a distribution system will need a barcode, whether it's a packet of gum, a book, or an automobile. In fact, barcodes have become so common, they have entered into our graphic language, appearing in logos and graphics whenever a retail theme needs to be suggested. But the technical standards to use barcodes, and other types of documents that need to be read by an automated scanner, are very strict, and designers should be aware of them.

These guidelines will help you meet the technical requirements needed for consistent scanning, while incorporating the barcode or other markers into your documents without them becoming an eyesore. It's worth noting that many large organizations, such as Wal-Mart or the US Postal Service (USPS), have their own standards and guidelines for automated document reading. Typically these standards are rigorously enforced to prevent wasted time and money. Those standards should supersede any information given here.

GETTING A BARCODE

Although there are many types of barcode, and subvariations, the most widely used ones are generated to a standard approved by the Global Standards 1 (GS1) organization, and they carry enough data to uniquely identify your product. Typically barcodes are supplied by the company handling the distribution of the product. Software to generate barcodes can be widely found online (BarcodeMaker from www.teacupsoftware.com works as an InDesign plug-in), but the data to generate one, usually in the form of a Universal Product Code (UPC) or a European Article Number (EAN), will still need to be supplied by the distributor.

ONE-DIMENSIONAL BARCODES

The most familiar of all barcodes, consisting of a series of fat and thin lines, can be found on just about anything and everything. Although there are many variations to one-dimensional barcodes, they usually contain just enough information to identify a product. In North America and Canada the 12-digit UPC is used, while the EAN has been adopted by the rest of the world and adds an extra digit to help with identifying the product's country of origin. There are additional variations for International Standard Book Numbers (ISBN) and International Standard Serial Numbers (ISSN), which append two or five extra digits to identify issue numbers, reprints, and other variations.

Postal services use their own one-dimensional barcode formats, in the form of tall and short lines or a series of dots.

STACKED BARCODES

When two or more one-dimensional barcodes are applied to the same product it is referred to as a "stacked" barcode. Typically used in wholesale distribution networks, each barcode refers to a different aspect of that particular product—for example, product type, place of origin, and destination.

TWO-DIMENSIONAL BARCODES

Looking like a square or rectangle of random pixels, two-dimensional barcodes are relatively new, but there are still dozens of formats and variations. As these barcodes store information vertically as well as horizontally, it is possible to encode far more data than on a standard barcode—the Quick Response Code, for example, can store up to 7,366 numeric characters. The most widely recognized of the two-dimensional barcodes is the Maxicode format developed by United Parcel Service.

USING BARCODES

There are many guidelines and standards for utilizing barcodes, all with slight differences, but there are many common recommendations. The standards presented here are in line with most high-volume outlets and are sufficient for general use. However, it is always worth testing and checking your implementation before sending a product to print.

CONTRAST AND COLOR

Barcode scanners need lots of contrast in order to read data. Black on white is recommended, but black on a very light color or image tint of no more than 10% is acceptable. Never reverse out a barcode, always print black on a light background.

Checking barcodes

If you have a webcam, the scanner at http://en.barcodepedia.com/ will check the accuracy of your barcodes for you, free of charge.

SCALING

To ensure reliable scanning, barcodes should be used full size and without truncation—the guide bars at the beginning and end of each barcode should be at least 0.5in (12 mm) high. Some standards permit horizontal scaling down to 80%, and 50% of the vertical axis. Many high-volume outlets are beginning to reject reduced barcodes so use with caution, especially on low-quality print surfaces, such as newsprint. There is no technical limit on scaling up a barcode as the operator simply holds the product further from the scanner, but there may be practical limitations that cause extreme examples to be rejected by outlets.

BARCODES AND DOCUMENT READERS

PLACEMENT

Barcodes need a clean margin, known as a quiet zone, to ensure accurate reading. This margin should be at least 0.08in (2mm) wide; EAN barcodes have a leading character and trailing chevrons to ensure these areas remain clear of interference.

Barcodes should be positioned well clear of any edges, folds, or other interferences, so allow a gap of at least 0.3in (7.5mm). Many retailers prefer barcodes to be positioned in the bottom left-hand corner of the product, but as long as the other readability guidelines are followed this is rarely enforced.

LETTERING

The digits on a barcode—known as Human Readable Characters—need to be clear and legible. Although scanners will not read the digits, an operator may have to key them in manually if there is a problem with the barcode. Use a clean uncluttered font. Arial Monospaced is a good example.

POSTAL ITEMS

Many postal services offer a Business Reply Mail facility (also known as Freepost or Reply Paid) whereby a preprinted envelope or card is supplied for a customer to return without the need for filling in addresses. The standards for designing these items are very precise, as the specifications shown here for USPS Business Reply Mail, and Royal Mail Freepost testify. Always check with the postal service in your region for specifications and amendments before designing such a document.

OPTICAL MARK RECOGNITION

The technology behind scanning and reading handwritten forms is known as Optical Mark Recognition (OMR). The standards for designing and implementing forms to be used for OMR are much more relaxed than for barcodes and preprinted mail, mainly because the end user will also usually generate the form as well. Companies such as Abbyy (www.abbyy.com) and Gravic (www.gravic.com) produce software for designing such forms, and also reading the data back in.

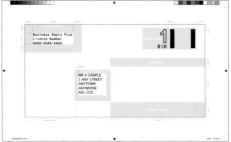

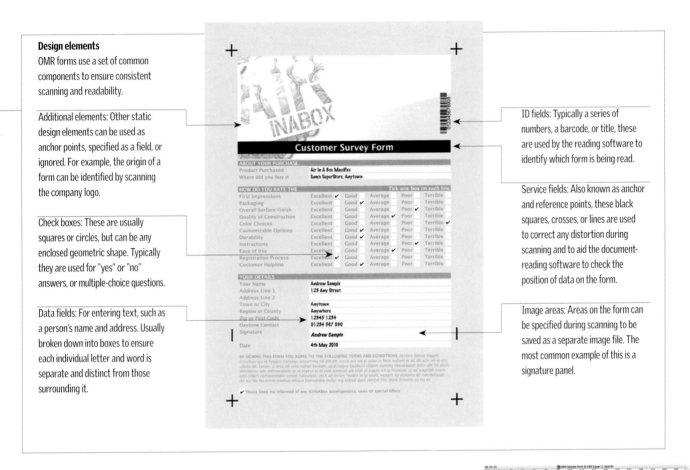

Design elements
OMR forms use a set of common components to ensure consistent scanning and readability.

Additional elements: Other static design elements can be used as anchor points, specified as a field, or ignored. For example, the origin of a form can be identified by scanning the company logo.

Check boxes: These are usually squares or circles, but can be any enclosed geometric shape. Typically they are used for "yes" or "no" answers, or multiple-choice questions.

Data fields: For entering text, such as a person's name and address. Usually broken down into boxes to ensure each individual letter and word is separate and distinct from those surrounding it.

ID fields: Typically a series of numbers, a barcode, or title, these are used by the reading software to identify which form is being read.

Service fields: Also known as anchor and reference points, these black squares, crosses, or lines are used to correct any distortion during scanning and to aid the document-reading software to check the position of data on the form.

Image areas: Areas on the form can be specified during scanning to be saved as a separate image file. The most common example of this is a signature panel.

TYPES OF FORM

The most advanced and versatile OMR form is printed using white panels in a field of pale color, known as a drop-out color. Once a form has been completed and scanned, the background can be removed leaving just the data and other desired elements ready for reading by the software. For example, a form printed in pale orange and written on with a black or blue pen will leave just the entered data when scanned in RGB mode and viewed only in the red channel.

Single color raster and linear forms use dots or frames to mark the areas for data entry, but as these frames appear in the scanned document, the reading software has to be "trained" to ignore certain parts of the form. Should a written letter or mark cross the boundary line, it may not be interpreted properly, or ignored altogether.

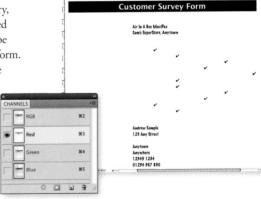

WEB-DESIGN BASICS

Web pages are usually made up of a combination of text, images, and styles. They may also include other media such as audio and video files, or interactive programs such as games. Web pages almost always include links to other pages. Because web pages are interactive (at the very least, they allow users to click on links), you need to know how to create a design that your visitors will understand. Ideally this design will work on a number of different devices and not just Macs and PCs.

Whether you create your web pages by hand, coding in HTML, or use a web-editing program such as Dreamweaver, the page itself will always be a data file containing HTML code. It is advisable to familiarize yourself with at least the basics of HTML, because sooner or later your web-editing program will produce unexpected results and you will have to fix the design manually. There are many good HTML tutorials on the Internet, including those at www.w3schools.com/html.

Traditional desktop-publishing software makes it easy to produce multicolumn layouts, but the same is not true with web pages. A popular way to create columns has been to use HTML's table feature. This is no longer considered a good idea, so disregard advice you will find in many online tutorials that suggests this. Use Cascading Style Sheets (CSS) instead.

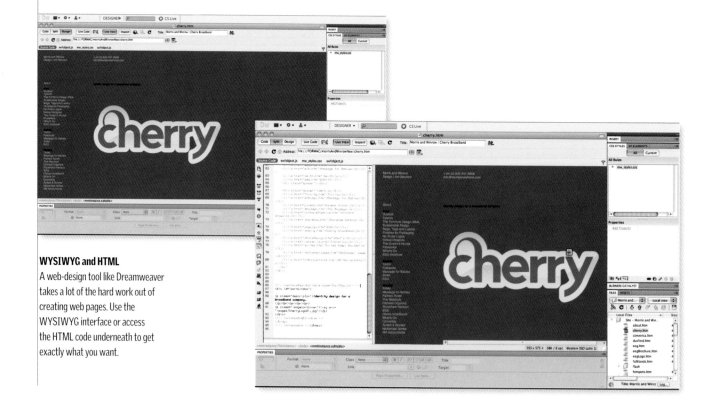

WYSIWYG and HTML
A web-design tool like Dreamweaver takes a lot of the hard work out of creating web pages. Use the WYSIWYG interface or access the HTML code underneath to get exactly what you want.

Linking pages
Select the text and type the page name that it should link to in the Link box below.

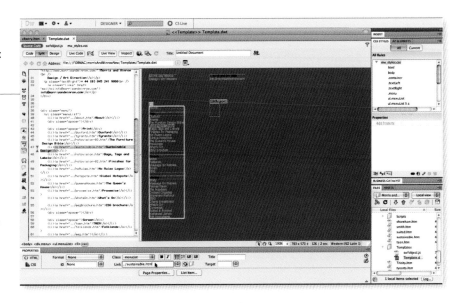

TEXT

Choose a series of fonts that will work well on a range of computer screens). Use CSS to set the size and color, and ensure that the fonts' colors contrast with the background for optimum legibility.

IMAGES

Before importing images into your web pages, remember that your visitors may attempt to view them using slow Internet connections. Use JPEG compression to reduce the file size, while maintaining reasonable levels of image detail.

LINKS

Convention states that textual links are underlined, and images that link to other pages have a border around them. You are free to defy convention for artistic purposes, but your pages may be less successful if your visitors fail to grasp your intentions.

STYLES

At first, using external CSS files seems like harder work than setting the colors, sizes, and other attributes of text and other page elements manually. However, using CSS means you can apply dramatic, site-wide design changes to hundreds of individual pages in one go simply by editing one file.

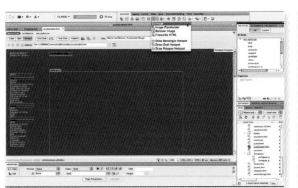

Placing images
Drag images onto the page or insert them using the menu options.

Managing design
Using CSS to manage your site's styles makes it easy to run out changes over multiple pages.

DESIGNING YOUR FIRST WEB PAGE

The first step when designing a web page is to decide on the hierarchy of the information you want to present. This is likely to include a heading of some sort, which could be a logo graphic and some text. You will also probably include a navigation device, such as a toolbar running across the screen under the logo, or maybe as a sidebar to the left or right of the main content. You may want a footer at the end to display copyright information and a summary of important links that appear in the navigation.

Don't worry too much about the layout at this early stage. Remember that your page may be viewed by basic devices with small screens that won't handle your main design concept very well. First, use your web-editing software to construct the page using as little layout as possible. Import the logo image; type the text that will sit next to it; create a list of links for the navigation; import the images and text for the main part of the page; and finally add the footer text. At this stage you should have a boring-looking page that will work with every computer on the Internet, from an top of the range Mac or PC to a basic cell phone.

USE LABELS

Allocate a unique description to each of these page elements, such as "header," "toolbar," "content," and "footer." HTML experts will type DIV tags into the HTML code to do this, while those using Dreamweaver will need to use the *Insert Div Tag* option to achieve the same results. At this stage the page will still look boring, although it now contains a labeled structure.

Link a CSS file to the page and edit it to list each of the elements you labeled earlier. Allocate each element with properties such as color, width, and position. There are many different

Design grids
Create a basic layout to hold the branding, content, and navigational elements of your site.

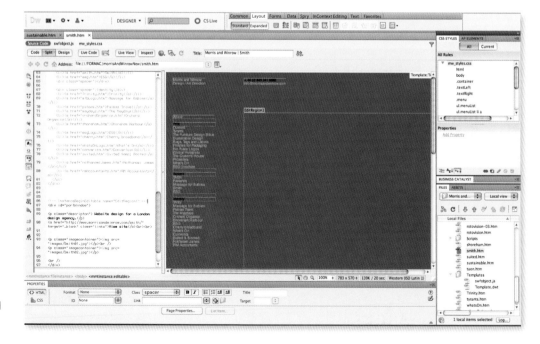

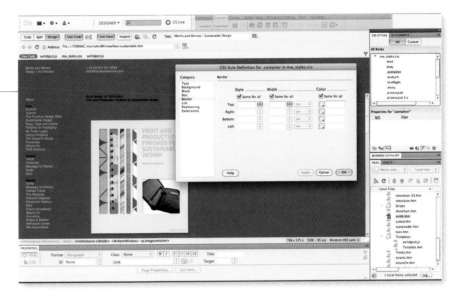

attributes you can use, and excellent examples are provided at www.w3schools.com/css. Your web page should appear on most personal computers more or less as you intended. However, it will probably now fail to work well with small-screened devices. To allow these to work, you need to edit the CSS file and add an entry for handheld media types.

Editing style sheets
Make changes to the site's appearance by editing the CSS file. Programs like Dreamweaver let you do this using a friendly interface.

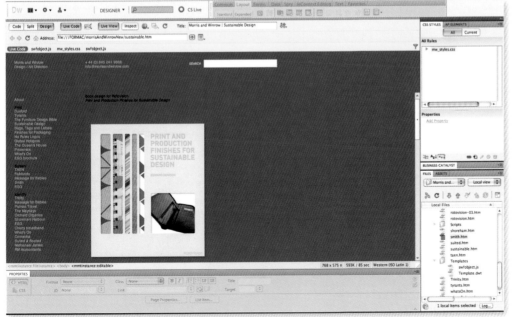

User-friendly sites
Adding forms such as the Search box will make your site more usable.

DEVELOPING YOUR WEBSITE

The web designer's job has evolved from simply generating great-looking pages to programming dynamic sites. The difference between a basic, static site and a dynamic one is that the former simply displays web pages that have been created manually, whereas a dynamic site builds the pages automatically whenever a visitor requests them. This makes it possible to have exciting sites that change as often as you like, perhaps allowing users to customize the results. In the long run it's also a lot less work to maintain a dynamic site than a static one because you don't have to edit every single page when you want to change the wording of a header or make a small change to a toolbar that appears on every page.

To create a dynamic site you'll need to extend your knowledge of web programming beyond basic HTML. Currently the most popular web programming language is PHP (Hypertext Preprocessor) which, when combined with the MySQL database, will allow you to create professional sites that can rival the biggest names on the Internet.

DYNAMIC CONTENT
It is possible to add some interactive elements to your site without getting too bogged down in programming. Image galleries, discussion forums, blogs, audio and video broadcasting, and many other features are all available cheaply if you choose to download and install free software written by others. You won't get the same level of customization that you would if you wrote it yourself, but it's a quick and easy way to create a professional-looking site.

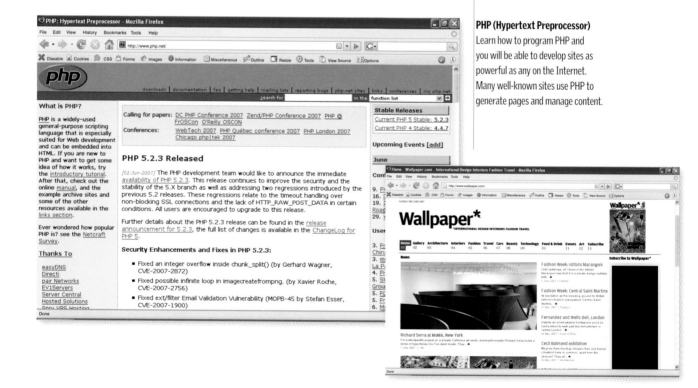

PHP (Hypertext Preprocessor)
Learn how to program PHP and you will be able to develop sites as powerful as any on the Internet. Many well-known sites use PHP to generate pages and manage content.

Content management
Use a free content-management system like Joomla! to create a dynamic site.

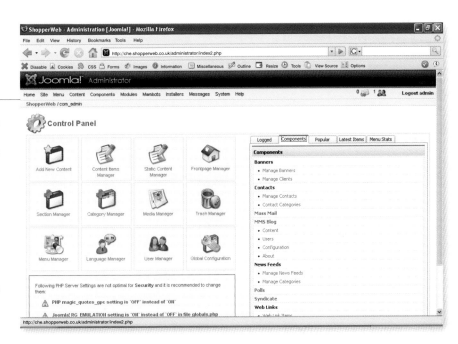

Using Flash can make your site stand out, although you should be careful how you use it or you many risk alienating some users. Most personal computers come with a Flash player, so you can be 90% sure that your designs will work for each visitor. However, try to avoid using Flash for critical elements that hold your site together, such as navigation toolbars.

A site that relies on a Flash menu system will be useless to some visitors, whereas one with a text-based navigation toolbar and an impressive Flash representation of some data will still work to a certain extent. Try to provide a text-based alternative for visitors without Flash.

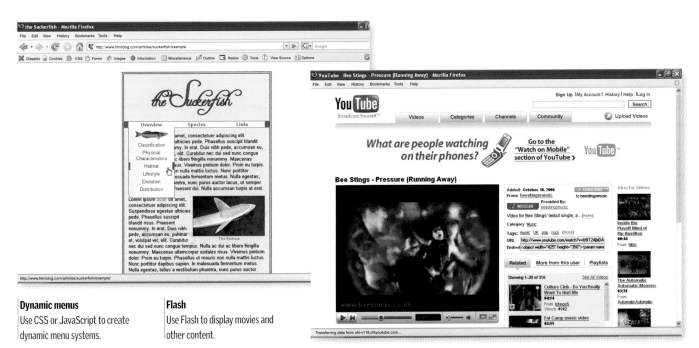

Dynamic menus
Use CSS or JavaScript to create dynamic menu systems.

Flash
Use Flash to display movies and other content.

PUBLISHING A WEBSITE

It is unwise (although technically possible) to run a live website on the same computer that you use for daily tasks. It is more sensible to subscribe to a web-hosting service, which will provide you with disk space and an Internet connection so that the public can access your web pages and other files. You will need a way to copy these files from your computer onto the web server, which the web hosting company uses to publish your site.

FTP

The most common way is to use an FTP program. FTP (File Transfer Protocol) lets you copy files over the Internet, both to and from a remote computer such as a web server. There are lots of FTP programs available, with common choices including the free FileZilla (http://filezilla.sourceforge.net) for Windows and Fetch (http://fetchsoftworks.com) for the Mac. These allow you to drag files from one window to another, just as if you wanted to copy files between folders. The difference is that with FTP they travel over the Internet.

A newer, more secure version of FTP is becoming increasingly popular. SFTP (Secure FTP) encrypts your connection so that hackers cannot intercept your file transfers and vandalize your website. FileZilla is compatible with SFTP and Mac users can use Fugu (http://rsug.itd.umich.edu/software/fugu), which is also free.

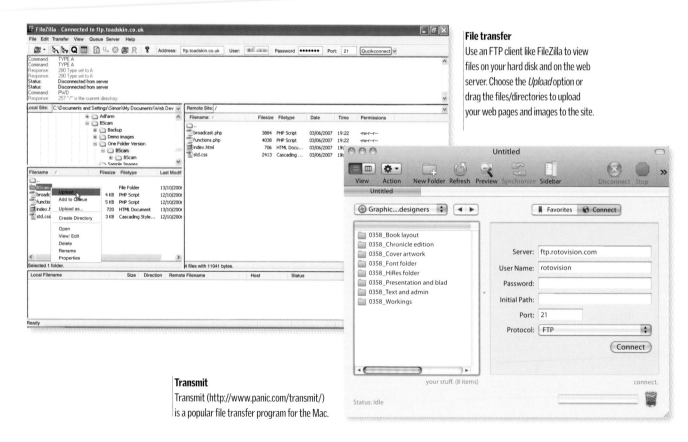

File transfer
Use an FTP client like FileZilla to view files on your hard disk and on the web server. Choose the *Upload* option or drag the files/directories to upload your web pages and images to the site.

Transmit
Transmit (http://www.panic.com/transmit/) is a popular file transfer program for the Mac.

Some web-hosting companies provide web-based tools to help you upload files. These can be easier to use for beginners, but in the long run most people will find them limiting. An FTP or SFTP program can automatically synchronize files on your hard disk with those on the server. This makes updating your site with new designs quick and easy, and also lets you download visitor log files quickly. You can use these to analyze which pages are the most popular.

TESTING

When you believe you have created your finished website, don't immediately upload the pages to the web and hope for the best. For a professional result, run a web server in your studio and use that as a test machine. Mac OS X server includes a web server, as does Windows XP Professional. Use as many different computers, devices, and web browsers to visit your test site and see how it appears in each. If you have to make changes, the public at large won't see your work in progress.

Testing site designs

Run a web server on your computer, to test a site design.

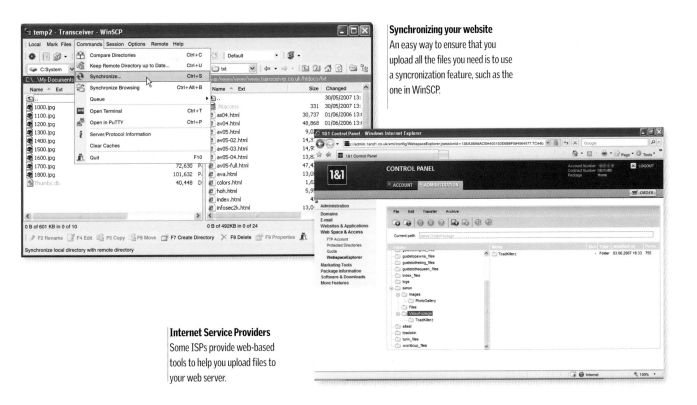

Synchronizing your website

An easy way to ensure that you upload all the files you need is to use a syncronization feature, such as the one in WinSCP.

Internet Service Providers

Some ISPs provide web-based tools to help you upload files to your web server.

Production

Not so long ago a design studio would hand layouts, transparencies, and illustrations to a reprographics house who would deal with the process of turning everything into a single file of use to the printers. The continuing evolution of desktop publishing has led to many of these skilled and technical tasks, previously managed by the reprographics company, now being the responsibility of the designer.

This section covers the information you need to turn your designs into finished, print-ready artwork, and getting it all to the printers with the minimum of fuss. Guides to the different print methods used, as well as the pitfalls of each are discussed, along with the effects different paper stocks will have on the finished results. Reference tables of the different international standards for paper sizes and print finishing round off the section.

SETTING UP A STUDIO PRINTER

Even with the advances made in soft-proofing work on-screen, the increasing use of on-screen delivery, and the falling prices for bureau printing, all studios still need an in-house printer to run out bills, test designs, or generate full-color proofs.

PICKING THE RIGHT PRINTERS

There are essentially two choices when it comes to printing technology: laser or inkjet. Laser printers are usually more expensive to buy, but cheaper to run; with inkjets it's the other way round. Inkjet printers are of most use when generating color proofs and other high-quality output, though note that the cost of specialist inkjet media is high.

Laser printers—even expensive, color-managed models—can, by contrast, print with usually good results onto even the cheapest, recycled papers, but the characteristics of the finish to their output makes them usually unsuitable for color proofing at the most critical level.

At the very least, a studio should have an A3 (297 x 420mm [c. 11¾ x 16½in]) mono laser printer for text and layout proofing, invoices, and the like, and an A3+ inkjet for finished work and color proofing, allowing A4 (210 x 297mm [c. 8⅛ x 11⅝in]) spreads plus bleed to be checked.

Printer choice

It could be that you only need an A4 consumer printer for image proofing, but it is likely that at the very least you will require a large-format printer that can handle A3 or A3+ to enable you to output design visuals at full size. There are dozens of models to choose from, so shop around and check specifications carefully to ensure you cover all your main output requirements.

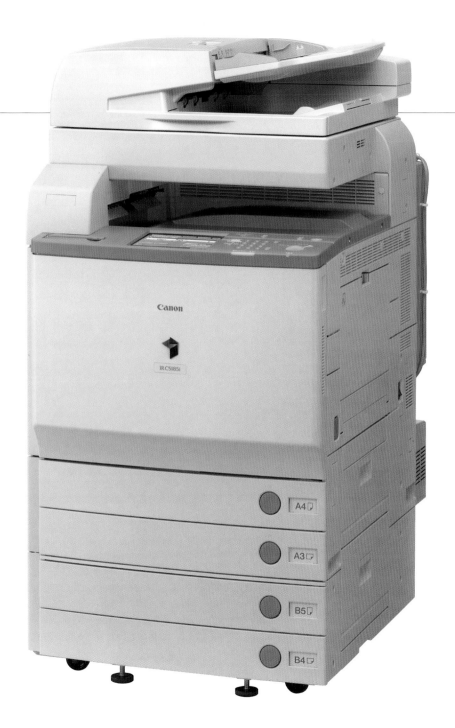

SETTING UP A STUDIO PRINTER

POSTSCRIPT AND RIPS

To get the best results possible in the least time, printers must include support for Adobe's PostScript page-description language; lasers usually boast this from the mid-range up, although it's found only in a very few high-end inkjet printers. If this is the case, invest in a RIP that will do the job for you. This can be in the form of a stand-alone box—essentially a small, moderately powerful computer—or as software that runs on the computer to which the printer is directly attached.

CONNECTIVITY

Both Macs and PCs can share printers, connected directly to them using USB, with other users on a local network. This is less than ideal, however; far better to get printers that have Ethernet ports to allow them to be connected directly to the network, accessible by all. This is now common even for mid-range inkjets; a color inkjet multifunction device—which includes printer, scanner, copier, and often fax—that features Ethernet would be a good, cheap choice for very small-scale color output and general office tasks.

One danger of using printers across the network is color reproduction; it's important to make sure that where printers are shared all the computers that you and your colleagues use are set up with the correct color profile.

Print presets
Setting up print presets—to include or exclude printer's marks, for example—makes life much easier for a team of designers.

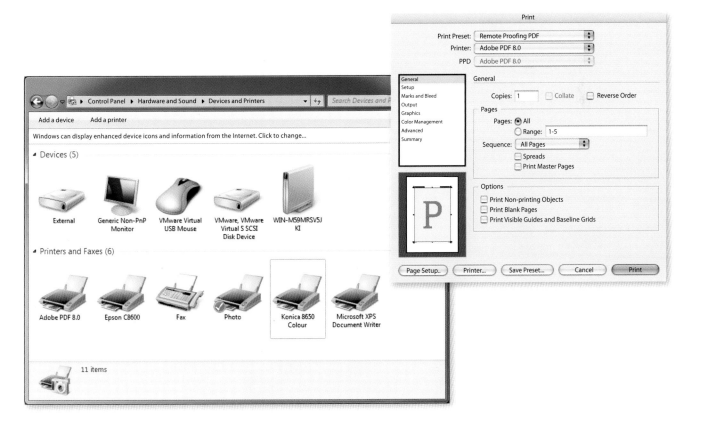

PREFLIGHT PROCEDURES

Whenever you send layout files to a reproduction company or printer, you should be able to rely on them to check the files carefully to ensure they're set up correctly for their system. However, it's also your responsibility to check files just as carefully before they leave your own workstation to avoid any problems or extra costs.

A TYPICAL PREFLIGHT CHECKLIST

This list represents what you should check as part of a standard preflight procedure for a typical print project—using the built-in features of InDesign, QuarkXPress, or Photoshop.

File formats and settings

Check with your reproduction company or printer to see if they have specific guidelines for their preferred file formats or preference settings. For example, if they have their own custom color-management settings, ask that a set be sent to you for use with any jobs they handle. Also, ask if they prefer files to be delivered as original packaged layouts or as repro-ready PDFs.

Document

The preflight stage is really too late to be checking document size and basic set-up issues such as bleeds and so on, but do it anyway as a small error made at the start of a project could spell disaster if it's missed and goes all the way through to print.

Images

• Flag images that aren't supplied in position and as high resolution. This can be done by creating a "notes" layer with virtual Post-its, which can be hidden prior to final output.
• Ensure there are no duplicate file names.
• Ensure all images are of a sufficient resolution for reprographic use, and resize any that don't fit this criteria. Also, check that digital images have been sufficiently sharpened and color balanced.
• If you include any screen shots in your layouts, at either 72 or 96ppi, do not be tempted to resample the originals, even though a repro company will flag them as incompatible with standard preflight parameters. They will reproduce cleanly if left at their original resolution and are reduced in the layout.

Notes layers

Add Post-it-style notes to a layout in order to flag up all positional images, and to include any other relevant notes to the repro house. Make sure they stand out clearly so that they aren't forgotten and left in the document for repro and print. It's also a good idea to keep them on a separate layer so you can show or hide them globally.

• Check that all images are CMYK, unless a mixed RGB/CMYK workflow has been agreed upon.
• Ensure no images contain spot colors that will create an extra unwanted separation.
• Check that there are no required images on hidden layers.

Fonts

• Check that all the fonts you've used are available to the reproduction company or printer.
• Check that all fonts have been set in the correct weight rather than "styled" in the layout software package.
• Check that there are no incompatible font formats as these may cause problems at the output stage.
• Delete any unused style sheets.

Colors

• Check that there are no spot colors set to separate out to CMYK.
• Strip unused colors from documents, in turn weeding out duplicates or color inconsistencies.

SPECIALIST PREFLIGHT SOFTWARE

Specialist software packages take preflight procedures to a much higher level than the built-in features of InDesign or QuarkXPress. FlightCheck Professional from Markzware (www.markzware.com) and Pitstop Professional from Enfocus (www.enfocus.com) are both well-regarded products—and both companies offering an online preflight product too. This kind of service is increasingly popular now that the

Internet can cope with the large file sizes that accompany this type of work. The huge selection of features will appear daunting at first, but if you preflight lots of documents, the investment in specialist software may well be worth it.

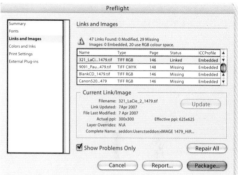

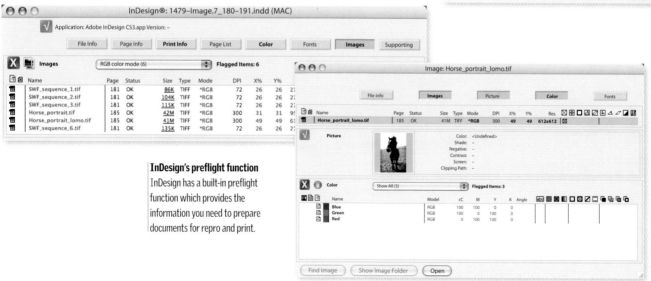

InDesign's preflight function
InDesign has a built-in preflight function which provides the information you need to prepare documents for repro and print.

THE TRANSPARENCY FLATTENER

Most users of Adobe's Creative Suite are familiar with the four main transparency effects available to them—namely soft shadows, feathered edges, blending modes, and opacity. However, it's also important to understand how "flattening" works during output.

FLATTENING BASICS

Any objects that have a transparency effect applied, including any linked graphic or image files that are affected by a transparency effect, must be flattened when output to a printer. This is also the case when files are exported as an Encapsulated PostScript (EPS) or saved as a PDF 1.3. Later versions of the PDF standard have built-in support for transparency.

In simple terms, flattening is the process by which all the areas in a stack of transparent objects that overlap are converted into separate objects while retaining the measure of opacity they were assigned when transparent.

FLATTENER PRESETS

Transparency Flattener settings must be specified according to the type of output you require when printing, saving, or exporting a file to PDF or EPS. Any settings you create can subsequently be saved as a preset and reused. There are three built-in transparency flattener presets available in both InDesign and Illustrator—*Low Resolution*, *Medium Resolution*, and *High Resolution*. These are suitable for the following uses:

Low Resolution

These presets are normally fine for output to black and white desktop printers for use as visuals or for quick in-house proofing.

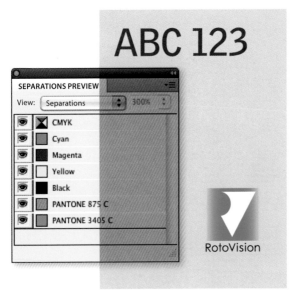

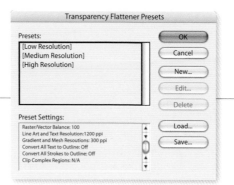

Medium Resolution

Stick to the *Medium Resolution* preset for color visuals output from a desktop printer. This is also a reasonable setting for the types of documents run through print-on-demand PostScript digital presses.

High Resolution

Use this preset if you're preparing material to send to an imagesetter or some other kind of high-resolution output device, including digital presses where the highest-quality output is required.

You can of course create your own presets, and it's a good idea to speak to your reproduction house or printer to find out what settings they themselves use. They can easily send you their saved presets, which you can add to your own applications using the *Load* button in the *Transparency Flattener Presets* palette.

Flattening

To illustrate how flattening affects a group of objects, let's take a look at this example. The background panel was drawn in InDesign. The screen shot is an imported .tif file set to *Multiply* and with a drop shadow applied. The shadow is also set to *Multiply.* The RotoVision logo is a vector graphic copied to the InDesign page as an editable object. The green panel has a gradient feather effect applied to it. Using the *Flattener Preview* palette, areas that are affected by flattening are highlighted by a pink overlay while unaffected areas are knocked back to a pale gray. You can see that the transparent objects—the screen shot and the feathered box—are highlighted in the first example, while everything except the type will in actual fact be affected in some way when flattening is applied to the group of objects as a whole.

EXPORTING PDFs

Although some of you may still be sending InDesign or QuarkXPress files along with the necessary images and fonts out to your service provider to generate PDFs prior to output, it's increasingly likely that you'll soon be supplying PDF files directly to the printer. It's an additional level of responsibility to take on board but, with some prior knowledge and through the use of software presets, generating press-ready PDF files is no

harder than printing layouts to a desktop printer. InDesign and QuarkXPress both have built-in functionality for generating PDFs, and if you use Acrobat Professional you can preflight your own PDF files. Remember, however, if you're not completely familiar with the procedure, it's a good idea to ask your printer to preflight PDFs for you until you gain enough confidence in this area.

INDESIGN PDF PRESETS

InDesign includes a number of presets for PDF export that are designed for specific uses. Incidentally these export presets are also available to the other components of the Creative Suite.

Smallest File Size: This is a good choice for PDFs that will be sent as e-mail attachments for review purposes, or are intended for use in websites. Image quality is relatively low to keep the file size down, and all colors are converted to the sRGB color space, which is good for general viewing on-screen.

InDesign presets

To export a PDF directly from InDesign, select a preset via *File > Adobe PDF Presets*. If you create custom presets yourself, these will also appear in this menu. Not all presets will work with all documents: a yellow warning triangle will appear next to any items that could cause problems during output.

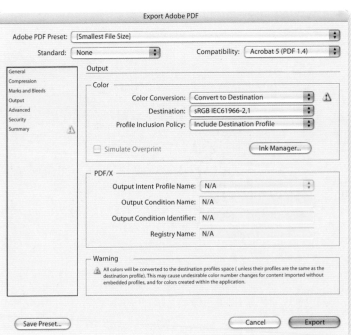

High Quality Print: This is a good choice for PDFs destined for output to desktop proofing devices such as inkjets or color laser printers, and image quality is high. Color conversion is not carried out using this preset, but Tagged Source Profiles are included. This means that device-independent colors are left unchanged and device-dependent colors appear as the nearest possible equivalent in the PDF.

Press Quality: This is the best choice for any prepress workflow that will be output as high-resolution color separations or to a digital press. This option produces a PDF that features "editable transparency," which means that the printer can "flatten" the files later and to their own specification . Colors are converted to CMYK or spot.

PDF/X-1a 2001: This option is designed for high-resolution output and creates a PDF/X-1a-compliant (see What is PDF/X? below) file. All fonts are embedded, color is CMYK or spot, and page boundaries and trapping are defined in the PDF file.

PDF/X3 2002: This option is similar to PDF/X-1a, but it supports a color-managed workflow and allows a profile to be specified for output intent. RGB and LAB colors can be included with this option, which is useful for a mixed RGB/CMYK workflow.

PDF/X4 2008: A newer ISO standard for PDFs which also supports a color-mamaged workflow but also allows 16-bit color, transparency, and the use of layers.

Press Quality preset

The Press Quality preset will create a PDF suitable for high-end printing requirements, but doesn't take into account any specific standards such as PDF/X. If your printers prefer to handle any flattening themselves, this is a better option than PDF/X. The example below is a press-quality PDF with all printer's marks switched on.

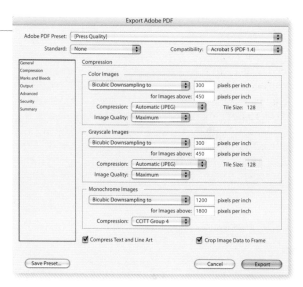

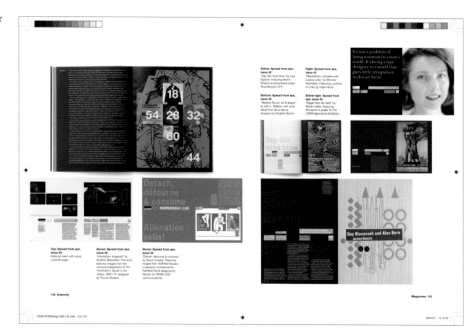

EXPORTING PDFs

QUARKXPRESS 8 PDF PRESETS

QuarkXPress 8 now ships with a number of preinstalled PDF presets similar to those found in InDesign. However, alternative presets that correspond to those described above can be downloaded from Quark's website (www.downloads.quark.com), and you can, of course, create your own custom presets via the *Output Styles* command (*Edit* > *Output Styles*), which will be familiar to all seasoned Quark users as its layout is identical to Quark's other *Edit* dialog boxes. The same principles for PDF generation apply when using QuarkXPress. Image-compression settings, transparency flattening, and color policy dictate how your own custom presets are used.

WHAT IS PDF/X?

PDF/X isn't an alternative format, it's a subset of the Adobe PDF specification. It was designed to help eliminate common problems that occur when PDF files are exchanged—such as missing images and fonts—and to minimize unexpected color reproduction through its support for a color-managed workflow. Using the PDF/X standard ensures your files will be output as you intended. Check with your printer before sending PDF/X files however. If they prefer to handle the flattening themselves you may get better results supplying them with a standard PDF.

Export Adobe PDF

Adobe PDF Preset: [PDF/X-1a:2001]

Standard: PDF/X-1a:2001   Compatibility: Acrobat 4 (PDF 1.3)

General
Compression
Marks and Bleeds
Output
Advanced
Security
Summary

Output

Color

Color Conversion: Convert to Destination (Prese...

Destination: Document CMYK - Europe IS...

Profile Inclusion Policy: Don't Include Profiles

☐ Simulate Overprint   Ink Manager...

PDF/X

Output Intent Profile Name: Document CMYK - Europe...

Output Condition Name:

Output Condition Identifier: FOGRA27

Registry Name: http://www.color.org

Description

Colors will be converted to the destination profiles space only if they have embedded profiles that differ from the destination profile (or if they are RGB colors and the destination profile is CMYK, or visa versa). Color object without embedded profiles and native objects (such as line art or type) are not converted, so that color numbers are preserved.

Save Preset...   Cancel   Export

PDFX-1a2001 option

Selecting the PDF/X-1a (or PDF/X-3) option helps to minimize unexpected color changes at output, as it supports a color-managed workflow. It also allows you to specifiy an Output Intent Profile, which is generally unavailable for alternative options.

WHAT IS PASS4PRESS?

Pass4press is a relatively new set of prepress PDF guidelines introduced by the Periodical Publishers Association (PPA) to help streamline the method by which digital files such as advertisements are supplied to magazine publishers. The guidelines describe the best practice for creating good-quality PDF files that will be compliant with a standardized preset and will be completely ready for print. If a PDF is supplied "pass4press" it shouldn't require any further work prior to output. All job option presets for Acrobat, InDesign, and QuarkXPress, can be downloaded at www.pass4press.com along with a good deal of additional information about pass4press and PDFs in general.

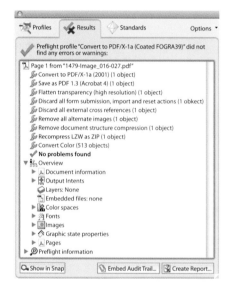

Preflight palettes

The results shown in the Preflight palette indicate that this PDF/X-1a-compliant file is free of any problems. With the extensive preflight function, it is possible to generate a detailed report that can be included as part of the artwork you send to your printer.

PREPARING FOR OUTPUT

Once a document has been run through the preflight process, it can be considered ready to be "packaged" (InDesign) or "collected for output" (QuarkXPress). This is the process by which all images, fonts, and any other items deemed necessary for successful output are pulled together for despatch to a reproduction company or printer. The principles behind how this works are very similar in both InDesign and QuarkXPress, but the interfaces differ slightly, so here is a brief discussion of the procedure for each application.

PACKAGE (INDESIGN)

Before beginning the process of "packaging" a job for reproduction, it's always worth looking at the *Links* palette to ensure that there aren't any missing or modified images within the document's pages. They would be flagged automatically during the package procedure anyway so there's no danger of them being missed altogether. Double-check the preflight panel to make sure all other elements are present and correct, and you're ready to go. When you click the *Package* button, you'll be prompted to fill in a *Printing Instructions* panel. This isn't absolutely necessary, but if you get into the habit of including it with the layouts, it can do no harm to add it to the disc with the rest of the job.

The final *Create Package Folder* panel includes a number of checkbox options. You're likely to always include *Fonts and Linked Graphics*, and it's good practice to keep the *Update Graphic Links in Package* box checked, as the original document is duplicated rather than moved to the *Package Folder*. Incidentally, "Except CJK" stands for Chinese, Japanese, and Korean. These font files are usually very large and are often copy protected. Do be respectful of font licencing issues too, and make sure that you are not breaking the law by distributing fonts illegally. A warning dialog box appears as part of the packaging process until you choose to dismiss it. Click the *Save* button automatically to create a folder containing a copy of the artwork file, the fonts, the linked images, and a report.

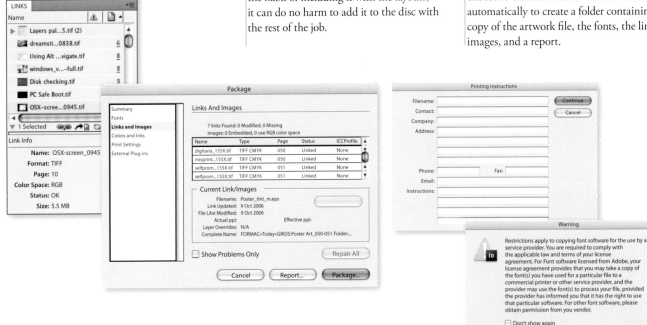

COLLECT FOR OUTPUT (QUARKXPRESS)

The "collect for output" procedure with QuarkXPress is very similar to InDesign's "packaging" process. Take a look at the *Usage* palette, paying particular attention once more to the images and fonts. Make sure everything is linked correctly, and that all the fonts have loaded correctly, then proceed to the *Collect for Output* stage.

Once again, clicking the *Save* button pulls all items together in one place for despatch to the reproduction company or printer. QuarkXPress doesn't automatically create a containing folder, so use the *New Folder* button if you need to. Note that QuarkXPress can also make copies of any color profiles that have been used.

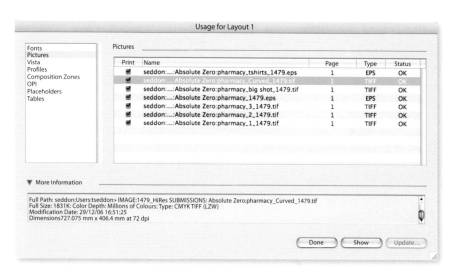

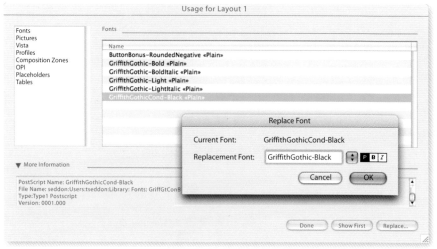

FILE TRANSFER

In a typical busy design studio 20 years ago, couriers would arrive at the front door every 10 minutes or so to collect or deliver a parcel or envelope. Now we send e-mails with attachments, or upload larger files to an FTP (File Transfer Protocol) server, and the courier, for this purpose at least, has become more or less redundant. A shame for them, but for those of us working to today's tight deadlines it's good news.

USING A COURIER

There'll always be a need for couriers, despite the advances offered by today's communication technology. Some things are just too big to send practically by electronic means, and there are still marked-up lasers or color proofs to consider as part of a typical design workflow. If you have a very large file to send, consider sending it by courier. It may well turn out to be easier in the long run, particularly if the schedule allows the time.

E-MAIL

E-mail is used extensively to transfer many different types of file as attachments. However, in a lot of instances it's not used effectively. It's common for people to send attachments that are far too large. This can not only jam up your own e-mail facility, but can also cause the recipient's e-mail server to grind to a halt. As a general rule of thumb don't send e-mail attachments that are more than a megabyte or so.

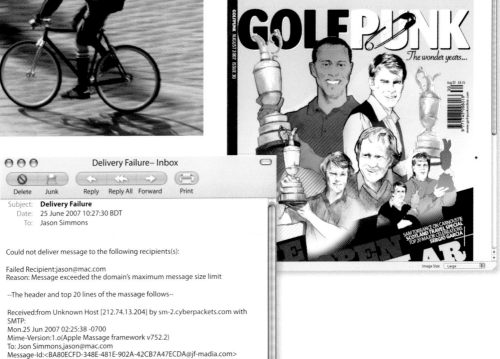

E-mail
To avoid delivery failures, keep e-mail attachments to a sensible size, normally a maximum of one megabyte is a safe bet. Your own e-mail system may be able to cope with large attachments, but your recipient's system may not.

FTP

File Transfer Protocol (FTP) is much better for the transfer of large files. Check to see if your clients have FTP servers to which you can upload material, or indeed collect material from if necessary. Alternatively you can set up your own server fairly easily, but you will need a dedicated workstation that can be kept permanently online.

WEBSITES

If you don't have an FTP server, take a look at one of several websites that allows you to send large files via their server. A current favorite of mine, www.mailbigfile.com, offers a free service which restricts file sizes to 200MB and a very inexpensive pro-service which allows 2GB files to be uploaded.

Footnote

Earlier I said that this was all good news, but in some ways the speed with which material can be transferred has created the culture of ever-shorter deadlines. Clients can now legitimately ask why it is that they can't see something "today." It's a good thing in one way that we have the facility to send material across the world almost instantly, but it does put pressure on designers to deliver the job that much quicker.

Online services

You don't have to rely on a dedicated FTP server if budgets are tight. Use one of the free or low cost online file transfer services to send any files that are too big to send as an e-mail attachment.

FTP software

There are plenty of well designed FTP software applications available. Transmit (www.panic.com) is one of the most popular choices.

CHOOSING PAPER

The choice of paper stock used for printed projects can make or break a job in terms of the quality of the final result. Here are a few of the more important points to consider when making that choice.

BASIC WEIGHT

Basic weight, sometimes referred to as substance, refers to the weight of a quantity of paper stock. In the USA it describes the weight of a ream (500 sheets) in a standard size. In most other countries, paper weight is specified using the metric system in grams per square meter (gsm). This refers to the weight of one square meter of the stock.

GRAIN DIRECTION

The grain direction is the direction in which the paper runs through and off the paper-making machine during its manufacture. The fibers in the paper tend to lie in this same direction. It's important to consider grain direction when specifying paper for a couple of reasons. First, during printing it's preferable to have the grain running across the direction of the printing. This helps prevent stretch and subsequently helps to maintain registration. Secondly, it's better to have the grain direction running parallel to the spine of a book or magazine. There'll be less strain on the bound edge and the end product will feel better when handled.

Add.48210

wel-encrusted, s of letters and or future gene-nvelope with a very young and and often failed with his writing lio of Rosenberg's envelope. Touching ed from the trenches velope that came to t found in the inside his stained envelope one of Britain's most

Isaac Rosenberg poem fragment on back of envelope All Pleasures Fly, 1917, from a collection of drafts, partly in pencil, including some typescript, 1905–1917. (F.33)

[illus. page 56]

Bible paper
This very thin paper, usually 40–60gsm, has clear show-through.

Glassine paper
Glassine paper, another thin, semi-transparent stock, is often used to provide protective sheets in albums.

WO WONDERLAND

Polypropylene
An alternative to paper, this flexible plastic is available in many colors, in both clear and frosted finishes.

BULK

Bulk is the thickness, or caliper, of the paper. Weight is obviously a factor in the amount of bulk that can be achieved with any one particular stock, but a high-bulk process can make some weights of paper stock bulkier without increasing weight. This means papers of the same weight will often bulk differently, depending on how they were manufactured. It's generally advisable to order a blank dummy from your printer made from the specified stock to ensure you're happy with the bulk before committing to print.

SHADE

Check samples carefully to be sure that the shade is acceptable. We're talking about white paper here of course, which can range from natural to blue white, and the brightness of the stock will greatly effect the quality of any color printing. To complicate things some paper stocks are "metameric," meaning they look different under varying lighting conditions. White paper is actually the hardest stock to specify because of its very exact qualities.

OPACITY

Show-through is the term used to describe the opacity of a paper, and is mostly used to describe paper through which images printed on the back of a sheet can be seen from the other side, which is usually unacceptable. Therefore, for high-quality book or brochure production, care must be taken to specify stock of a sufficient opacity to prevent show-through.

Simulator paper
Another thin paper with clear show-through, this is more commonly known as tracing paper.

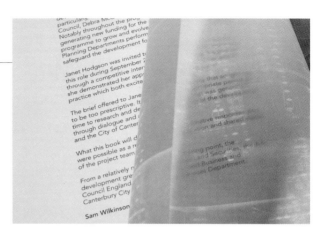

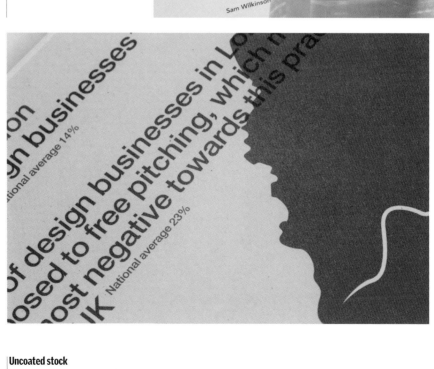

Uncoated stock
Paper that has not been coated has a rougher surface than coated paper, and is both bulkier, and more opaque.

PAPER SIZES

Standard US sizes, trimmed sheets

	Imperial (in)	Metric (mm)
ANSI A (Letter)	$8^1/_2$ x 11	216 x 279
ANSI B (Ledger)	11 x 17	279 x 432
Super A3/B	13 x 19	330 x 483
ANSI C	17 x 22	432 x 559
ANSI D	22 x 34	559 x 864
ANSI E	34 x 44	864 x 1,118
ANSI F	28 x 40	711 x 1,016

Other common sizes, trimmed sheets

	Imperial (in)	Metric (mm)
Quarto	8 x 10	303 x 254
Foolscap	8 x 10	203 x 330
Executive	$7^1/_4$ x $10^1/_2$	184 x 267
Government letter	8 x $10^1/_2$	203 x 267
Legal	$8^1/_2$ x 14	216 x 356
Tabloid	11 x 17	279 x 432
Post	$15^1/_2$ x $19^1/_2$	394 x 489
Crown	15 x 20	381 x 508
Large Post	$16^1/_2$ x 21	419 x 533
Demy	$17^1/_2$ x $22^1/_2$	445 x 572
Medium	18 x 23	457 x 584
Royal	20 x 25	508 x 635
Elephant	23 x 28	584 x 711
Double Demy	$23^1/_2$ x 35	597 x 889
Quad Demy	35 x 45	889 x 1,143
Statement	$8^1/_2$ x $5^1/_2$	216 x 120
Index Card	5 x 3	127 x 76
Index Card	6 x 4	152 x 102
Index Card	8 x 5	203 x 127
International Business Card	$3^3/_8$ x $2^1/_8$	85.6 x 55
US Business Card	$3^1/_2$ x 2	88.9 x 63.5

US envelope standards

	Imperial (in)
Commercial/official window	
6	$3^3/_8$ x 6
$6^1/_4$	$3^1/_2$ x 6
$6^3/_4$	$3^5/_8$ x $6^1/_2$
7	$3^3/_4$ x $6^3/_4$
$7^3/_4$	$3^7/_8$ x $7^1/_2$
Data Card	$3^1/_2$ x $7^5/_8$
$8^5/_8$	$3^5/_8$ x $8^5/_8$
9	$3^7/_8$ x $8^7/_8$
10	$4^1/_8$ x $9^1/_2$
$10^1/_2$	$4^1/_2$ x $9^1/_2$
11	$4^1/_2$ x $10^3/_8$
12	$4^3/_4$ x 11
14	5 x $11^1/_2$
Booklet	
$2^1/_2$	$4^1/_2$ x $5^7/_8$
3	$4^3/_4$ x $6^1/_2$
$4^1/_4$	5 x $7^1/_2$
$4^1/_2$	$5^1/_2$ x $7^1/_2$
5	$5^1/_2$ x $8^1/_2$
6	$5^3/_4$ x $8^7/_8$
$6^1/_2$	6 x 9
$6^3/_4$	$6^1/_2$ x $9^1/_2$
7	$6^1/_4$ x $9^5/_8$
$7^1/_4$	7 x 10
$7^1/_2$	$7^1/_2$ x $10^1/_2$
8	8 x $11^1/_2$
9	$8^3/_4$ x $11^1/_2$
$9^1/_2$	9 x 12
10	$9^1/_2$ x $12^5/_8$
13	10 x 13

	Imperial (in)
Catalog	
1	6 x 9
$1^3/_4$	$6^1/_2$ x $9^1/_2$
2	$6^1/_2$ x 10
3	7 x 10
6	$7^1/_2$ x $10^1/_2$
7	8 x 11
8	$8^1/_4$ x $11^1/_4$
$9^1/_2$	$8^1/_2$ x $10^1/_2$
$9^3/_4$	$8^3/_4$ x $11^1/_4$
$10^1/_2$	9 x 12
$12^1/_2$	$9^1/_2$ x $12^1/_2$
$13^1/_2$	10 x 13
$14^1/_4$	$11^1/_2$ x $14^1/_4$
$14^1/_2$	$11^1/_2$ x $14^1/_2$
Announcement	
A-2	$4^3/_8$ x $5^5/_8$
A-6	$4^3/_4$ x $6^1/_2$
A-7	$5^1/_4$ x $7^1/_4$
A-8	$5^1/_2$ x $8^1/_8$
A-10	$6^1/_4$ x $9^5/_8$

International A series, trimmed sheets

	Imperial (in)	Metric (mm)
4A0	$66^1/_4$ x $93^3/_8$	1,682 x 2,378
2A0	$46^1/_4$ x $66^1/_4$	1,189 x 1,682
A0	$33^1/_8$ x $46^3/_4$	841 x 1,189
A1	$23^3/_8$ x $33^1/_8$	594 x 841
A2	$16^1/_2$ x $23^1/_8$	420 x 594
A3	$11^{11}/_{16}$ x $16^1/_2$	297 x 420
A4	$8^1/_4$ x $11^{11}/_{16}$	210 x 297
A5	$5^7/_8$ x $8^1/_4$	148 x 210
A6	$4^1/_8$ x $5^7/_8$	105 x 148
A7	$2^7/_8$ x $4^1/_8$	74 x 105
A8	2 x $2^7/_8$	52 x 74
A9	$1^1/_2$ x 2	37 x 52
A10	1 x $1^1/_2$	26 x 37

International R and SR series, untrimmed sheets

Sheets in these formats will be cut to the trim size after binding.

	Imperial (in)	Metric (mm)
RA0	$33\frac{7}{8} \times 48\frac{1}{8}$	860 x 1,220
RA1	$24\frac{1}{8} \times 33\frac{7}{8}$	610 x 860
RA2	$17 \times 24\frac{1}{8}$	430 x 610
SRA0	$35\frac{1}{2} \times 50\frac{3}{8}$	900 x 1,280
SRA1	$25\frac{1}{4} \times 35\frac{1}{2}$	640 x 900
SRA2	$17\frac{7}{8} \times 25\frac{1}{4}$	450 x 640

ISO B series, trimmed sheets

	Imperial (in)	Metric (mm)
4B0	$78\frac{3}{8} \times 111\frac{5}{16}$	2,000 x 2,828
2B0	$55\frac{11}{16} \times 78\frac{3}{4}$	1,414 x 2,000
B0	$39\frac{3}{8} \times 55\frac{5}{8}$	1,000 x 1,414
B1	$27\frac{7}{8} \times 39\frac{3}{8}$	707 x 1,000
B2	$19\frac{5}{8} \times 27\frac{7}{8}$	500 x 707
B3	$12\frac{7}{8} \times 19\frac{5}{8}$	353 x 500
B4	$9\frac{7}{8} \times 12\frac{7}{8}$	250 x 353
B5	$7 \times 9\frac{7}{8}$	176 x 250
B6	5×7	125 x 176
B7	$3\frac{1}{2} \times 5$	88 x 125
B8	$2\frac{1}{2} \times 3\frac{1}{2}$	62 x 88
B9	$1\frac{3}{4} \times 2\frac{1}{2}$	44 x 62
B10	$1\frac{1}{4} \times 1\frac{3}{4}$	31 x 44

ISO C series, trimmed sheets

	Imperial (in)	Metric (mm)
C0	$36\frac{1}{8} \times 51$	917 x 1,297
C1	$25\frac{1}{2} \times 36\frac{1}{8}$	648 x 917
C2	$18 \times 25\frac{1}{2}$	458 x 648
C3	$12\frac{3}{4} \times 18$	324 x 458
C4	$9 \times 12\frac{3}{4}$	229 x 324
C5	$6\frac{3}{8} \times 9$	162 x 229
C6	$4\frac{1}{2} \times 6\frac{3}{8}$	114 x 162
C7	$3\frac{1}{4} \times 4\frac{1}{2}$	81 x 114
C8	$2\frac{1}{4} \times 3\frac{1}{4}$	57 x 81

ISO envelope standards

	Imperial (in)	Metric (mm)
C3	$12\frac{3}{4} \times 18$	324 x 458
B4	$9\frac{7}{8} \times 12\frac{7}{8}$	250 x 353
C4	$9 \times 12\frac{3}{4}$	229 x 324
B5	$7 \times 9\frac{7}{8}$	176 x 250
C5	$6\frac{3}{8} \times 9$	162 x 229
B6/C4	$5 \times 12\frac{3}{4}$	125 x 324
B6	5×7	125 x 176
C6	$4\frac{1}{2} \times 6\frac{3}{8}$	114 x 162
DL	$4\frac{1}{4} \times 8\frac{3}{4}$	110 x 220
C7/6	$3\frac{1}{4} \times 6\frac{3}{8}$	81 x 162
C7	$3\frac{1}{4} \times 4\frac{1}{2}$	81 x 114

Japan Industrial Standard (JIS) B series, trimmed sheets

JIS A series trimmed sheets are identical to their ISO A series counterparts. JIS B series sheets are slightly larger than the ISO B series.

	Imperial (in)	Metric (mm)
B0	$40\frac{9}{16} \times 57\frac{5}{16}$	1,030 x 1,456
B1	$28\frac{11}{16} \times 40\frac{9}{16}$	728 x 1,030
B2	$20\frac{1}{4} \times 28\frac{11}{16}$	515 x 728
B3	$14\frac{5}{16} \times 20\frac{1}{4}$	364 x 515
B4	$10\frac{1}{8} \times 14\frac{5}{16}$	257 x 364
B5	$7\frac{3}{16} \times 10\frac{1}{8}$	182 x 257
B6	$5\frac{1}{16} \times 7\frac{3}{16}$	128 x 182
B7	$3\frac{9}{16} \times 5\frac{1}{16}$	91 x 128
B8	$2\frac{1}{2} \times 3\frac{9}{16}$	64 x 91
B9	$1\frac{3}{4} \times 2\frac{1}{2}$	45 x 64
B10	$1\frac{1}{4} \times 1\frac{3}{4}$	32 x 45

Dimensions

It is standard practice for dimensions in North America and mainland Europe to be described as width followed by depth. In the United Kingdom and the Far East, depth is followed by width. For clarity, the North American system has been employed in this book.

FOLDS AND BINDINGS

Folding and binding is a fundamental aspect of book or magazine manufacturing. There are many ways paper can be folded, and each finishing shop will have its preferred method of folding and trimming sections, but generally speaking they all achieve the same result. Spend some time making a dummy if you plan to use a single sheet folded to make a booklet, and make sure you understand what goes on each page and its orientation—it's surprisingly simple to mistakenly place a page upside down!

Before committing to producing anything with a complex fold, discuss your requirements with the people who will be doing the work, especially for a long production run. Your design may be easy enough to fold by hand, but the automated process will probably be far more complicated.

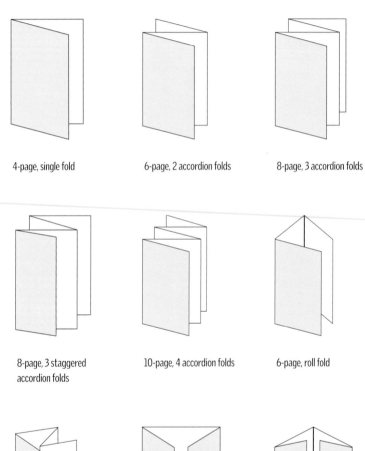

4-page, single fold

6-page, 2 accordion folds

8-page, 3 accordion folds

8-page, 3 staggered accordion folds

10-page, 4 accordion folds

6-page, roll fold

8-page, roll fold

6-page, parallel fold

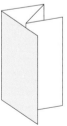

8-page, 2 parallel folds

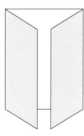

8-page, gate fold

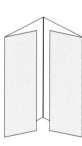

8-page, closed gate fold

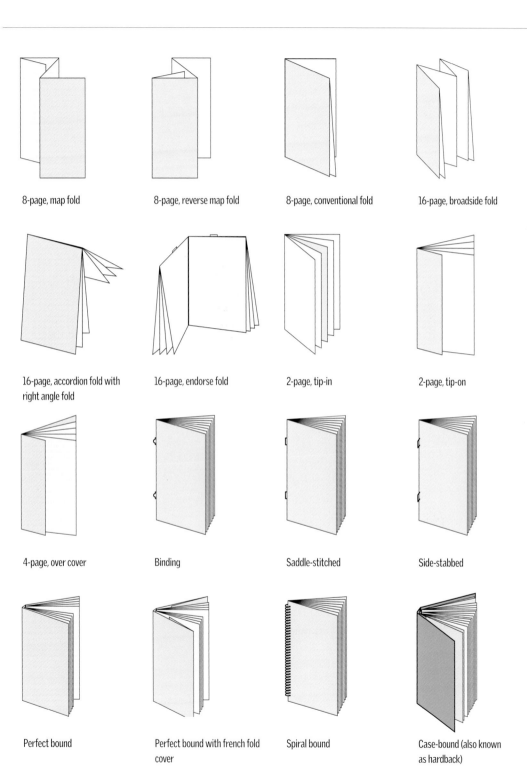

8-page, map fold

8-page, reverse map fold

8-page, conventional fold

16-page, broadside fold

16-page, accordion fold with right angle fold

16-page, endorse fold

2-page, tip-in

2-page, tip-on

4-page, over cover

Binding

Saddle-stitched

Side-stabbed

Perfect bound

Perfect bound with french fold cover

Spiral bound

Case-bound (also known as hardback)

IMPOSITION

To enable printers to print pages that will run consecutively on one large sheet of paper, they use a process known as "*impositioning*." Pages are arranged in a specific order which depends on how the sheet will be folded and trimmed, meaning that all pages will eventually be placed in the correct sequence when bound together as a book or brochure. It's not something that designers generally have to think about, but there are aspects of imposition that can affect design and print decisions.

Unless you actually require some pages to be blank, all publications must contain a page extent that's divisible by at least 4, but more usually 8 or 16. Printing machines normally print pages in multiples of either 4, 8, 16, 32, or 48, depending on the size and type of press. It's usual to work on multiples, or sections, of at least 16 when calculating the extent of a book, like this one for example. If you take a look down a book's spine, you can clearly see each section where it's attached to the binding. It's up to the printer to decide how to arrange the pages when imposed, basing their decision on the most economical way to use the sheet size for the printing press to be used.

While it's the printer's responsibility to take care of the imposition, it's sometimes useful to take the imposition scheme into account when designing spreads. This is particularly relevant if you wish to print some pages using the four-color process and some in black and white or with spot colors. If all four-color pages appear on the same imposed sheet, and all single-color pages are limited to another, there'll be a cost saving.

A common phrase that you'll come across when dealing with imposition is "work and turn," also known as "half-sheet." This basically means that all the pages in a book or brochure are printed on just one side of a sheet. The sheets are then turned over and printed with the same pages on the other side, then cut in half before being folded and gathered into complete books.

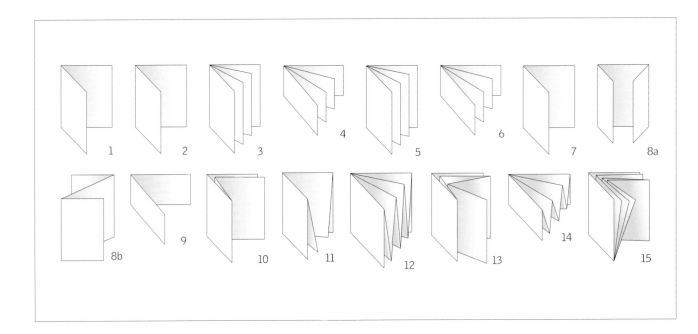

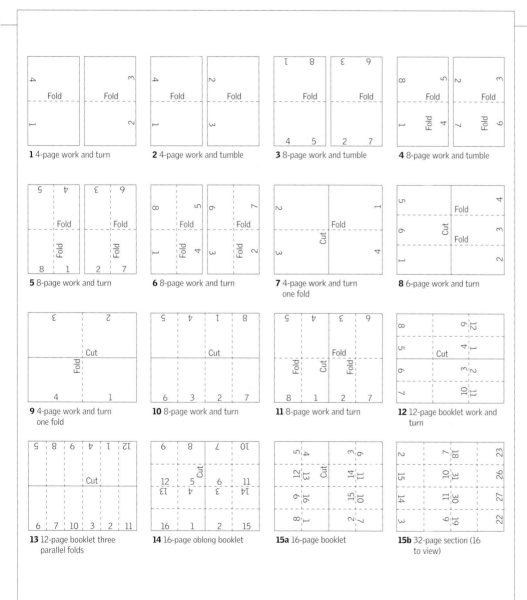

1 4-page work and turn

2 4-page work and tumble

3 8-page work and tumble

4 8-page work and tumble

5 8-page work and turn

6 8-page work and turn

7 4-page work and turn one fold

8 6-page work and turn

9 4-page work and turn one fold

10 8-page work and turn

11 8-page work and turn

12 12-page booklet work and turn

13 12-page booklet three parallel folds

14 16-page oblong booklet

15a 16-page booklet

15b 32-page section (16 to view)

Imposition

The arrangement of pages on each side of a printed sheet determines the order in which they will appear when the sheet is cut, folded, and trimmed. The most commonly used imposition schemes and folding methods are shown here. To allow for folding and trimming, a margin of $^1/_8$–$^1/_4$in (3–6mm) is left all round.

PRINT FINISHING

There are a number of print finishing techniques available for specialist printing applications. Extra finishes invariably represent an extra cost, so make sure this is factored into your budget—but the right choice of finish can add a great deal to the final result.

DEBOSSING

This term refers to the technique of pressing a design or pattern into the surface of the paper stock. It's also known as blind embossing, and requires the manufacture of a forme, or die, to make the impression. No ink is printed during this process.

DIE-CUTTING

Complex shapes can be cut from pages or board covers using this technique. It also involves the manufacture of a die from prepared artwork, but in this case the die has a sharp steel edge instead of a flat or textured surface. The technique is carried out using either a specialist die-cutting machine, or by placing the die in the bed of a modified letterpress machine. Laser die-cutting is now also used, removing the need for a metal die to be manufactured, and can produce intricate cutouts that are beyond the capabilities of traditional die-cutting.

EMBOSSING

At the risk of stating the obvious, this is the opposite of debossing. The technique uses a male and a female die to create the raised impression, with the stock being pressed between the two.

forty-eight posters
josef müller-brockmann

Debossing
Also known as blind embossing, this technique produces the opposite effect of embossing; the pattern is pressed into the printed surface.

Die-cutting
For this technique, a custom-made die is used to cut shapes from the page.

Embossing
Embossing produces a raised design on the surface of the paper or board.

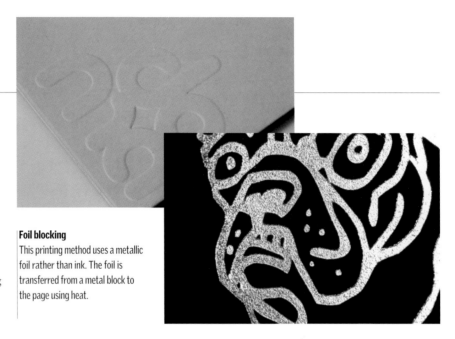

FOIL BLOCKING

To achieve this finish, metallic foil is pressed onto the stock by the application of a metal die that has been heated. Advances in the technology used to make the dies mean that techniques such as this are becoming more affordable, and are therefore experiencing something of a renaissance in terms of popularity, encouraged by the sympathetic use of foil blocking by today's designers.

LAMINATION

This involves a clear matte or gloss film being applied to the surface of a printed sheet on a specialist laminating machine. Lamination offers long-term protection and is often used on book covers.

PIGMENT BLOCKING

This process is similar to foil blocking, but uses colored rather than metallic film.

THERMOGRAPHY

This is a relief effect produced by sprinkling a special powder onto a printed image that is still wet. The sheet is then passed through a device that heats the powder, baking it to the surface of the paper.

UV VARNISH

There are several types of varnish used in printing, some of which can be run as an extra color on offset litho printing presses. UV, or ultraviolet, varnish requires the use of a special ultraviolet drying device. UV varnishes can be applied as an overall coating or as a spot varnish, and are normally applied using a screenprinting technique.

Foil blocking
This printing method uses a metallic foil rather than ink. The foil is transferred from a metal block to the page using heat.

Thermography
Another process involving the application of heat, this produces a relief effect. A special powder is dusted onto a printed image while it is still wet, then passed through a heating device.

UV Varnish
UV varnishes are available in matte, satin, and gloss finishes. They are applied by screenprinting, either over the entire surface of the page, or over a specific section (known as a spot varnish). A spot varnish is often used to highlight particular elements on a page.

SOLVING COMMON PRINT PROBLEMS

Printing, binding, and trimming are complex process with many variable factors. Despite the wealth of guidelines and standards, many things can still go wrong. Some will be errors made by the printer, some will be bad luck, while others may be your mistake.

The problems listed here represent some of the more common issues that designers can unwittingly create. Discuss the problem with your printer: they are usually more than happy to help you find the best solution.

Text is in a different font or has reflowed
This is probably down to a missing font during the PDF generation stage, or not embedding fonts to the file itself.

Blurred body text
Check your body text is set to black, and not registration or another black mix. If using InDesign, check your *Color Settings* are on *Emulate Adobe InDesign 2.0 CMS Off.*

Images are pixelated
Either you have used a low-resolution image in your layout, or the image was missing during the PDF creation stage (for InDesign use the *Links* palette to check for missing images; in QuarkXPress check the *Usage* dialog box and select *Pictures*. Now look down the *Status* column to see if any images are marked as *Missing*).

Colors don't match your expectations
Inaccurate colors are nearly always down to poor monitor or proofer calibration. Invest in professional calibration equipment for your display or proofer.

Murky shadow areas
Too much ink is causing the large, shadow dots to fill in. Increase the dot gain value in Photoshop's *CMYK Settings* (*Edit > Color Settings*).

Washed-out images
Either your dot gain settings are too high, or your maximum ink limits are too low for the paper you are using. Adjust your CMYK conversion settings appropriately.

Rippled paper
The paper stock you are using has become overloaded with ink and has warped. Upgrade your paper stock, adjust your Photoshop *CMYK Settings*, and ensure your colors do not have a total ink value of more than 300%.

Pixelated

Filled-in shadows

Text reflow

Blurred body text

Unexpected colors

Washed out

Show through

Moiré effect

Disappearing into gutter

The reverse side of the paper is showing through

The only real solution here is to upgrade your paper stock. Reducing the *Total Ink Limit* allowed by the *Color Settings* in Photoshop may help in some cases.

Solid blocks of color are streaky

There is only so much ink a press can put down at a time, and a dense image or tone farther up the sheet may be taking all the ink. Be aware of any imposition issues and the problems they may cause, and adjust your color selection and/or flatplanning accordingly.

Misregistration

Color plates going out of register is an almost unavoidable aspect of printing. You can either increase your print run and discard the imperfect sheets, take greater care with your color selection, or adjust your trapping tolerances to allow for a greater margin of error.

Halftones have a moiré effect

Moiré is usually caused by the halftone dots used to generate the colors being incorrectly set. If you have supplied finished film directly to the printers this is an error of whoever produced the film, if supplying PDFs it is a printer error. The problem may also be caused by a fine pattern or texture in an image.

Text or images disappear into the fold

For perfect binding almost ½in (13mm) of page can disappear into the binding of a magazine, more for books, and less for saddle-stitched titles. Any images that are positioned across a gutter should be split and spread out slightly to compensate for this. It is good practice to avoid placing text across the gutter.

Poor trimming

Most printing is a mass-production factory process, so there will always be margins of error and the most noticeable of these is on the trim area—pages will wander slightly, and won't always be cut perfectly square. Always extend bleed areas by ⅛in (3mm), and keep important elements ¼in (5mm) or more from the trim line.

Print problems

These examples are simulated, and have been exaggerated to clearly illustrate a point. The point at which an inherent weakness of the printing process becomes a problem is a judgement you must make yourself, along with the solution most appropriate for your budget.

Duplicated or missing pages

When you are under pressure, it is an easy mistake to make a PDF of the wrong page, or name the file incorrectly. Get a second person to double-check your PDFs against a flatplan.

Under- or overruns

If you need a specific number of copies of your document clearly state this to your printer early on. Trade standards allow for a certain number of copies to be wasted during setup. Typically this is around 3% of the total print run, but can be as much as 10%.

Streaky image

Misregistration

Poor trimming

Duplicate page

Underun

DEALING WITH PRINTERS

The printer you use to produce your job is an integral part of your team, and although you may never meet him in person you should treat him or her as a valuable resource. Like you, printers want to do the best job possible, as the final product reflects the quality of their work, and good products ensure their customers are happy. There are a few things you can do to ensure the relationship with your printer is as happy as possible.

NEVER ASSUME ANYTHING

Whatever the job, it's likely your chosen printer has produced something like it before. They will have a good idea of what you want and be able to advise you of the best way to achieve it. But that prior knowledge also brings with it some assumptions, which may or may not be correct—so get everything in writing and state it clearly. Ensure you specify even the smallest detail, and be precise. For example, if you want to use four spot-color inks, ensure your request isn't mistaken for four-color process printing (CMYK). If you are printing using film rather than Computer To Plate (CTP) technology, specify if you want to keep the film for future reprints.

PLAN AHEAD

If you are planning a large print run, ensure you make arrangements with your printer well in advance. Not only is this to ensure you have the press time booked, but also to ensure the appropriate paper stock can be ordered in time. Specific orders can sometimes take up to a month to arrive.

Before you begin to produce your designs, ensure you have the right technical specifications and are using the correct CMYK separation settings. Your printer contact will be able to supply the correct data for you. Once you have a few layouts ready, create some PDFs or file packages to the correct standards and send them as test files so you don't get any nasty surprises at the last minute.

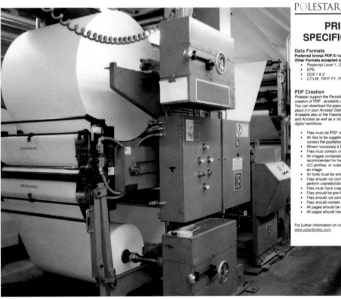

MEET YOUR DEADLINES

Deliver your files on time, or a little early if possible. Don't, however, send them too early, or your job will get lost in the hundred other jobs waiting to go on press.

If possible, send proofs of every page or layout. Even better is to get the printers to produce the proofs for you, so you're checking the actual files you have sent for printing. If you don't have the time or budget for professional hard proofs, many print shops now offer online soft-proofing options. Use the proofs to illustrate any unusual pages that you want to bring to the printer's attention. Intentionally printing images, or whole pages, upside down is a typical example of something that may stop the presses and get you an expensive phone call in the middle of the night.

DON'T DISAPPEAR

Once you have finished and sent the job don't go on holiday. Make sure the person running the press has your contact details and can get hold of you day or night. When you leave your studio, take a laptop or hard drive with all your files on it in case you need to fix a problem quickly.

Even better than staying in contact with your printer is to actually go and see the job being printed. Not only will you be on hand for the press check, you will also begin to build a valuable relationship with the people actually on the shop floor, not just the people on the sales team.

GETTING THE JOB BACK

Once you get the job back, look at it in detail as soon as possible. If there are problems, discuss it with the printers as soon as possible, and also put your complaints in writing for future reference. Bear in mind that you need to be realistic about what a printer can achieve given time, budget, and material restraints—and remember some of the problems may well be of your own doing.

If you are happy with the results let the printers know—they will appreciate your feedback. It's always courteous, and sometimes a contractual obligation, to provide the printer's details in the credits for a magazine or the imprint page of a book.

REPURPOSING PRINT FOR THE WEB

Whether it's to open up new markets for your publication, or as a bonus for subscribers, it is becoming increasingly popular for printed journals also to be distributed over the Internet. Adding interactive links to a document designed for print is relatively simple, but for large documents it can be a time-consuming and laborious process.

BASIC HYPERLINKS

At the simplest level, Acrobat will interpret any web addresses on your document as hyperlinks. Click on the www. text and your preferred web browser will take you to the link.

CREATING URL LINKS

To add hyperlinks to any object within InDesign choose *Window > Interactive > Hyperlinks*. With your element selected, click the *Create New Hyperlink* button to bring up a dialog box in which you can name and define the link behavior. Choosing *URL* as the *Destination Type*, and inputting your target URL will set the link up. The *Appearance* settings are for adding borders and highlights to set your link apart from a regular item. Choosing *Invisible Rectangle* keeps the link unobtrusive—the most appropriate setting for a repurposed print document, although the mouse pointer will still change to a pointing finger when placed over your link to indicate it is interactive.

OTHER TYPES OF LINKS

In addition to *URL*, the alternative link types include *page* and *Text Anchor*. By adding *page* hyperlinks to folios and page references within your document, a simple click will jump between pages. *Text Anchor* allows you to jump to a specific part of the text, or a box-out within the document. The most logical application of these tools are contents pages, where clicking an article name takes you directly to the story.

BOOKMARKS

Bookmarks can also be added in a similar manner. Choose the element to be marked, and on the *Bookmarks* palette click the *Create New Bookmark* button. Once named, the bookmark will appear in the bookmark list of your PDF reader, acting as a hyperlink directly to the chosen object.

Left: Adding a hyperlink; Center: Acrobat click link; Right: Adding a bookmark

TAKING IT FURTHER

Using the options found in InDesign under the *Object* > *Interactive* menu, it is possible to create layouts that have more in common with websites than printed documents. Adding movies, buttons, and other live objects is handled in a similar way to static objects. Choose the source file, fit it to the box, and define its behavior from the drop-down menus.

The release of InDesign CS5 has seen a whole raft of new features designed to enable the easy conversion of print layouts to interactive media formats, including ePub. Check the latest features at www.adobe.com. It's still preferable to design complex websites using a dedicated application such as Dreamweaver, but in many instances you'll not have to leave the familiar environment of InDesign to achieve impressive results.

EXPORTING TO PDF

Once you have added your interactive elements, you will need to export your document for on-screen viewing, using *File* > *Export*. A double-page spread usually fits well on a screen, but the detail will be lost. To resolve this, keep the resolution of images to around 144dpi or higher to allow for zooming in. Use JPEG compression to reduce the size of the PDF files, and change the destination color space to RGB, not CMYK. The *Security* panel allows you to add a password to restrict viewing, and limit the user's ability to print or edit your document. This won't restrict the distribution of your document though, as it is a simple matter for someone to send a password with it, allowing anyone to open and read it.

BESPOKE OPTIONS

There are a number of companies that offer dedicated distribution options and online viewing of print magazines. Once you have produced a set of screen-resolution PDFs, these companies will do the hard work for you, and add all the interactive elements. Additionally, their services prevent the unauthorized reading of your magazine, and allow you to control its distribution to genuine subscribers only. Look at www.zinio.com or myvirtualpaper.com for two established companies—but more are appearing all the time.

Adobe Export and Document Security palettes/windows

ARCHIVING

When a design job, whether book, magazine, or newsletter, is printed, it's important to archive so that it is both safe and easy to access. Traditionally, this practice was carried out using tape drives—these provided the best balance between capacity and cost—but it was fiddly to retrieve specific data, such as a page or chapter from a book. Now, though, we have many more media options.

More important than the media you store on is implementing a proper archiving strategy—and much of what we say here applies equally to backup of current work.

DEVELOP A STRATEGY

Belt and braces

Don't fall into the trap of thinking that your archiving is done when you've burned a DVD. Everything from media failure to fire and flood can destroy your archive. Archive in as many ways and to as many different media as is practical and within budget. It's definitely worth considering storing a duplicate archive "off-site," to guard against natural disasters or vandalism.

Make it part of the workflow

Force yourself to archive jobs when they're done; it keeps your work area neat and will reduce computer bottlenecks.

Verify integrity

Check archives periodically (consider setting a reminder) to ensure they're still accessible and aren't in danger of degrading. Optical media such as CDs and DVDs are particularly susceptible to damage by sunlight.

Fight obsolescence

Save documents in a way that will still be accessible in years to come. Avoid bespoke compression systems and exotic file formats, as in the fast-paced world of computers, you can quickly find you're locked out of your own files.

Track

Make sure you know where everything is archived. Depending on your organization's complexity, this can range from simply labeling a DVD to tracking archive locations with a full-blown management system.

PICKING THE BEST MEDIA

When it comes to deciding what media to archive to, you have four main options.

External hard disk

There's no simpler way to archive work than simply to copy it to an external hard disk. It's relatively secure, can easily be moved off-site, and is very accessible. Hard disks are expensive, though, and aren't ideal for very long-term storage.

Apple backup options

LaCie external hard drive

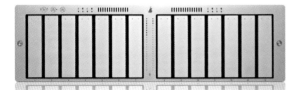

Local RAID server

Local server

Most design studios will have at least one server providing centralized storage capacity. Simply copying work to be archived to the server is certainly easy, but it does mean that a significant investment has to be made in the capacity of the server. A RAID system usually provides higher capacity, faster, centralized storage, and, depending on configuration, can provide a high degree of data redundancy to ensure no work is lost.

Remote server

Copying data across the Internet to a server in another physical location provides insurance against local disasters, but if you're relying on a third party–hosted service, you're likely to find that it's expensive and offers meager storage.

Removable media

DVDs and CDs are convenient and cheap, but can degrade with surprising speed. Never trust your archives to unbranded media, and duplicate the archives onto fresh discs every 12 months. As capacities increase, and new technologies such as HD-DVD and Blu-ray become available, consider consolidating multiple smaller-capacity discs onto a single, larger disc.

Iomega's removable hard disk system, dubbed "Rev," is now available in 70GB capacities, and is a natural successor to tape.

Backup to remote server

Iomega Rev, removable hard disk

GLOSSARY

A

ASCII (American Standard Code for Information Interchange) A digital text file format used to transfer data. It does not include any formatting.

Achromatic A method of color correction used on a color scanner to achieve an extended degree of undercolor removal (UCR). In conventional UCR, most of the color and tone is still contributed by the three primary colors, with the black lending only deeper shadow tones. With achromatic reproduction the very minimum amount of color required is computed and the black is added to produce the required depth of color.

Aliasing When "jaggies," or visual stair-stepping effect, becomes apparent in an image. Caused by a low-resolution file. Can occur when an image is enlarged beyond its capacity to be viewed as smooth edged.

Anti-aliasing The addition of increasingly lighter pixels to a jagged edge to smooth the visual effect.

Aqueous coating A coating applied after initial printing, but usually in-line from a water-based solution to further enhance the visual printing effect.

Ascender The portion of a lower case letter that extends above the x-height, e.g., b, d, and k.

B

Back step (collation) marks Black numbers or letters on the spine of a signature/section. When the signatures are gathered, the marks appear in a staggered sequence on the spines indicating the order.

Banding An undesired printing effect when the graduation from one tone to another is not smooth, causing a band effect at the transition point.

Bitmap Any image formed in monochrome or color by pixels in a rectangular grid. Contrast with vectors.

Blad Book Layout and Design. A small booklet featuring the front cover of a book plus sample pages to provide advance promotion or sales interest at trade book fairs, and to help secure commitments for reviews.

Bleed (1) When an illustration or image is designed to run off the page. A term also used by book binders to describe overcut margins. **(2)** Ink that changes color or mixes with other colors, sometimes caused in lamination.

Blind (1) Book cases or covers that that are stamped (US), or blocked/embossed (UK), or without the use of ink or foil. **(2)** Term applied to a litho plate that has lost its image.

Block (UK) (1) A binding term describing the impression or stamping of type or a line image on the cover. This can be achieved with metallic or pigment-based foil, or gold leaf. **(2)** In printing, a letterpress block (cut, US) is an etched copper or zinc printing plate mounted on wood or metal.

Bolt Any folded edge of a section other than the binding/spine fold.

Book block The printed, gathered sections/signatures of a book or publication ready for the application of glue, prior to paperback binding, or casing in hardcover books.

Bottom out (US) The arrangement of type to prevent widows. See also Orphans.

Brightness A papermaking term to define the level of blue light reflected by the paper. Contrast with whiteness, the degree of which is achieved by varying the chemical mix in the pulp.

Bronzing A process for obtaining a metallic finish by the addition of a hand- or machine-applied bronzing powder to a wet, adhesive ink.

Bulk The relative thickness of a sheet or sheets, e.g., a bulky paper and a thin paper may have the same weight.

Bulk factor (US) The number of pages of a paper equal to one inch. (UK) Volume.

Bull's eye A printing defect caused by dust or lint, usually from the paper or board's surface causing a white spot on the printing surface that should be ink.

Bullet/bullet point (UK) A heavy, centered dot (•) used to make a piece of text stand out, or to identify items in a non-numbered list.

Burst binding An unsewn binding method whereby the spine fold is burst with perforations during the folding, enabling the glue to adhere to each leaf without having to grind off the usual 3mm, or 1/8in.

C

CMYK Abbreviation for Cyan, Magenta, Yellow, and BlacK, or Key, used in four-color process printing. Combined they approximate colors in the spectrum, within the color gamut of printing inks.

CTP Computer to Plate. The prepress or imaging process in lithographic printing where a finished digital layout or image file is output direct to a printing plate, rather than to film. Most book and magazine publishers now use this system, which is more efficient and usually more accurate

than Computer to Film (CTF), although there are some disadvantages.

Cap height The vertical space taken up by a capital letter. The top may be below the top of the font's ascender, while the foot always aligns with the baseline.

Carbonless paper (NCR) No Carbon Required Paper that has been coated with microscopic chemicals allowing the transfer, under written or typed pressure, of whatever is being written on the topmost surface.

Case In binding, the cover for a book using cloth, paper, or synthetic material, or a combination of these, over board. Can be one or three piece.

Center line/centered A line of type with an equal amount of space at each end. Contrast with ragged right or ragged left, or justified composition.

Chalking A drying problem with offset printing leaving a loose pigment on the surface of the paper.

Character set The complete suite of letters, numerals, symbols, and punctuation marks, plus any special characters, in a font.

Choke See Spreads.

Coarse screen A halftone screen of up to 35lines per cm (85 lines per inch). Used to reproduce photographs on newsprint or similar grade papers.

Coated paper Paper that is coated either one or two sides in matte, semi-gloss, or gloss finish.

Cockling A wave effect on paper caused by changes in the humidity while in transit or storage. Can result in severe problems on press.

Cold set Printing by web offset litho that does not require heat for drying the ink. It has limitations on the fineness of a halftone screen and suitable paper.

Collation marks See Back step marks.

Collotype A planographic process of printing. Gelatine is applied to a sensitized plate onto which the type and images are exposed, and without a screen. This is a slow and expensive process. It reproduces flowers and art with a high fidelity of color balance and detail.

Color control bar A strip at the back edge of a sheet consisting of color and grayscale measurements to assist the press operator in determining a variety of controls are working correctly for the job on press.

Color profile Establishing a profile on a prepress device, or for a printing press that conforms to an agreed set of parameters.

Color separation In color reproduction the method whereby an original image, e.g., a transparency, print, or digital file, is separated into the primary colors, plus black. This can be achieved on desktop computers running programs such as Photoshop, or on high-end scanners. Once approved, the separations are converted into film or go direct to plate from the digital file.

Color swatch(es) A set of color reference guides, e.g., the Pantone Matching System®.

Comb binding A method of binding a publication. Small rectangular holes are punched into pages and covers followed by the feeding of the plastic "comb" through the holes. The spine of the comb can be printed.

Continuous tone, or Contone An image, such as a photograph, composed of graduations of tone from black to white. Contrast with line work, such as drawings.

Convertible press A printing press that can print either a single color on both sides of a sheet of paper or board in one pass, or two colors only on one side.

Copy Author-supplied text and supporting material ready for editing and production. Can be supplied as hard copy or in electronic form.

Copyright The right of the legal party in the contract (author, photographer, artist, or publisher) to control the use of the work being reproduced. International agreements exist to protect the copyright holder. However, intellectual property rights are an increasingly complex area in the Internet age, with local legislative systems often at odds with the global, file-sharing impetus of the Internet.

Corner marks Serve as the location in finishing for where the sheet is to be cut or trimmed.

Cromalin DuPont-patented high-quality, off-press, four-color proofing system from color separations, used to provide a good indication of final color reproduction.

Cut flush A binding style where the book block and the cover are trimmed flush to each other. Usually achieved with a guillotine, or in-line with a three-knife trimmer.

Cut in Index Also known as a thumb index. An index to a book, e.g., dictionary, where the alphabet divisions are cut into the fore edge of the book in a series of steps.

Cut marks (US) Printed marks on a sheet to indicate the edge of a page to be trimmed. (UK) Trim marks.

Cutoff The maximum length of a sheet that can be printed on a web-fed press and equivalent to the circumference of its impression cylinder.

Cyan The special shade of blue in the four-color process inks, known collectively by the abbreviation CMYK. The pigment shade may vary between countries.

D

DAM (Digital Asset Management) Now print production is largely digital, DAM describes the strategy of managing these digital assets collectively and individually on central servers and in terms of version control, archiving, and easy retrieval for reprints and new editions. A logical DAM strategy can be an asset in itself.

DCS2 (Desktop Color Separation) A robust format for transmitting five EPS files—one for each color image, plus a master file—from the prepress stage to the final output device, preventing any intervention or changes.

DPI (Dots per inch) A measure of the output resolution of a laser printer or imagesetter. See also pixels per inch.

DTD (Document Type Definition) A specialized coding system that prepares documents for XML searching and display. It identifies the various elements in the document and establishes a hierarchy by the use of machine-readable tags. The results are invisible to the end-user.

Deckle edge The ragged or frayed edge on the edges of a sheet of handmade paper.

Descender The part of a lower case letter falling below the X-height of the character as in g, q, and p.

Descreen Removal of the original screen value on a previously printed image or film to prevent the creation of a moiré pattern. The image is then rescreened to the desired new halftone screen value. Can be applied to one-color or four-color images. Also see rescreen.

Diacritic A typesetting term applied to a mark placed over, under, or through a letter to distinguish it from one of similar form, or to indicate pronunciation or stress.

Digital printing (DP) An impression printed from a digital prepress file via plateless application of text and images using ink-jet, fused toner, or liquid ink.

Die cutting The use of a die to cut holes or irregular shapes in display work or on book covers.

Die stamping An intaglio process whereby the image is in relief on the surface of the material, either in color or blind (without ink).

Direct to plate (or CTP: Computer to Plate) The process of transmitting digital layouts and instructions from a file to the plate without the interim step of creating film.

Discretionary hyphen Also known as a soft hyphen. This specially noted hyphen in a computer file will disappear in the event of editing or reformatting.

Dot See Halftone.

Dot gain An on-press condition where the dot size of an illustration or text increases, making type appear heavier and images less clear. Some papers, such as newsprint, are more absorbent and thus can cause increased dot gain. All presses have a dot gain capacity, and software can compensate for the problem. Excess pressure exerted on the blanket, or use of an overly worn blanket during the press run can also add to dot gain.

Dry proof Any proof that is prepared off press. Cromalin, Matchprint, Epson, Approval, Waterproof, etc., all fit into this category of proof. Various systems use powders, films, ink-jet, or thermal transfer to achieve the proof.

Duotone Two halftone plates made from the same original image, usually a black-and-white photograph, but to different tonal ranges. When the image is printed a duotone will have a greater tonal range than is possible from one-color reproduction. One color in a duotone is usually black; the other can be any color.

E

EPS (Encapsulated PostScript) A file format often used for images generated in object-orientated drawing applications, e.g., Illustrator or Freehand, and also for scanned images. Contains a postscript file, which describes the image, and a preview image for display on computer.

Em The area occupied by the capital letter M. It will be wider or narrower than square, all depending on the style of the letter in a specific typeface. An em space is twice the width of an en space. Ems and ens are referred to, respectively, as "muttons" and "nuts."

Embossing, blind The process of raising or recessing an image using an uninked block.

Emulsion Normally, a light-sensitive coating on film or a printing plate, but it may also include encapsulated aromas or flavors in promotional printing.

Emulsion side The matte side of a film that is placed in contact with the emulsion of another film or plate when printing to ensure a sharp image. As in "right-reading emulsion down."

Endpapers Lining paper used for the front and back of a casebound book. They adhere to the first and last signatures of the book and attach to the front and back covers of the case. Also known as endsheets.

Extenders See Ascenders and Descenders.

Extent The complete number of pages in a printed work, which will normally be a multiple of four or eight.

F

F&C/F&G Folded and Collated/Gathered. Sheets of a book that have been folded and gathered and/or collated in preparation for binding.

FPO (For Position Only) A low-resolution image in a digital document to indicate the size and placement for the eventual high-resolution image.

FTP (File Transfer Protocol) A data transmission and communication protocol for sending large amounts of data between remote locations, either via a Web browser, or using dedicated FTP software. (Compare with HTTP [Hypertext Transfer Protocol], used to allow remote computers to connect to a website.)

Feet/foot margin The white area at the bottom of a page between the type area and the trimmed edge.

Feint Lines, usually ruled and printed in a pale blue on account book pages and in school exercise books.

Film lamination A polypropylene or other synthetic film laminate applied in one of a variety of finishes (gloss, matte, silk, lay-flat) to the printed surface of a dust jacket, paperback cover, or item piece. Used both for visual effect and protection.

Finish The surface given to a grade of paper from calendering, coating, or embossing.

Finishing (1) All operations performed after printing. **(2)** The hand lettering or ornamentation on the cover on a handbound book.

Fixed space The space between words or characters not variable for justification purposes. Used in ranged left, ragged right, centered, and tabular typesetting.

Flat back Bound sections or signatures having a square spine, as opposed to a rounded and backed spine; normal in limp bindings, but less common in case binding. More common in short-extent children's books.

Flexiback/Flexibind (UK/US) A binding style with sewn signatures. Often used for guide books.

Flexography A relief printing process using rubber or plastic plates on a web-fed press and solvent-based liquid inks. Mainly used for packaging, and for some newspapers.

Flop When an image is reversed (or flipped) from its intentional appearance, usually in error.

Flush left/right Type that aligns vertically to the left or to the right. Also described as ranged left or right. Contrast with ragged left or right.

Foil (1) Film with either a metal or color pigment used to block type and images on book covers and packaging. **(2)** Clear film used as a backing during film assembly.

Folio (1) A page number, and consequently a page. **(2)** A large page in which the full size sheet only needs to be folded once before binding.

Font Software that contains the data necessary to generate the characters or glyphs for a particular typeface.

Footer Recurring information at the foot of a page in a book or magazine, often repeating the title, subject matter, or chapter heading. Also see Headline.

Fore edge The edge of a book or publication that opens.

Fount (1) A fountain or duct on a press. **(2) (UK)** A set of type characters of the same design, now more commonly referred to as font.

Four-color process Color separation from original art, transparencies, or files followed by printing the three primary colors, cyan (C), magenta (M), and yellow (Y), plus black (K, standing both for "key plate" and also instead of "B" to distinguish it from blue).

Four-color inks The pigmented inks used to reproduce the four-color process.

French fold (1) A sheet of paper with four pages printed on one side only, then folded twice with right-angle folds into quarters without cutting at the head. The inside pages are blank with an image appearing on pages 1, 2, 3, and 4, but actually on pages 1, 4, 5, and 8 of the imposition. **(2)** A dust jacket that has a fold over at the top and bottom to provide extra strength. Usually reserved for large art books.

Frontispiece The illustration placed facing the title page in a book. Maybe printed on text stock or tipped in as a separate page printed on coated stock.

Full color Interchangeable term for four-color process.

Full out Type that is set to the specified full measure.

Full point/stop (.) (US) A period.

G

Gatefold Two parallel folds toward each other, in which the fold can be opened from the left and right.

GSM or G/M2 (Eur) Abbreviation for grams per square meter. A method of indicating the substance of paper on the basis of its weight, regardless of the sheet size.

Ghosting (1) When an image re-occurs in a faint appearance by mistake alongside the required image. **(2)** Due to ink starvation the image is reproduced to a lighter (and unacceptable) degree.

Grain (1) In photographic film, the structure of its light-sensitive emulsion. **(2)** In paper, the direction of fibers during the papermaking process.

Grayscale A line of gray tones in varying percentages ranging from white through black and used by printers as a measure to an industry standard.

Gripper edge The allowance of extra space on a sheet of paper for the grippers to hold it.

Gutter The margin closest to the spine of a publication.

H

H&J See Hyphenation and justification.

HTML (Hypertext Markup Language) A markup language used to format digital text and graphics for use on the web, in which links can be embedded.

Half up Art prepared 50% larger than final reproduction size. Allows it to be reproduced at 66%, thereby reducing any initial flaws in the original.

Halftone screen An original photograph reproduced on press following the prepress application of a screen value in a series of dots varying in number per square inch depending on the paper to be used.

Hard copy Printed page(s), as opposed to digital files.

Hash Symbol used in computing to stand for the word "number," but in UK typography it is used primarily by proofreaders to indicate a space.

Headline The display line(s) of type denoting the title of a news story, article, and so on. Followed by a white space before commencement of the main text. In the US, running heads (UK) are referred to as headlines.

Head/tail band A narrow band of plain or striped sewn cotton, glued to the top and bottom of the book block's spine in a casebound book. They cover the ends of the signatures or sections. Primarily a cosmetic, inexpensive addition with minimal addition to the binding strength.

Head trim The usual allowance is 3mm or 1/8in (or twice this between pages) for the removal of folds and clean edges. Bleeds must compensate for this.

Hexachrome Also known as Hi-Fi color printing when two additional inks are used with the CMYK—usually a green and an orange to heighten the visual impact on selected images.

Hickie/Hickey See Bull's eye.

House style Standard spellings, writing styles, and abbreviations used by different publishing houses. House style guides are usually given to writers and editors.

Hue The part of a color that is its main attribute, e.g., its redness or blueness, as compared to its shade (lightness or darkness), or its saturation.

Hyphenation and Justification/H&J A system, usually software-generated, that determines the accepted end of line breaks in justified typesetting. Preprogrammed word-break dictionaries with publisher's approved exceptions or alternative are core to such a system.

I

ICC (International Color Consortium) An internationally recognized and accepted method for achieving consistent color management throughout the prepress and printing stages. Scanners, monitors, proofing devices, and printing presses can all be calibrated to conform to a device-independent ICC standard.

ICC Profile When a device has been calibrated to conform to a given ICC standard and will operate with similarly calibrated devices.

ISBN International Standard Book Number. A unique (once 10- and now 13-digit) serial number that identifies a book from all others, with its title, author, and publisher, plus a check digit.

ISSN International Standard Serial Number. A unique eight-figure number that identifies the country or publication of a magazine or journal and its title, referring to the run of a publication instead of a specific edition.

Imagesetter A device using either a solid-state or gas laser to record text and images at high resolution on special paper, film, or direct to plate.

Impose/Imposition The arrangement of pages to fit the press being used and to provide the correct margins such that when the sheet is folded after presswork, the pages appear in their correct sequence.

Imprint The printer's name and location of printing. Often a legal requirement for overseas printing to comply with customs, i.e., country of origin. As distinct from a publisher's imprint which comprises their name and often a "mark" or symbol, appearing inside and on the spine of a book. For example, the imprint (UK) or copyright (US) page contains the printer's and the publisher's name, an ISBN, credits, and the British Library (UK) or Library of Congress (US) CIP (Cataloging in Publication) information.

Indent (1) Short line (or lines) of type set to the right or left of the standard margin, often used at the beginning of new paragraphs, and to draw attention to specific pieces of information within a larger text. **(2)** The special making of a paper order from the mill for a particular publication or book.

Inferior characters Letters or numbers smaller in point size than main text, and set on or below the baseline.

Insert (1) A signature/section of a book printed separately, often on a different paper—e.g. uncoated for the main text and coated for an illustrative insert—and bound into the book between signatures, as opposed to wrap. **(2)** A piece of paper or card placed loose inside a book or magazine by hand or machine. A blow-in.

Italic Letters in a type family that slope forward, as distinct from roman upright letters and numerals. Text or individual words are set in italic, thus, for emphasis or reference purposes, and also occasionally when foreign-language words are used during the course of a text. If the italic type formatting function (rather than the italic version of a font) is used within a page layout application such as QuarkXPress, it is not a true italic and may not reproduce. Within InDesign, false italics can be created by sloping highlighted text by a few degrees.

J

JDF (Job Definition Format) An XML-based "job ticket" standard that permits easy exchange of information and specifications between the various parties involved in the production of a printing job.

JPEG (Joint Photographic Experts Group) One of several bitmapped compression methods for storing images in a lossy format. In some applications, quality can be set on a scale from high (for print), to low (for web, or layout positional purposes). Resaving JPEGs recompresses the file, losing further data.

Jaggies The visible stair-stepping (aliased) effect on raster images and type, that should instead appear as smooth edges and curves. See aliasing and anti-aliasing.

Justification See Hyphenation and justification.

K

K (US) Key (or blacK). Indicates black in the four-color (CMYK) process, preventing confusion with "B" for blue.

Kerning The adjusting of the space between individual characters in a line of type, nowadays within programs such as InDesign and QuarkXPress.

Key/line (1) Any block, forme, plate or artwork fitting into the register with other colors. **(2)** A line on artwork indicating an area for tint laying. **(3)** A component on a printing press that controls the degree of ink flow onto the rollers. Adjustable by the press operator, usually by computer control.

Kiss cut A light touch of a knife blade on label stock with peel-off to the required size. Sufficient pressure is applied to allow the label to easily detach from the backing sheet without cutting into it.

L

Lamination (1) The application of a transparent gloss- or matte-finish thin film from a variety of materials, e.g., polypropylene, mylar. Available in a lay-flat finish for paperback books to prevent warping of the cover. **(2)** Manufacture of paste boards (see board, duplex, and triplex) by pasting sheets or reels together.

Leading The vertical space between lines of type, expressed using the point system—10 on 12 point (meaning 10pt type with an additional two points of leading added). Originally, leading was a literal term describing thin strips of metal used in hot metal typesetting as spacing. Today, leading is set within page layout programs, such as InDesign and QuarkXPress.

Leader A type character having two or more dots in line. Used to assist the eye's movement across blank space to the next type item, especially on lists, tables, and so on.

Lenticular printing A series of optical-grade, ribbed plastic lenses that sit above two or more printed images giving the impression of movement, or a 3D effect. Also known as auto-stereo images. Not to be confused with a hologram.

Ligature Two or three letters joined together to make one typeset character, e.g., "fi," "fl," "ff," and "st."

Light fast An ink or colored material whose color is not easily affected by light, specifically sunlight. Often used for point of purchase and window display printed matter, e.g., showcards.

Linen tester A magnifying lens used to check halftone dot patterns.

Lining figure Numerals that are the same height as the capital letters in any given typeface.

Literal (UK) A typographical error (US/UK). Also known colloquially as a typo.

Lithographic printing A printing process where the image and non-image areas are on the same surface plane of the plate. As water and grease do not mix, the surface of the plate is treated to attract ink and repel water.

Logo/type Graphical symbol, or stylized piece of typesetting, representing a company or organization.

Loose leaf Individual sheets of paper placed in a binder for easy removal or addition.

Loose line A typesetting term applied to a line where the space between words is excessive.

Lower case Small letters (not caps).

M

Magenta The red pigment based ink used in four-color process printing.

Magnetic ink character recognition A form of machine readable character.

Marbling A decorative multicoloring applied to book edges and commonly used on endpapers in bookbinding.

Mark-up Directions to a typesetter or prepress house for the composition treatment to a manuscript.

Masking The area of an illustration required for reproduction with extraneous material "masked" out.

Matchprint A proprietary prepress proofing system prepared from film, or in digital form. A dry proof.

Measure The length of a line in typesetting, normally determined in picas or points, but sometimes in inches or millimeters.

Medium (1) The substance (usually linseed oil or a varnish) in which the pigment of printing ink is carried. Also known as a vehicle. **(2)** The weight of a typeface midway between light and bold. **(3)** A standard size of printing paper (18 x 23in; 455 x 585 mm).

Metallic inks Inks whereby the regular pigments are replaced by very fine metallic particles, typically gold or silver in color.

Micron 10 and 20 dots assigned in stochastic or FM screening for process color reproduction. 10 micron is finer, but it is more difficult to adjust color in track when on press, and special equipment is required to bake the plates prior to exposure.

Middle tone The range of tonal values between highlights and shadows.

Moiré The undesired screen pattern caused by incorrect screen angles of overprinting halftones.

N

Negative Exposed photographic film or image in which all the tonal values are reversed.

Network A group of interlinked computer or communications devices through which information can be exchanged, either via cables, hubs, and routers, or wireless protocols via a wireless hub.

Newsprint A relatively inexpensive paper made for newspaper presswork – mostly from groundwood/mechanical pulp. With its high acid content, it quickly yellows when exposed to daylight.

Notch (burst) binding A form of adhesive binding. Pages are not cut into individual leaves, but instead are notched with slots to facilitate the penetration of glue.

O

OCR (Optical character recognition) The use of a scanner to scan a printed text and turn it into an editable text file.

Octavo A standard book format obtained by folding a sheet three times at right angles to create eight leaves. Sometimes abbreviated to 8vo or 8mo.

Offset (1) A mainly lithographic method of printing, in which the ink is transferred from the printing plate first to a blanket cylinder, and then onto the paper or other material—rather than printing direct from plate to surface. **(2)** When the pages of a previously printed book are photographed into bitmap form and the file is used to print a new edition. Also referred to as "shoot from the book." Often used to bring previously out of print titles back into print.

Old-style face Typefaces from a period between Venetian and Transitional, e.g., Bembo. Capitals tend to be shorter than lower case ascenders and slightly more contrast in the stroke weight.

Opacity A state of a material that determines its relative ability to inhibit the transmission of light. In papermaking this determines show through, i.e. whether or not text or images printed on one side of the paper can be seen from the other.

Optical media A disc, such as a DVD, encoded by light.

Original Any artwork or copy to be reproduced in print.

Orphan An unacceptably short line length on the last line of text on a page, or paragraph, which needs correcting. Contrast with Widow. Also known as a club line (US).

Overmatter Typesetting that will not fit in the available type area space. Options are to edit to fit or cut.

Overprinting (UK) To print a second image (not always in an additional color) on a previously printed sheet.

Over-running To turn over words from one line to the next (or for several successive lines) after an insertion or other correction. The opposite is to run back.

Overs The percentage of additional copies above the agreed contract quantity. The percentage is negotiable and may be chargeable. The opposite of unders.

P

PDF (Portable Document Format) Adobe Systems technology that enables layouts (for example) to be viewed on-screen and printed outside of the original application that created them, and without the need to have the original files and fonts. When a PDF is made of a document, by using Adobe's Acrobat Distiller on the original QuarkXPress or InDesign file (for example), all of the fonts and images are embedded into the file, which can then be published online, or sent as an e-mail attachment, or via FTP. Printers can produce separations from prepress-quality PDFs, while low-resolution PDFs have relatively small file sizes but are of sufficient quality to be viewed on screen (using the free Acrobat viewer) or published on a Web site. When combined with CTP, the workflow from origination through to printed article can be relatively swift and manageable.

PLC (Paper Laminated Case) Instead of a cloth over board, paper is printed, laminated, and glued over the board.

Pantone Matching System® Pantone Inc's. proprietary check standard for color reproduction and color reproduction materials. Each color bears a description for its formulation in percentages, for use by the graphic arts and printing industries.

Packager A company that sells book ideas to publishers, who will then commission an agreed quantity of the book from the packager and publish it under their imprint when the packager delivers the completed book. The packager does not publish or distribute the book, and is guaranteed the sale of the printed quantity at an agreed unit cost, while the publisher sells at the full cover price for a profit.

Page makeup The organization of text and graphics into the desired design and format.

Pagination Making a publication into its paged form with page numbers, includes any blank pages.

Pass (for press) (1) Instruction to printer approving the project for press. **(2)** When a sheet or roll of paper is running through the press.

Perfect binding A binding method, most popular in magazine publishing, in which all of the sections are glued into a separate cover, with a flat spine.

Perfecting The printing process whereby the sheet/roll is printed on both sides in one pass.

Perforation Very small holes or slots in continuous lines made through the paper or card. Can be done to achieve easy removal of part of the form or document, or to facilitate easier folding of heavier-weight paper or card.

Peripheral Any device not essential to a computer's operation, but connected to it for a specific additional function, e.g., a printer, scanner, or external drive.

Pi characters (Pies) (1) Any character such as fractions or musical symbols, not normally included in the regular font. Also called a special sort. **(2)** A mixed or disordered collection of printing type.

Pica A unit of typesetting measure. Twelve points equals one pica in the Anglo-American system with 6 picas to the inch.

Picking Damage to the surface of the paper, card, or board during presswork.

Pixel (Picture Element) The smallest element of a picture captured by a scanner or displayed on a monitor.

Pixels per inch/per centimeter The measure of resolution of a scanner, scanned image, or monitor screen. The ppi or ppm system is used to describe the resolution of a scanned image to distinguish from the frequency at which it is printed. The accepted ratio for conversion is 2:1, e.g., 300 ppi = 150-line screen.

Plate Metal, plastic, or even paper, image carrier used to transfer ink to paper in letterpress and litho printing, or to the blanket in offset litho. In color separation for full-color or two-color printing, a separate plate is made for each process color.

Plate cylinder (1) The cylinder on a press that holds the printing plate in position. **(2)** An illustration in a book. Can be printed with main text, or more usually, separately on a different (perhaps coated) paper, and tipped in.

Platesetter A laser operated device that records text and images directly from the file to the printing plate.

Point (1) One thousandth of an inch. **(2)** Used to refer to the thickness of board, e.g., 98pt board.

Point system Type measurement systems; 12 points make a Pica Em.

Positive A photographic reproduction on printing film, made from a negative, or on a duplicating film in which the highlights in the original are clear and the shadows are deep.

PostScript The device and resolution-independent page description language, which is used to describe the appearance of a page prepared on a computer to a laser printer, imagesetter, or digital press.

PostScript file A data file containing all the information required to print a single or stream of pages. Contains all picture and text data and may also include fonts.

Posterization The condition of using a limited number of gray levels creating a special effect to a halftone, i.e., reduced number of tonal shades.

Preflight Before a completed application file is sent for proofing/printing one of several desktop programs can run a series of checks to ensure the content is correct and all fonts and additional items are included. Printers also run preflight checks prior to platemaking.

Press proof A proof prepared on a press with ink on paper, often the actual paper to be used on the final pass, as compared to a prepress proof. A machine proof.

Primary colors Used in the four-color process printing, comprising cyan (blue), magenta (red), and yellow, plus black, to reproduce four-color separations.

Print down To use a vacuum frame to transfer a photographic image from one film to another, or to a printing plate.

Printability The ability of a specific paper from a particular making to successfully accept the ink without causing on-press problems, especially picking.

Process color See four-color process.

Progressive proofs A succession of proofs utilizing all of the inks in the four-color process, shown individually and in gradual combination.

Proof The representation on paper of the final printed product. This can be at any interim stage, or at final layout, showing text and images in paged form. Some proofs can be used for color reproduction checking, and others purely for positional purposes.

Proof correction marks Standardized symbols used to mark errors in text or illustrations on proofs that require correction. Usually, these are marked by hand by a proofreader, or an editor, but software exists to allow these to be marked electronically on PDFs. Corrections will then be "taken in," either by the project editor, on interim, internal proofs, or at the printer on completed layouts.

Proofreader A person who reads typeset proofs and marks appropriate corrections.

Proportional spacing System used in typesetting by which all the letters in the alphabet occupy an appropriate amount of space for the best fit within that typeface's design, with an "m" being wider than an "i."

Q

Quarto A page size typically about A4 and obtained by folding a sheet once in each direction.

R

RGB (Red, Green, Blue) The additive primary colors used to create the image on a monitor. Most scanners capture their image in RGB values with a subsequent conversion to CMYK for print reproduction. A device-dependent color space with a color gamut in RGB that is greater than that of CMYK inks and, therefore, cannot be exactly matched. Used for scanning and color separations

RIP (Raster Image Processor) A computer device which converts the postscript data describing pages into bitmap format for imaging on an imagesetter, platesetter, digital press, color photocopier, or other imaging device. Often includes specialized technology for the rendering of different types of halftone screen. Also used in phototypesetting and electronic page composition systems, processing the digital information passed to them relating to individual letters, numerals, and images both line and halftone, before preparing pages for output in the correct position and orientation.

Ragged right/left Use of a fixed word space in typesetting to prevent the type from aligning vertically on either the left or right hand side. Also known as unjustified composition. The opposite of flush left, or right typesetting.

Range To cause type or illustrations to line up on or to a certain point, either vertically or horizontally.

Raster (graphic) A bitmap. An image formed from a grid of pixels, or points of color, on a computer monitor, or printed onto a surface. Contrast with Vector graphics.

Rasterize To turn into a bitmap.

Ream 500 (originally 516) sheets of paper.

Recto A right-hand page.

Register/Registration To print two or more impressions that fit together without overlap or causing a moiré effect. Also to backup accurately if printed on opposite sides of the sheet with the intention of maintaining register and preventing possible show through.

Register marks Marks on sets of overlays, artwork, typeset pages, film, plates, or formes so that when they are superimposed during printing the rest of the work is in register.

Reprint Any printing of a work (with or without corrections) subsequent to the initial printing.

Repro house (UK) A prepress house, who take application files or PDFs from clients and ready them for print production, making color separations, and so on.

Rescreen When a previously printed halftone has to be treated as an "original." To avoid the creation of a moiré pattern with conflicting screens the image is first descreened and then rescreened. See Descreen.

Retouching (1) Hand treatment on litho film negative or positive to change tonal values or correct imperfections. **(2)** In a digital context the modification in Photoshop of an original image to comply with the photographer's or designer's preference for the final visual effect.

Reverse out When type or an image appears in white out of a black, or other color background.

Right reading Paper or film in positive or negative that can be read in the usual way, i.e., from left to right.

River A series of word spaces (usually occurring in badly justified typesetting) that form a noticeable pattern of white space down many lines of type.

Roman The standard characters of a font in which the letters are upright, as opposed to italic sloping.

Rosette The locations on a color separation where all four colors intersect.

Rough An unfinished design/layout. Also known as a comp (US).

Run on Sheets or signatures printed in addition to ordered initial quantity.

Runability The resistance of paper to curling/waving, or web breaks and other problems associated with the paper, as opposed to printability.

Runaround To lay out type on a page whereby the line beginnings or endings follow the shape of an illustration, which may be regular or irregular.

Running head/foot Recurring lines of text—usually a book or magazine title, or a chapter heading—at the head or foot of every page of a publication. Also see Headline.

S

Saddle (wire) stitching Similar in effect to stapling, achieved on a saddle-stitching machine which feeds a continuous wire to form staples of the required length to be fired into the publication and folded on the inside.

Sans serif A category of typeface without the serifs, e.g., Helvetica.

SGML (Standard Generalized Markup Language) A meta language used for coding a digital manuscript to facilitate eventual searching of the document.

SWOP (Standard Web Offset Printing) (US) A standard for printing color on web offset presses. An alternative is a sheet-fed color space with more density than the high speed SWOP version.

Scale To calculate the percentage of enlargement or reduction of an image. To resize an image in proportion.

Screen (1) See Halftone screen. **(2)** The material used in screen printing that contains the text and images.

Screen angle When halftones are printed in one or more colors there is a risk of a moiré pattern appearing on the printed sheet. If the angle used for each screen is not correctly selected the result can create a moiré effect In the four-color process. The angles are commonly black 45 degrees (as in monochrome), magenta at 75 degrees, yellow at 90 degrees and cyan at 105 degrees.

Screen clash See Moiré.

Screen ruling (or frequency) A measure of the quality or fineness of the dot structure used to reproduce a halftone image or tint expressed in lines per inch or centimeter. Do not confuse with PPI.

Screened negative / positive print Any film or print of a color or monochrome subject that has been reproduced using a halftone screen.

Script A typeface that imitates any handwritten style.

Scumming Effect caused in litho printing when the non-image areas of the plate do not repel the ink resulting in a dirty image being printed.

Sections/Signatures A folded press sheet. Paper is folded to form part of a book or booklet. Sections/signatures normally comprise sheets folded to make 4, 8, 16, 32, or 64 pages.

Self cover A publication whose cover is the same paper or material as the inside pages.

Self ends A binding in which the endpapers are part of the first and last section of the book, as opposed to being tipped in separately. Rarely used.

Separated artwork Artwork prepared as a series of overlays, each one providing the portion of the overall separation for the relevant color to be printed.

Separation See Color separation

Serif The small ornamentations/terminating strokes on individual letters/characters of serif typefaces, as opposed to Sans serif.

Set solid Type which has been set without any leading or line feed between the lines. The result is usually difficult to read.

Sheet-fed press A press on which the printing plate surface is fixed around a cylinder and is fed with single sheets, as opposed to a web-fed press.

Side sewing/stitching To stitch through the side of a book or booklet from front to back at the binding edge (spine) with a thread or wire. A method of binding leaves as well as sections. The publication will not lay flat and extra spine margin should be allowed for.

Signature Interchangeable term for Section.

Signature numbering A consecutive number or letter printed at the foot of the first page of a Section/signature to enable the binder to check the correctness of the sequence and completeness of a binding. The letter or number may be accompanied by a rule on the back of each section so that when they are folded and gathered these appear in a stepped pattern, one out of sequence indicating incorrect gathering.

Slug line A line on a color proof that indicates if any of the colors are clogged (filled-in) on the proof.

Small caps Type fonts, especially those used for book typesetting which include an extra alphabet whose cap height is the same as the x-height, but without the strokes being thinner than the rest of the font, as occurs when ordinary capitals are reduced to their x-height. There are no true italic small caps.

Soft proof A digital proof for viewing on a monitor screen.

Spine The binding edge of a book.

Spiral binding A publication bound with spiral width of varying diameter and often coated with a colored plastic. Pages are punched with small holes to accept the coiled wire.

Spot color When a color is printed using a specific color of ink, usually from a special guide, in coated or uncoated version, instead of creating it via a build of percentage tints from process color inks.

Spot varnish The application of a gloss or matte varnish to a specific area on the page or cover. Can be a press varnish applied in-line or a separate pass.

Spread (1) Reproduction. A variety of terms, e.g., "lock-on," "overdraw," and "spread and choke," are used to describe the need to make two adjoining images slightly thicker than on the original artwork to facilitate register when printing in two or more colors. **(2)** A double-truck/page spread (DPS) (US/UK) occurs when an illustration occupies two opposing pages. Strictly speaking, this only occurs on the center spread of a signature—elsewhere it is a "false double"—however the term is commonly used in book and magazine publishing, advertising, and design

Stamping (US) See Blocking.

Stet Leave as set. Instruction to return to the original intention in a typeset proof and to ignore a previous correction or deletion mark.

Stock Any material to be printed on.

Stochastic screening Also known as FM, or random dot screening. Unlike AM screening where dots are placed in a pre-determined line screen per inch, e.g, 150 lpi and vary in size, with stochastic screening the microns at either 20 or the even finer level of 10 micron dots are the same size and vary where they are positioned, i.e, clustered heavily in shadow areas and fewer in highlights.

Strip and rebind To take unsold casebound books (for example), strip off the covers, and then rebind them as paperbacks to achieve further sales.

Stripping (1) To insert, i.e., "strip-in," any correction in film or paper during phototypesetting. **(2)** To glue a strip of cloth or paper to the back of a paperback book or pad as reinforcement.

Subscript /inferior characters Any letter, numeral or character appearing below the baseline in typesetting. The opposite of superscript.

Substrate Interchangeable term with stock.

Suitcase A method of managing fonts in which all the elements needed to display and print a font, or font family, are included within a single, protective file.

Superscript/superior characters Any letter or numeral smaller than the text-size and are positioned above the x-height of the type body.

Surprinting (US) See Overprinting.

Swash characters Italic letters with exaggerated strokes.

Swatch (book) Samples of binding cloths, inks, endpapers, head/tail bands, or text papers to show the designer and print buyer the available selection.

T

TIFF (Tagged Image File Format) A high-quality bitmap file format for images, especially photographs, that is ideal for print production purposes.

Tabulate To arrange type and other elements in regular columns, usually of figures.

Tailband Same as headband but at the foot of the spine on a casebound book.

Thermography An imitation of die stamping. The finished effect of a similar raised look is achieved by a combination of ink, powder and heat.

Thread sealing A method of book binding in which the sections are "stabbed" with thread, the loose ends then being sealed with adhesive.

Thumb index An index where the dividers are cut into the fore edge rather than stepped as in a cut in or tab index.

To view The number of pages appearing on one side of a sheet. e.g., 16 pages to view would equal a 32-page signature.

Tone The gradation, usually expressed in percentages, from light to dark in ink on paper, contrasted with line work that has no tonal values. Measurable with a instrument known as a densitometer.

Tranny A photographic transparency.

Trapping The technique of slightly overlapping one |image on an adjacent one thereby preventing unsightly small white gaps appearing between the two colors. A misregister will only exacerbate the problem by either increasing the gap or overlapping the trap.

Trim marks (UK) See Cut marks (US).

Turned in The cloth or other material used on the case of a book that is turned in round the edges to prevent the board's edges being exposed.

Type area The area on a page determined by the designer to be allocated for the placement of type and illustrations, excludes margins.

Typo Abbreviation term for a typographical error.

U

UCR See Undercolor Removal.

USM Un-Sharp Mask. A photographic darkroom process, available in digital form within software such as Photoshop. It uses a blurred positive to create a "mask" of the original image, which, when combined with the negative, creates an illusion of increased sharpness. Like all sharpening techniques, it does not improve poor focus, but creates the perception of sharper detail.

UV (1) Ultraviolet. **(2)** A coating on top of a previously printed product to enhance the visual effect.

Undercolor removal A technique used in the color separation process that removes unwanted or excess color, either to reduce the amount of ink to be used on press (for economy but more often to reduce trapping), or where these colors cancel each other out in the various achromatic systems.

Underline/underscore A typesetting term to indicate a fine rule being placed just below the baseline and used to indicate emphasis.

Unjustified setting When lines of type align vertically on one side and are ragged set on the other. The amount of indent on the ragged edge can be specified to prevent an ugly appearance. The word space is usually kept to a constant value to enhance the visual effect.

Upper case Capital letters (caps). From the portion of the type case that held the capital letters in the days of hot metal typesetting.

V

Variable data printing When every digitally printed piece varies from its predecessor and successor. Used extensively for direct mailing pieces to target perceived individual preferences in product, but can also be just the name and address that vary.

Variable space The space inserted between words to justify them. This can be controlled with acceptable minimum/maximum amounts of allowed space, defined as being "to the em", as in "5 to the em". See Hyphenation and justification.

Vector graphic Graphic (drawing) format that uses mathematical calculations to reproduce lines and curves on screen. When an image is scaled up, the calculations are redone so that the image displays without image degradation. Vector graphics are different from pixel graphics, which degrade or "pixelate" when blown up beyond the resolution and image size they were saved at.

Verso A left-hand page.

Vignette A halftone with etched, gently fading edges, as opposed to being cut out or squared up.

W

Watermark A design impressed by a dandy roll into a newly-formed web of paper containing a unique logo or symbol, which is visible when held up to the light. Digital files, such as images, can also be "watermarked" digitally, either invisibly, to trace the route of piracy, or visibly—such as in the widespread use of copyright messages embedded within low-resolution positional images from commercial image libraries, prior to the purchase of, and permission to reproduce, high-resolution versions for print reproduction.

Web offset Reel-fed offset litho printing. There are three systems: blanket to blanket, when two plate and two blanket cylinders on each unit print and perfect the web; three-cylinder systems, in which plate blanket and impression cylinders print one side of the paper only; and satellite or planetary systems in which two-, three-, or four- plate and blanket cylinders are arranged around a common impression cylinder printing one side of the web in as many colors as there are plate cylinders.

Weight (of type) In any given font, light, medium, black, bold, or ultra versions of the same basic typeface, affecting its overall blackness and visual impact on the printed page.

Widow A single word, or a short line, appearing at the top of a page.

Wire-O binding A binding method for publications. The pages and covers are punched with rectangular holes and a double-loop wire is then inserted through the holes. The loops are crimped to keep the wire in place. A strong, lay-flat binding. Allow for a deeper spine margin.

Word spacing The amount of space allowed between words by the typographer's/designer's specifications.

Wraparound (1) A plate that wraps around a plate cylinder. The normal condition in litho printing, but not universal in letterpress. **(2)** One sheet or signature wrapped around another in the binding stage.

Wrong reading Film that has been made such that it reads from right to left from the side in question.

X

XML (Extensible Markup Language) A metadata (data about data) markup language used to code and identify the different elements of text, graphics (and any other digital data) within a file for searching and also for use on the Internet. XML is "platform agnostic," in that any computer device can read it, regardless of the operating system it runs on. Anyone can write their own XML "tags" to describe the format of a piece of data. It is at the heart of the idea of "web services," the seamless and intuitive creation and flow of online applications and information to and from the user, and is therefore a vital tool in cross-platform publishing.

x-height That part of a letter with no ascender or descender, e.g., an "a," or an "x."

INDEX